Aspects of Paris

Aspects of Paris

PETER DE POLNAY

W. H. ALLEN
LONDON
1968

© PETER DE POLNAY, 1968

PRINTED AND BOUND IN GREAT BRITAIN
BY T. & A. CONSTABLE LTD
EDINBURGH
FOR THE PUBLISHERS
W. H. ALLEN & COMPANY
ESSEX STREET LONDON WC2

491 00301 3

Contents

Illustrations

A section of pictures appears between pages 128 and 129. All appear by courtesy of the Bibliothèque Nationale de Paris. The two endpaper maps were drawn specially by Beatrice Manson and Jean Maxim Perramon.

Introduction

In the Neolithic Age elephants lived on the slopes of Belleville, huge mammoth-like creatures nearly twelve feet high and fifteen long. They used to go down to drink in the Seine, taking the road that today roughly corresponds with the avenue Mathurin-Moreau and the rue de la Grange-aux-Belles. In 1903 during the construction of the Métro Porte-des-Lilas-Villiers, the molar tooth of an elephas primigenius was found; pre-historians completed the pattern. If the elephants did indeed take the shortest cut to the river, then they must also have lumbered along the future rue Saint-Denis, the road the kings of France were later often to take.

Blaise Pascal said: "Rivers are roads that move." Paris was born in the Cité, where two roads meet, one the East-West river road, the other the North-South land road. When the Cité became too small, the inhabitants grouped themselves on both banks of the river along the North-South road, which became the rue Saint-Jacques on the Left and the rue Saint-Martin on the Right Bank. The North-South road was joined together by two wooden bridges across the river, Le Grand-Pont (now Pont-Notre-Dame) and Le Petit-Pont, still on the same site with the same name. Over the two bridges passed the great road connecting the Loire with the plains of the North. From the start Paris remained a circle crossed by two perpendiculars: the river road and the land road.

Today, as in the days of the Romans, all the routes nationales begin in the Place du Parvis-de-Notre-Dame in the heart of the Cité, which is the heart of France.

In 50 B.C. when Caesar came to conquer Gaul, the Cité was inhabited by the tribe of the Parises or Parisii who hailed from Asia. Labienus, Caesar's lieutenant, marched on the Parisii, his legions vastly outnumbering the tribesmen. Before joining battle with the Romans, Camulogène, the chief of the Parisii, burnt all the bridges and the houses of the settlement; then he perished in the fight. Thus Paris was born out of defeat and fire, for that burnt-down village was its first ancestor. Not for nothing is "Fluctuat Nec Mergitur" the motto of the town.

Between the second and the fourth centuries an entirely Roman town stood on the site of the burnt village. On the distant hillock of Montmartre (Mons Martis to the Romans, Mons Martyrum to the Christians because of the martyrdom of SS Denis, Rustique and Eleuthère) stood temples of Mercury and Mars. Inside the Roman town, which spread on the Left Bank from the Seine to Mons Lencotitius (Montagne Sainte-Geneviève), lived about fifteen thousand souls. The town was called Lutetia. The Right Bank remained marshland. The rising little city took the fancy of the Emperor Julian the Apostate, who lived there from 351 to 361 A.D. It is said that he built his palace on the site nowadays known as Les Thermes de Julien; but that is not certain.

Within the town the Romans built a theatre (the site of the Lycée Saint-Louis), an arena (rue Monge), and baths, the ruins of which are beside the Cluny Museum in the rue du Sommerard.

"I was in winter quarters in my dear Lutetia," wrote Julian in a letter. "Here winter is less rigorous than elsewhere. The people have it that this is caused by the sea breeze that reaches Lutetia.... Sea water is less cold than fresh water. In this land you find excellent vineyards and fig trees, which are protected with straw in winter. The natives take the gifts of Bacchus because he is the father of joy. Their usual drink is water from the river, which is clear and limpid. As they live on an island, it would be difficult for them to procure any other water."

Fig trees are still to be found at Argenteuil, and straw is still used as protection against the cold.

After the invasion of the Franks, the town lost the name of Lutetia and was called Paris after the long-extinct, small tribe of the Parisii.

During the reign of the Franks, the Parisians suffered heavily from their cruelty and treachery. Chilpéric II outdid his kinsmen. In August 584, envoys appeared in Paris sent from Spain by the Visigoth ruler whom Grégoire de Tours, the great chronicler, refers to as the King of Spain. The emissaries came to arrange a marriage between the Visigoth king and Rigonthe, Chilpéric's daughter. Chilpéric ordered a large number of Parisian families to leave their homes so as to accommodate the envoys in a dignified manner. The poor people were herded together, put into four-wheeled wagons and driven out of town. Those who clung to their homes were put to death. It was rather modern in conception and execution.

Chilpéric agreed to the marriage, and gave his daughter a fine dowry. Queen Frédégonde added a large quantity of jewels, gold and silver. Fifty wagons were needed to carry the daughter's baggage south. The escort consisted of four thousand men. Ducs Domegisellus, Ansoalde and Bladaste, along with Wadon the High Chamberlain, were sent with the bride to guide and protect her. The cortège left Paris through the southern gate. The axle of one of the carriages broke and the superstitious populace cried out: "Mala hora!"

Having travelled the distance of three leagues, tents were pitched for the night. When darkness fell, a group of soldiers stole about a hundred horses and disappeared into the forest. The horses all wore gold chains and bits. On the second night, still more horses vanished. On the fourth, some of the gold and silver went too. The nobles who were there to protect their princess set the example, and, wherever Rigonthe and her suite passed, the cottages of the poor were destroyed and their beasts driven away. In Poitiers several noblemen abandoned her, taking a fair share of the dowry with them. None the less Rigonthe continued on her journey. On arrival in Toulouse she heard of her father's death. He had been assassinated on the order of his wife Frédégonde. On hearing the news, the three dukes and the High Chamberlain decamped with the rest of the treasure. Rigonthe had to give up the idea of marriage, and all that was left for her was to seek refuge in the convent of Sainte-Marie-de-Toulouse.

Such was life under the Franks.

After the dismemberment of Charlemagne's empire, Paris became the capital of the kingdom which from then on was called France. The town continued to expand along the North-South road, the Cité still remaining the centre of the town. On the Right Bank the North-South road cut across the new East-West road (rues Saint-Antoine and Saint-Honoré), and where the two roads crossed became known as la Grande Croisée de Paris. Churches rose, among them Saint-Julien-le-Pauvre and Saint-Germain-des-Prés, the oldest surviving churches of Paris—building started on both before 1170 —unless one considers Saint-Pierre of Montmartre, started in 1134 and finished in 1147, when Montmartre was well outside the boundaries. Notre-Dame, though begun in 1163, was finished only in 1330. The little church of Saint-Julien-le-Pauvre, without belfry and transept, was one of the twenty churches built in the vicinity of Notre-Dame during the Middle Ages which, with the exception of Saint-Julien and the remains of the chapel of Saint-Aignan in the rue des Ursins, have all disappeared.

Already in Roman times Paris was a walled city, but the town continued consistently to expand beyond the walls. It was King Philippe-Auguste who in 1188 decided to construct a final wall round Paris, a wall intended to give the town its definitive size and shape, and which became known as the Enceinte de Philippe-Auguste. Excavations in 1896 in the rues Clovis and Cardinal-Lemoine revealed a section of this wall, about nine feet thick; at regular intervals of about two hundred yards stood a tower. (One such tower can still be seen at 29 rue Guénégaud.) The wall had five gates on the Right Bank. Starting from the Quai des Célestins, it reached as far as the Portes Saint-Denis and Saint-Antoine; then in a half-circle it enclosed the Louvre and stretched back to the Seine.

The western end of the wall was on the Left Bank, somewhere near the French Academy, where at the time stood the Tower of Philippe-Hamelin, later known as the Tour de Nesle, of sinister reputation. The wall was carried as far as the Porte Saint-Jacques and joined the river at the height of the Port-de-Saint-Bernard. On the Left Bank the enceinte had about thirty towers and six gates.

Remains of the Enceinte de Philippe-Auguste can be seen at the Palais de Justice (Tour de l'Horloge), the flagstones of the Cour Carrée of the Louvre between the clock and the south entrance giving on the Quai du Louvre, in the rue de Rivoli behind the statue of Coligny, at 135 rue Saint-Denis, at 11 rue du Temple and elsewhere.

Paris refused to stay put. The next attempt to halt it was the Enceinte of Etienne Marcel, completed by Charles V, who took the wall more to the east to join up with the fortress of the Bastille. As Paris continued to outgrow its walls, new ones were built. For instance, the Portes Saint-Martin and Saint-Denis are part of the Enceinte of Louis XIV. From the time of Julius Caesar until 1841 when the fortifications were built, Paris had nine different walls, each trying to contain the town; but whenever outlying places and villages were officially included within the city in an attempt to give it a definite limit, new agglomerations sprang up beyond them. In brief, the effect was contrary to aim and expectation, as though the walls were in constant pursuit of the expanding town. Such is also the story of the suburbs, which are still on the move and, it seems, will never stop.

Neither walls, ramparts, bastions, fortifications nor octrois (toll-gates) could stem the tide; the town expanded, pushing all obstacles out of its way. The reason for this was aptly put by E. Babize in 1930. "England," he said, "goes to India, Germany to America, Italy colonises Africa, and France immigrates to Paris."

In the eighteenth century, in accordance with the Plan of Bretez, also known as the Plan of Turgot, a new enceinte was thrown round Paris, the Walls of the Fermiers Généraux, the "tax-farmers" who did very well for themselves in their work of collecting the revenue. One evening, after a game of chess in Voltaire's drawing-room at Ferney, the guests told stories about robbers, and Voltaire was asked to tell one too.

"Mesdames," he said, "once upon a time there was a fermier général . . . ma foi! I forget the rest."

Those walls were to stay until 1860.

One generally pictures old Paris as a dark, sordid town with dark houses clustered round the churches and dark crimes committed in narrow alleyways. In the sixteenth century Torquato Tasso, the Italian poet, visited Paris as a member of the suite of Cardinal Luigi d'Este. The spoilt son of Renaissance Italy did not think much of the city. In letters to his friends in Ferrara he complained of the awful climate, the monotonous fog and the inhabitants who were as changeable as the weather. A few church spires attracted him; the houses not at all; and the only things he praised and admired were the gay windmills of Montmartre.

On the other hand, Rodolphe Boutenais, a lawyer from Château-dun who became advocate to the Great Council of Paris towards the end of the same century, wrote a poem in Latin in praise of Paris, entitled *Lutetia*:

"Here on the summit of the mountain where Saint-Denis and his companions were put to death"—he was alluding to Montmartre —"still flourishes a village that took its name from the martyrs, the friends of Christ. Here stone is quarried to which is added plaster, so useful in the construction of our houses, whose brilliant whiteness transforms Paris into a town wearing a cloak of snow. The constant use of this mixture keeps the flames away, and to it we owe the peace of our town, its beauty and resistance to fire."

You have only to look at the buildings that have recently been cleaned to be able easily to visualise Boutenais's Paris as a town wearing a cloak of snow.

In the days of Philippe-Auguste, clothes and horses' harness were covered with gold, silver and jewels, but people lived poorly at Court and even more poorly elsewhere. The royal palaces had neither marble nor polished floors; carpets were unknown: the king and his courtiers walked on straw.

"For the salvation of our soul and the souls of our forebears," wrote Philippe-Auguste, "we hereby give the usage of all the straw of our room and house to the poor who dwell in the Maison-Dieu in front of the great church of Notre-Dame, whenever we leave the town and sleep in some other place."

The same monarch shared with the Provost of Paris the spoils of the condemned, including the clothes they wore at their executions; supervised the gaming houses and brothels, which paid him toll; and attached women to the Court, who, known as the Royal Prostitutes, wore special dresses to distinguish them from other harlots, and whose main task was to keep the bodyguard happy.

The people paid tolls and taxes on practically everything. Already in the time of Saint-Louis, at the toll-gate of the Petit-Châtelet payment was exacted in respect of the rare monkeys that entered the town. If a merchant imported a monkey for sale, he paid 4 deniers, but a laudable exception was made in the case of jugglers. If the monkey danced for the toll-collector in the Passage du Petit-Châtelet, no duty payment was demanded, and if on top of that the juggler sang a song that pleased the collector, he too was exempted from tax.

Pigs abounded in the streets of Paris. They roamed the town, eating all the filth and offal for which they could wish. These scavengers were very useful, for they fed well, cleaned up some of the mess in the streets and, once they had become fat and appetising, provided succulent food for the people, who thus doubly benefited from them, until one day, near Saint-Gervais, a pig unfortunately found itself between the forelegs of a horse ridden by Philippe, the eldest son of King Louis-le-Gros. The horse threw the prince, who died of his fall, and the bereaved king stopped the pigs' free progress and forbade them to wander in the streets. An exception was made for the pigs of the monks of Saint-Antoine; as long as each carried a bell, they were free to run about, though never more than twelve were allowed out together. They became known as the Privileged Pigs.

Another and often more dangerous obstacle to free circulation was the number of streams running in the middle of the streets. There were no pavements and no gutters. When it rained, the streams turned into torrents, especially down the streets dropping from Montmartre and on the Left Bank from the Montagne Sainte-Geneviève. The streams, of course, swept filth and dirt along. They were still running in the middle of the eighteenth century, and Restif de La Bretonne, that inexhaustible chronicler of the Paris of his day, relates a scene he witnessed in the rue Montmartre where he saw such a torrent. (One wonders whether Restif ever slept, since he seems invariably to have been at hand whenever and wherever anything happened in Paris.)

It was night: he preferred to stroll about at night. The torrent in the rue Montmartre was in full flow. Although there was a moon, the town was in darkness. It was an old, barbarous custom, as he says, not to light the street lamps when there was a moon, in spite of the fact that its light could not penetrate into the narrow streets because of the high houses. Few people were abroad in the night· Fearlessly, he walked on, his aim the rue des Vieux-Augustins (now rues d'Argout and Hérold), his intention to cross the covered sewer there. He called out to two women on the other side of the torrent, busybody that he was, not to cross the stream before they reached the sewer. They were mother and daughter. The daughter did not listen to his wise words—so few people seemed to—but tried to wade across. She fell, and the torrent took her along. The mother shrieked. Restif entered the mire, which was the messy stream from the Halles, risking being thrown over by its force. Restif of course, who always emerged victorious, pulled the girl from the torrent, and, seeing that she had fainted, carried her home to her lodgings and modestly vanished before the grateful mother could thank her daughter's saviour.

The custom of not lighting the street lamps when there was a moon was still in existence when street lanterns were changed to street lamps in the 1770s. By 1780, twelve hundred street lamps shed their light every moonless night. Householders had to pay for their lanterns, and later their street lamps, every twenty years. The citizens complained that this tax was greater than the expense of lighting the town.

The streets were covered in mud, which turned black and smelly at mealtimes when water was discharged from the pitchers, in spite of the sulphur and salt used against mud and stench by the municipality. The mud was now and then carted away in wheelbarrows by private contractors. When it snowed, the mud froze, and the streams were covered in ice. It was bitterly hard work to clean the streets when it thawed.

Until the eighteenth century, houses were known after their ensigns. If they had none, then they were referred to as the house next to such and such an ensign, or the second or third house after the ensign. In 1726 street numbers began to be used. Noblemen objected to them, for they found it humiliating to live, say, at number 10 with a tradesman at number 11. Tradesmen did not care for street numbers either: they feared new taxes. In 1797 street numbers became obligatory. All houses were given numbers, starting on the right side of the street and ending on the left. For example, in the rue Saint-Honoré the house on the right corner of the rue de la Lingerie was number 1, on the left corner number 730. Street names were given officially only from 1726 onwards: until then tradition alone had kept their names alive.

Paris under the kings was poor in public gardens but rich in private ones, especially on the Ile-Saint-Louis (Ile-des-Vaches in the Middle Ages). True, there were the public squares of Grève (now de l'Hôtel-de-Ville), Chevalier-du-Guet (rue Jean-Lantier), Sainte-Opportune, Sorbonne, Parvis-de-Notre-Dame, and Croix-Rouge among others, but they were cluttered with the stalls of fishmongers, butchers and bakers, leaving little room for the strolling Parisian. Henri IV and Richelieu were each moved by the poverty of open space, but the contributions of the good king and the great cardinal amounted only to the Place Dauphine and the Place Royale. Still, the Parisian had the laughing countryside just beyond the walls, and there he repaired to drink, eat and dance in the guinguettes* that surrounded the town like the enceinte.

The Revolution, the Empire and the Restoration all contributed to the growth of Paris, but the great feverish impulse came with the Baron Haussmann, Prefect of the Seine for seventeen years, who was led, guided, helped and pushed by his sovereign, the Emperor Napoleon III. The Walls of the Fermiers Généraux were demolished, and the outlying villages of Montmartre, Batignolles, Belleville, Ménilmontant, Reuilly, Les Gobelins and Montrouge attached to the capital; and thus in 1860 the Paris of twelve arrondissements turned into the Paris of twenty. The Emperor was happy. Once the walls were gone and the villages swallowed, the town sprawled, as it were, all over the place, and the villages quickly lost what little rusticity they still possessed.

To the Emperor and his indefatigable Prefect, progress seemed the answer to all ills. "Du petit au grand" was their motto. By the 1860s they could boast of new, large, beautifully paved streets and boulevards, flanked by new houses of equal grandeur. New buildings rose daily. The rue de Rivoli and the Place de l'Opéra were conceived. The Hôtel de la Paix (now Grand-Hôtel) and the Hôtel du Louvre were erected with their hundreds of rooms for the foreigners who flocked to admire the new Paris with its modern

---

* Guinguettes: taverns with gardens where one danced, named after Guinguet who owned such an establishment in the 1670s in Ménilmontant.

cafés, some with twenty-four billiard tables, rightly calling themselves the biggest in the world. On top of all this appeared the large stores like the Louvre, Pygmalion, the Belle Jardinière, and the Bon Marché, which revolutionised commerce and brought in a new era in shopping which Emile Zola ecstatically praised in his *Au Bonheur des Dames*.

The lovers of old Paris still grind their teeth when speaking of the baron. The "haussmannisation" of Paris remains a deadly sin in their eyes. "Think," they say, "of all the old streets that vanished, the old stones that were destroyed and the squares and the private gardens that had to disappear." They forget one thing, that the wide boulevards of the Baron with their trees and the houses that flank them are not as ungainly a sight as the huge lifeless barracks and skyscrapers that would have sprung up if the prefect and the emperor had left the matter to our age. Anyway, many old streets are left as witnesses of the past of Paris.

Paris has several times been invaded, yet little physical damage has been caused to the town by enemy hand. Its worst ordeal, and the worst destruction it suffered, was caused by the Parisians themselves during the violence and horrors of the short-lived Commune of 1871.

"You cannot govern against Paris; you cannot govern without Paris," observed Léon Gambetta to Louis Andrieux, Prefect of Police, who, remembering the Commune, was of the opinion, however, that if one day a government ruled France according to the wishes of only the Parisians, they would govern against France.

I

The Halles I

The district of Les Halles lies in the first arrondissement and dates back to the twelfth century when it belonged to the new parish of Saint-Germain (Saint-Germain-l'Auxerrois). In the reign of Philippe-Auguste a chapel was built in the Halles dedicated to St Agnès, and paid for by Jean Alais, a burgher of Paris and chief of the mystery players. Alais had lent money to the King who did not repay him in cash but gave him the right to levy 1 denier on every panier of fish brought into the Halles. Alais did so well that he donated the chapel out of sheer remorse. The chapel received relics of St Eustache from the Abbey of Saint-Denis. It soon changed its name to Saint-Eustache, and the newly created parish took the same name. The population of the Halles grew so fast that Saint-Eustache had several times to be enlarged. It was eventually pulled down to make room for a much larger church. The foundation stone of the present church was laid on August 19, 1532, by Jean de la Barre, Comte d'Etampes, Provost of Paris. Saint-Eustache is to the Halles what Notre-Dame is to the Cité, and in dignity ranks next to it.

At the time when St Louis was in the Holy Land, a strange personage arrived in the Halles who took the church by force. He was a Benedictine monk called Jacob, who came from the Abbey of Cîteaux (Côte d'Or), leading thirty thousand men, a miscellaneous horde consisting of shepherds, beggars and ordinary people who had joined him on his progress. Most of them were armed. Jacob evicted the priests and anointed himself bishop. The clergy of Paris did not dare intervene. Was he a visionary, a plain adventurer, or a madman? Nineteenth-century socialists liked to think of him as a revolutionary and a social reformer.

Jacob, whose followers camped and lived around the church, was a preacher of strength. He, the simple monk, had seen the angels, and the Blessed Virgin had visited him in his cell in the Abbey of Cîteaux. He was at Saint-Eustache to execute her holy commands. He and his aides used the confessional to discover which of the parishioners had worldly goods. The people of the Halles, who were already known for their good humour and gaiety, were delighted with the monk until his armed men began to take their money and possessions, including wives and daughters.

As suddenly as he had arrived, Jacob and his flock left Saint-Eustache and set out for Orleans. No more was heard of him. The priests of Saint-Eustache returned to the relief of the population. When there was no fear of his return, the Bishop of Paris excommunicated him and his followers.

During the reign of Charles VI, the English, the Burgundians and the Armagnac faction took their turn in ill-treating and killing the people of France. The Parisians suffered most, and the Armagnacs were the worst offenders. The merchants of the Halles preferred to be put to ransom by the English and the Burgundians, and the Armagnacs used to say to them, "If it were the English or the Burgundians you would not complain so bitterly."

The Armagnacs wore armbands. They wanted, as a chronicler put it, to enrol the saint, and went to Saint-Eustache and put a band round the arm of his statue. A young Parisian pulled off the band, then destroyed it. The Armagnacs cut off his hands and banished him from the capital. In May 1418, when the Burgundians entered

Paris, many Armagnacs were massacred. The overjoyed people of the Halles rose against the defeated foe, women and children calling them treacherous dogs while they were put to the sword.

Their hands still dripping with the blood of the Armagnacs, the parishioners of Saint-Eustache formed the confraternity of Saint-André. Its members wore garlands of roses. Their purpose was to butcher the prisoners who were behind lock and key in the several prisons of Paris. With the shout of "Kill the Armagnac dogs!" the brotherhood, followed and assisted by their women and children, burst open the prison gates. Great carnage took place inside. They murdered the Armagnac prisoners in the prisons of Saint-Eloy, For l'Evêque, Saint-Magloire, Saint-Martin-des-Champs and the Temple. They were a tough lot, the good humoured people of the Halles.

The Provost of Paris tried to stop the slaughter, but they answered him, "In spite of your justice, sir, your pity and your motives, God curse all who feel for those false Armagnac traitors." They were as good as their words. In less then twelve hours, five hundred and eighteen prisoners were killed, among them five bishops, several magistrates, Chancellor de Marle and the Constable of Armagnac, for whom they made an armband out of his own skin.

The address of the Church of Saint-Eustache is 2 rue du Jour. This is a short street of wholesale butchers, and the gutters often flow with blood, though nowadays only for a legitimate reason. In the old days it skirted the Enceinte of Philippe-Auguste and was named rue Raoul Raisolle.

The Place du Pillori du Roi was in the centre of the Carreau de la Halle, as the Halles Centrales were known until 1775. From the thirteenth century onwards, butter, cheese and bread, laid out on straw, were sold in the Carreau. Fish was laid on wooden boards, hence the fishmarket was known as Parquets.

The Royal Executioner, who lived in the House of the Pillory, received—indeed, collected in person—the revenues for the booths and sites of the Carreau. Followed by his lackeys, he took the rent from every vendor, and as each stallholder paid, a lackey marked the back of his smock with a chalk, the colour of which was changed every day.

Between the pillory and the gibbet stood a high stone cross, beside which bankrupts and debtors received their green bonnets from the executioner. The pillory, which was inside a one-storey-high tower with casement windows, consisted of a wooden post and frame, fixed on a platform raised several feet from the ground. In the centre of the platform was placed an iron wheel full of holes, into which were pushed the heads of the "patients" who on market days spent three hours there for the edification of the populace. Every half hour the wheel turned, and the patients, of course, with it. The practice was abolished by Louis XVI.

The first pillory was built in the thirteenth century. The gibbet was often in use. Even an executioner perished on it. In 1418, Capeluche, Royal Executioner who had struck the Duc de Bourgogne, a Child of France, was hanged in the Place du Pillori; he himself explained to his late assistant how to set about his task.

On April 1, 1516, Fleurant, another executioner, beheaded a condemned man rather clumsily, having several times to strike his blows. The awful sufferings of the victim caused indignation among the onlookers, who started stoning the executioner. The petrified man rushed down into the cave under the pillory, to which the populace set fire, burning him to death. A new pillory had to be erected.

Jean Montagu, Superintendent of Finance to Charles V and Charles VI, was beheaded in the Halles on October 17, 1409, and his body hanged at Montfaucon, a locality between La Villette and the Buttes-Chaumont, then outside Paris, famous for its gibbet erected in the thirteenth century. On November 12, 1411, were executed Colinet de Pirex and his six accomplices for having let the Armagnacs cross the bridge at Saint-Cloud which they should have defended. Five of the traitors were beheaded, the sixth hanged;

Pirex himself was drawn and quartered, and what was left of him hung from the gallows. The heads of the accomplices were exposed on spikes in six different places in the Halles.

The most spectacular execution was that of Jacques d'Armagnac, Duc de Nemours, which took place on August 4, 1477. He had been judged by Parliament for lese-majesty to Louis XI, who was not a man with whom to trifle. Nemours awaited the day of his execution in an iron cage in the Bastille. The preparations took eight days and a large crowd camped out in the Halles so as not to miss the entertainment. On August 4 the heat was intense. Taken from the iron cage, Nemours was hoisted on a horse caparisoned in black, then led to the Halles. The fishmarket was hung with black cloth. It had been scrubbed with vinegar to remove the smell of fish. There Nemours made his confession, while a meal of wine, white bread and pears was served to the officers of the King and the gentlemen of Parliament. After Nemours had received absolution, he was led to the gibbet and beheaded. By order of Louis XI, Nemour's two young sons were tied to the scaffold so as to be the first to receive their father's blood.

With lighted torches, one hundred and fifty Cordeliers (Franciscans) approached the gallows, and the bleeding remains were put into a coffin. Then chanting De Profundis, they carried the coffin to their church on the Left Bank (now 15-21 rue de l'Ecole de Médicine). The unfortunate sons were led back to the Bastille where they were fustigated once a week and had a tooth torn out once a month. One went mad and died in prison; the other was released and later killed in some obscure battle.

The people of the Halles loved their church, but also their amusements. Their Sunday entertainment was going to the Théâtre de l'Hôtel de Bourgogne in the rue Mauconseil, which they rightly regarded as their theatre since it was in their district. Vespers in Saint-Eustache had to end at three o'clock to give them time to walk to the theatre. That tradition dates back to the end of the sixteenth century when Jean du Pourtalais, an actor of the Hôtel de Bourgogne, beat the drum announcing the play too near the church walls. The priest objected. The following Sunday the actor behaved even more rashly, beating the drum during the sermon. Annoyed at the disturbance, the priest raised his voice; the drum beat louder and the congregation lost interest in the sermon. The priest sallied out and said to Pourtalais, "How dare you drum while I preach?"

"Who authorised you to preach after the play has begun?" Pourtalais riposted.

The congregation left the church and gathered round, enjoying every second of the argument. When it became heated, the priest drew a knife with which he split the drum. He turned back to continue the sermon. The actor ran after him and pushed the drum over his head. Retaining his dignity, the priest entered the church and told a deacon to free him. Then he looked round. Not one member of the congregation was left: they were all at the theatre. Next Sunday, services finished at three sharp, and thereafter no drum beat outside Saint-Eustache before the end of vespers.

The best loved priest of Saint-Eustache was called Merlin, who before his death called the fishwives to his sickbed and recommended his nephew, who was also a priest, as his successor. The Archbishop of Paris designated another priest for the position, which so enraged the people that they stopped him from entering the Halles. This happened during the reign of Louis XIII, whose Queen was Anne of Austria. Soldiers were sent to escort the new priest into the church, but the public resisted, and since the parishioners were known for their temper, the soldiers withdrew. (The Halles were always treated with leniency in the days of the Kings.) The parishioners had won, but they had no priest.

The fishwives of the Halles had their own corporation, and were officially known as the Dames des Halles. Vulgarly, they were called poissardes. They did not enjoy a good reputation; they were noisy, foul-mouthed, jealous of their privileges, and not loath to fight. The police often had to warn them. A police ordinance dated August 22, 1738, threatened them with large fines and prison if they continued insulting the passersby. The Ladies of the Halles took no notice. They were privileged to go in a body to congratulate the King, the Queen and the royal Princes, and to present the monarch with a bunch of flowers when a Child of France was born, or on the occasion of a royal marriage or a victory; also on New Year's Day, when they were served with a huge dinner, presided over by a Court official who gave them a money present in the King's name. When Saint-Eustache found itself without a priest, they decided to put their case before Anne of Austria.

When those hefty women came into the august presence, one of them said in a loud, excited voice, "Our good priest Merlin named his nephew as his successor. In any case, the Merlins have always been the parish priests of Saint-Eustache, son following in the father's footsteps." The Queen laughed, then referred them to the Archbishop, who did not give in until the population of the Halles was on the point of revolt. Thus was the nephew appointed parish priest.

Nowadays, on New Year's Day, the Dames des Halles bring their bunch of flowers to the President of the Republic and are duly photographed for the press.

The shop at 2 rue Sauval, known as the Pavillon des Singes, belonged to Jean Poquelin, Upholsterer to the King. Above the shop on January 15, 1633, was born his son Jean-Baptiste. Eleven years later the upholsterer bought another house at the corner of the rue des Petits Piliers, which disappeared when the new pavilions were constructed in the last century, and the rue Jean-Gilles (today rue de la Réale), where he moved with his family. His son, though hereditary Upholsterer to the King, did not follow in his father's footsteps, but went on the stage, taking the name of Molière. Yet he was buried as Jean-Baptiste Poquelin.

Molière died on February 17, 1673, his last performance being in *Le Malade imaginaire*. Because of their immoral profession, actors were not buried in consecrated ground; none the less Molière received the sacrament of Extreme Unction. Two nuns from Annecy were staying, guests of the actor, his wife and their daughter, in his house at 40 rue de Richelieu. The Archbishop of Paris, François de Harlay de Champvallon, did not know how best to act. Molière headed the King's troupe of players, and the King had admiration and affection for him, yet an actor remained excommunicated even in death. The parish priest of Saint-Eustache refused to have the funeral service in his church, though Molière had been one of his parishioners. In vain the Abbé Benjamin, Molière's confessor, declared that he had died a good Christian. The priest remained adamant and the Archbishop did not force the issue.

Armande, Molière's wife, Michel Baron, Molière's pupil, and the Abbé Benjamin went to Versailles to see Louis XIV, who was well acquainted with Saint-Eustache, where he had made his first communion. The argument they put to the King was that the parish priest of Saint-Eustache was denying justice to Jean-Baptiste Poquelin, Upholsterer-Valet to His Majesty, therefore a Crown official. In short, the priest was showing lack of respect for the King. Louis XIV "recommended" to the Archbishop that Molière be given a Christian burial.

"We have," the Archbishop notified the priest of Saint-Eustache, "given permission for the late Molière to be buried according to Christian rites in the cemetery of his parish, on condition that it should be without pomp, with only two priests and not during daylight. No solemn religious service is to be permitted in the parish or anywhere else."

Molière was buried on the night of Tuesday, February 21. An immense crowd assembled in front of the house in the rue de Richelieu, which frightened Armande, who, on the advice of her friends, threw a hundred gold coins through the window, begging the people to pray for the soul of her husband. She spoke in so touching a voice that the cortège was able to move off in respectful silence. The coffin was accompanied by a hundred torch-bearers.

As the procession reached the Halles, an onlooker enquired who was being buried. "Molière," a fishwife replied.

"Monsieur Molière to you," shouted one of her colleagues from her window.

In the year 1684 Paris was full of strange rumours. Within four months twenty-six young men between the ages of seventeen and twenty-five had disappeared. Gossip had it that they had been killed by assassins in the pay of some foreign princess who, on her doctor's recommendation, took a bath of blood every day to help cure the liver ailment from which she suffered. The story reached the ears of Louis XIV who spoke to de La Reynie, his police lieutenant, who in turn put one of his agents called Lecoq on the case. Lecoq had a smart son, a broad-shouldered, intelligent fellow of the right age. Father decided to use his son as the bait. L'Eveillé, as the son was nicknamed, was dressed up as a rich young man; he had a gold chain round his hat, and two gold watches protruded from the pockets of his silk breeches.

L'Eveillé strolled along the streets, the quays, and visited the gardens of the Tuileries and Luxembourg. On the fifth day he saw a remarkably pretty girl, accompanied by an old woman, in the Tuileries. They entered into conversation, then the duegna took him apart and told him in a whisper that the girl was the illegitimate daughter of a Polish prince and a milliner of the rue Saint-Denis. The prince had been murdered by brigands during a journey to Poland, and the girl had inherited all his substantial worldly goods. The old woman suggested that L'Eveillé should marry her.

The young man said he was the son of a rich physician and it was arranged that he should meet the old woman that same night after dark outside the church of Saint-Germain-l'Auxerrois, when she would introduce him to the girl's mother. In fact, she took him to the rue Courtalon in the Halles. There was no mother, only the girl, who received him in "deshabillé galant". She was such a lovely sight that he forgot all about his mission. His father and his men were outside the house, awaiting his signal. The son was too busy cuddling and kissing.

The princess left the room, promising to return. L'Eveillé was intrigued by a screen, which he tried to move but which seemed to be nailed to the floor. He shook it hard, and it collapsed, revealing a wardrobe which he threw open. There on twenty-six silver salvers lay twenty-six human heads. Worried by the silence in the house, the father and his men burst in; and just in time, for the girl had reappeared, accompanied by six armed bandits. The policemen swiftly disarmed them.

The girl belonged to a business association run by a rich English-woman, who was never caught. Young men were enticed to the house and killed. Their heads were cut off, and sent, dried and embalmed, to Germany, where they were used for the study of phrenology. The bodies were sold to medical students in Paris.

The so-called princess, the duegna and their henchmen were sentenced to death and hanged.

The Halles wake up when others sleep. The maraîchers (market gardeners) in their huge two-wheeled carts used to be the first to arrive; the meat porters began work soon after midnight; and all the odd hands needed by the Belly of Paris were hired long before day-break. It has always been the custom of the Halles for goods and work to be paid for on the spot and in cash, so there was plenty of ready money. Already in the Middle Ages, the Halles were famous for their cheap eating places, open all night. They drew the reveller, the crook, the deserter, the escaped convict and all who preferred dark-ness to light. Prostitutes were part and parcel of the way of life. The night was theirs. Those in the Halles were the cheapest in Paris. Some of them would give themselves for even a plate of soup and boiled beef. (The tradition of the low sums paid to prostitutes in the Halles has not died out. A streetwalker, say, of the Madeleine district, who there would accept nothing under 60 francs, drops her price to one-third if she goes to the Halles to add a little more to her earnings.)

A porter received a tip every time he delivered meat, and it was by no means rare to spend part of it on a woman between errands. In that noise, bustle and gaiety, the prostitute felt at home. Besides, if business were bad she could pick up vegetables fallen from a basket or a bit of offal dropped from a panier. At dawn the prostitutes withdrew, for at dawn came the Dames des Halles to open their stalls and booths. The fishwives were warm-hearted, willing, generous women, always ready for a temporary husband or lover. The prostitutes would have had little chance with them around.

Restif de La Bretonne liked strolling in the Halles—naturally at night. That assiduous chronicler of Paris-at-night was drawn by all he deplored. He was horrified by the debauchery in the Halles; therefore he could not keep away. He shuddered at the sight of men smoking or sleeping in corners, of fallen girls hobnobbing with cardsharps and billiard players. There were fights, and insults rent the air.

One dark night he caught sight of a fair-haired girl, practically the prisoner of an old bawd trying to ply her with eau-de-vie. The girl refused, the bawd insisted. "You both come with me," Restif addressed them sternly, and taking the girl by the hand, he led her out of the Halles. Following hard on their heels, the bawd suggested that he take the girl for himself, but he was too pure a man for that. They crossed over to the Left Bank, where lived the Marquise. (This good lady whose name was never divulged spent her time saving the fallen women whom he brought her. She was probably a figment of his vivid imagination.) The Marquise, having just finished writing a letter, appeared on the balcony. Restif made the usual sign, the door was opened, and the girl was ushered in. Immediately, a bed was made for her, a proof that the Marquise had taken her under her protection. Meanwhile the bawd was still waiting outside in the street.

"Fly," said Restif when he reappeared, "or the Marquise who lives here will have you arrested."

The bawd fled.

On another occasion he saw the Night Watch arresting a woman, who was young and good looking. A crowd surrounded them, and Restif felt pity for her. "I am an honest woman," she protested. "Anyone can check on that. I will give my name and address."

The unfortunate woman was sobbing loudly. Restif, however, knew how to treat the Watch. He was probably himself a police spy. "Gentlemen, I know this lady and will accompany her home," he said. The Watch withdrew. "Why did they arrest you?" Restif asked, walking beside her.

She was, she explained, a married woman. An unpleasant and ugly man had fallen in love with her and, because she scorned him, the man became angry and decided to avenge himself. She had been on business to the Palais Royal, and had run into him as she was crossing the Halles on her way home to the Faubourg Saint-Antoine. He followed her until they met the Watch, when he shouted for all to hear, "Mon Dieu! Here is the Watch! Run!" She stood her ground, however, and the man denounced her to the Corporal of the Watch, saying she had attacked and wanted to rob him. He had then disappeared in the crowd. Restif formed the conclusion that she was an adventuress, but none the less took her home. She lived near the church of Saint-Paul. She told her husband a similar story, though this time she turned the ugly man into a complete stranger whom she had never seen before. She whispered into Restif's ear that it was preferable thus to describe him to her husband.

When Restif left, he found the man himself waiting for him in the street. The man said terrible things about the woman. Restif called him a liar and a calumniator, addressing him from such moral height that the man had no answer. Restif returned to the house, where the woman was now alone, and begged her to tell the truth. She swore that she had already done so.

"You tried to seduce the woman," he said to the man, who was still outside. "If you dare to molest her again, I will speak to her husband."

The man drew his knife.

"You have been judged," Restif said. "Look out, calumniator."
Never again was the man seen in the neighbourhood.

One night in the 1750s the Duc de Foix, the Duc de La Ferté
and Monsieur de Camardon were in a place of debauch in the
Halles. Monsieur de Camardon suggested to the Duc de La Ferté
that he should bring his wife to the Halles to have a look at the
brothel of either Louise Darquin or Madelon Dupré, both of whom
had a high reputation in whoring circles. The Duc de La Ferté did
not find the proposition acceptable, in fact considered it in bad
taste. His wife, he said, was not the woman to visit places like that.
Camardon replied that not only the Duchesse de La Ferté but also
the Duchesse de Foix would come to one of the brothels. He was
willing to bet 100 pistoles. The bet was accepted.

Five days later Camardon went to see the Duchesse de Foix, who
was his sister, to tell her that he had arranged to take Madame de
La Ferté to the fair of Saint-Germain, but not a word would be said
to her husband. Would his sister join him on the same condition?
She agreed, and Camardon set out in a carriage with the two ladies.
In the Halles a wheel broke. Camardon offered to take them to the
house of a decent bourgeoise with whom he was well acquainted,
while they waited for another carriage. He took the duchesses into
a clean, well-furnished suite of rooms where they were received by
a dignified lady. By messenger Camardon sent a letter to the ducal
husbands, asking them to come to the brothel of Madelon Dupré
where there were new girls, each one a fresh discovery.

The husbands arrived post haste and nearly collapsed when they
saw their wives being entertained by the Dupré. The wives themselves became furious when their outraged husbands explained
where they were. Camardon, however, soothed their feelings when
he explained why he had taken them there. He beckoned to the
Dupré, who at once had an excellent dinner served. Camardon had
attended to that detail too.

The duchesses began to enjoy themselves and, after the meal, asked to be shown the girls. The Dupré called them in one by one, and made each walk past the table, displaying her charms; some of them even paraded again at the request of the husbands, who were laughingly scolded by their wives. Before they left, the duchesses congratulated the Dupré on her taste, and for the rest of their lives boasted of the pleasant day they had spent in a brothel.

In the early part of the reign of Louis XV, a market gardener from Orleans introduced red cabbage to the Halles. Nobody seemed to want it. People then were as conservative in their habits as they are today. A cabbage was green and not red. All their lives they had eaten green cabbage, and they would not change their habits just because a maraîcher from Orleans had the stupid idea of growing that red stuff. However, the Orléanais had a genius for publicity. He awaited the right moment.

His opportunity came in 1721 when the old Duchesse d'Orléans, widow of Monsieur, Louis XIV's brother, died. On the next Sunday, as the ladies of society arrived at the still not completely finished church of Saint-Sulpice (begun in 1646, façade finished only in 1745), a lackey in black approached them, handing each a sealed envelope and announcing in a mournful voice, "Her Royal Highness the Duchesse d'Orléans died last night. With her last breath she charged me to hand a letter to each of her friends who comes today to Saint-Sulpice."

There was one lady who could not resist looking at the letter during Mass. On her knees, she tore it open, and with bowed head surreptitiously read the contents.

"Tender friend," the letter said, "I cannot render a better and more valuable service than to leave you my favourite recipe on how to use red cabbage in cooking.

"Cook a medium sized red cabbage in four pints of bouillon with two slices of cooking apple and an onion stuck with clove, and add two glasses of good red wine. Sprinkle generously with spices and let it simmer for several hours."

The letter was signed, "Charlotte Elizabeth of Bavaria, Duchesse d'Orléans."

The lady tittered, for it was the sort of last gift that one might expect from a German princess. The other ladies could resist no longer, and read their letters too. They were identical. Of course, there was no lackey in black at the door when they came out.

The "Chou rouge à la d'Orléans" made the maraîcher's fortune. The story reached Versailles, the King tasted the red cabbage and grew to like it, and it was to become one of Madame de Pompadour's favourite dishes, which she often prepared herself for the King.

II

The Halles II

The Church of the Innocents was built in the twelfth century, and though it was demolished in 1786, the church and the adjoining cemetery, which was condemned at the same time, remain the symbol of Paris of the Middle Ages. Their memory seems to lift one back into the dark alleyways that twisted round the church, the cemetery, the charnel house and the arcades, and to conjure up a picture of Death leading the way in a Danse Macabre to the grave, kicking his legs with equal gusto whether his partner was mighty or poor.

The fifteen arcades on the site of numbers 1, 3, 5, 7 and 9 of the rue de la Ferronerie were painted in their whole length with frescoes representing the Danse Macabre. They were known as the Arcades des Charniers. The first charnel house was built in the fourteenth century. It was several times rebuilt, the last occasion being when the rue de la Ferronerie was reconstructed around 1668.

There were fifteen frescoes, seventeen with the introduction and the conclusion, and each contained two groups, each group consisting of two figures, one of them invariably Death with his grinning skull. Death was in animated conversation with thirty living creatures: in the first with the Pope, in the second with the

Emperor, in the next with the Cardinal, then the King, the Patriarch, the Constable, the Archbishop, the Knight, the Bishop, the Squire, the Abbé, the Magistrate, the Schoolmaster, the Burgher, the Canon, the Merchant, the Carthusian, the Sergeant, the Monk, the Usurer, the Physician, the Lover, the Lawyer, the Minstrel, the Parish Priest, the Labourer, the Cobbler, the Child, the Clerk, and finally the Hermit. Under each picture were verses containing the dialogue between Death and the living person. The verses were by Jean Gerson, Chancellor of the University of Paris. The frescoes were painted in vivid colours.

Paradoxically, the cemetery was the hub of life in the Halles. People on their way to the Carreau stopped with their beasts, lovers met beside the tombs, and, in spite of the putrid smell, fashionable folk took their evening stroll within the high walls that Philippe-Auguste had thrown round the churchyard.

Not only the parishioners of the Holy Innocents but also those of the adjoining parishes were buried in the cemetery. Most churches dumped their dead there. The dead belonged mostly to the poorer orders. From the sixth century onwards, the privileged classes were buried in their own parish churches, or in the chapels of abbeys, priories, convents, colleges, seminaries and hospitals. The Cemetery of the Innocents in general catered for those who were thrown into the fosses communes, the paupers' graves, each grave, shaped like a long trench, remaining open until it was full. The pestilential stench can be imagined. It was said, in praise of the cemetery, that its earth was of such excellence that it devoured a corpse in nine days. There were those who maintained that it took only twenty-four hours. Louis de Beaumont, Bishop of Paris, who died in 1492, insisted in his will that earth from the Cemetery of the Innocents be placed in his coffin.

The fosses communes were about sixteen to twenty feet deep. The dead lay in them, covered in shrouds. They could not afford coffins. When the trenches were full, earth was shovelled on the bodies and when the bones had been eaten dry they were taken to the charnel house. The galleries and cloisters all served the same purpose. The empty ditches were filled in, then new paupers' graves were dug. And so it went on. Each patch was either part of a grave or would soon become so. In winter the criminals and ruffians of the cours des miracles (thieves' kitchens) used to warm themselves by burning bones in the cemetery. As if emphasis were needed, a marble skeleton sculptured by Germain Pilon stood in the middle of the cemetery. Neither bones nor stench deterred the crowds. Haberdashers had booths under the arcades; public letter-writers sat on the tombs, waiting for customers; and prostitutes hung around for the same reason. The bereaved, after all, needed consolation.

Women who wanted to retire from the world often took up their abode in the cells of the Church of the Innocents. Each cell was walled up after the recluse had entered, leaving only a small aperture through which she could contemplate either the church or the cemetery, depending on the site of her cell. Once a day a few crumbs were pushed in through the hole. Once in, you stayed for life. Alix la Bourgotte, a nun of the Hospital of Sainte-Catherine entered a cell of the Innocents in 1420 in which she died forty-six years later. Louis XI paid for her tombstone in the cemetery, and the epitaph ended with:

> Elle trépassa céans en son séjour
> Le dimanche vingt-neuviesme jour,
> Mois de juin, mil quatre cent soixante et six.
> Le doux Jésus la mette en Paradis.

The record goes, however, to Agnès du Rochier, daughter of a rich Paris merchant who, in 1403, was walled up in a cell of the Church of Sainte-Opportune nearby in the Place Sainte-Opportune. (The Church was demolished in 1790.) She remained thus entombed from the age of eighteen to her death at the ripe age of ninety-eight.

Not all who were walled up chose that existence because of their devoutness. Renée de Vendômois, who in the reign of Charles VIII married the Seigneur de Souidai, fell in love with one of the

King's archers whom she loved with such fierce passion that she had her husband murdered. Parliament condemned her to death but Anne de Beaujeu, the King's sister and Regent of France, changed the punishment to perpetual reclusion in a cell of the Innocents, where she remained until her death.

"In the name of Our Lord and the Blessed Virgin, let me speak with you!" cried a man from the cemetery as Henri IV rode past in his coach. The man was François Ravaillac who had several times tried to have speech with his King.

Ravaillac was the son of humble parents. Born at Angoulême in 1578, he was as a child already drawn to religion, and was happier in church than in his father's cottage. He wanted to become a priest but his parents' resources were inadequate; they lived mostly on the alms of the neighbours. The son had to earn his living. He started as a valet de chambre, in time he managed to set up as a petty provincial solicitor, "solliciteur de procès", and he also taught children to read and write. He was thrown into prison by creditors. He had visions in his cell, and when he came out he sought to join the Society of Jesus, but was rejected. He took to writing madrigals and sonnets.

Slowly, he reached the conclusion that it was his destiny to save the Pope from the convert from Navarre who now ruled France and who sooner or later was bound to declare war on His Holiness. He, poor François Ravaillac, was sent by Heaven to enact the part of the Church's principal champion and protector. He made no secret of his views and spoke of them to all and sundry. He went to Paris with the half-formed intention to kill Henri IV. But, by temperament, he was no murderer. He appeared in the Louvre and asked to be admitted into the King's presence. His request was refused; he insisted, and was thrown out. He came back, and the Marquis de La Force ordered that the strange, uncouth fellow should under no condition be admitted. The King was within earshot and said to the Marquis, "Do not treat him badly." Ravaillac left, ready to return to Angoulême, but in a tavern in the Halles he had over-heard some priests and soldiers discussing the King. They had, quite wrongly in fact, thought that his conversion was only skin-deep and that he might one day turn against the Pope. In Angoulême Ravaillac remembered that conversation and decided that it was his duty to return to Paris to save the Pope from the King.

The angel of revenge arrived in Paris unarmed, but when he was refused a room at the inn of the Cinq-Croissants in the vicinity of the Hospital of the Quinze-Vingt near the Porte Saint-Honoré, he picked up a knife from a table and hid it on his person. He hung around the Cemetery of the Innocents, called to the King when he drove by and made other efforts to see him. What he really wanted was to explain to him that he was misguided, that he should repent and leave the Pope alone. As he found no opportunity to speak to the King, he decided once again to leave. He took the road to Angoulême. (All his journeys were made on foot.) When he reached Etampes, he stopped before a Crucifix at the entrance of the town. The Crucifix spoke to him and told him that he was shirking his duty. So Ravaillac turned round and retraced his steps to Paris.

There had already been fifteen attempts on the life of Henri IV. In spite of his vitality and laughter, he had the presentiment that he would die by the hand of an assassin. Foreboding lay heavily on him on the morning of May 14, 1610. Sully, his minister, was ill. He desired to see Sully, yet he could not bring himself to leave the Louvre.

"You must not go," the Queen (Marie de Medici) begged him. None the less he set out for the Arsenal to visit Sully. "I have much to tell him," was the reason he gave.

Ravaillac, who had spent the night at the Inn of the Trois-Pigeons at the corner of the rue Saint-Honoré and the cul-de-sac Saint-Vincent (now rue Saint-Roch), was already roaming the Halles.

The royal carriage was an open one with its floor so near the ground that nobody could have crawled under it. Above it, sup-ported by eight pillars, was a canopy. The curtains were thrown outside the carriage and almost brushed the ground as it bumped along. The Duc d'Espernon sat on the King's left, in front of him by the doors were the Duc de Montbazon and the Comte de Roquelaure, next the Marquis de La Force, the Maréchal de Lavardin, Monsieur de Liancourt, the Marquis de Mirebeau and finally the principal squire. Thus the carriage was pretty full. The King had his arm around the shoulder of the Duc d'Espernon. The coachman asked the King which way he wanted to go to the Arsenal.

"Go past the Cross of Trahoir," replied the King, "then through the streets of l'Oratoire, Saint-Honoré and de la Ferronerie."

The carriage arrived at the end of the rue Saint-Honoré and turned into the rue de la Ferronerie, where it had, however, to stop because of a cart loaded with straw which had broken down and which almost took up the width of the street in front of the cabaret known as the Salamandre. One of the two footmen who walked beside the coach had dropped behind to tie his garter. The King was reading a letter from the Comte de Soissons which Espernon had handed him. Trying to pass the cart, the coachman drew close to the shops which were tenanted by ironmongers. Before one of the shops (now 8 rue de la Ferronerie), which had for its sign a crowned heart pierced with an arrow, was a mounting-block, and from it jumped Ravaillac, who, with the stolen knife, struck the King between the armpit and the left breast. Then he struck again, this time the knife reaching the King's heart. The Duc de Montbazon clasped him in his arms. "Sire, what is it?"

"It is nothing," said the King. "It is nothing," he repeated, almost inaudibly.

France lost a great king and Ravaillac was executed a fortnight later.

Louis-Sébastien Mercier, the author of *Tableau de Paris* and many other works, often repaired to the Cemetery of the Innocents. Mercier evokes Paris of the second half of the eighteenth century with the same force as does Restif de La Bretonne, but while Restif speaks mostly of himself, Mercier sees only Paris. He writes with such detachment of his native city that one imagines him as a foreign visitor, preferably a Swiss, glaring at Paris from the outside, uninfluenced by any affection.

The public letter-writers of the Charniers, he says, had to lead the lives of theologians, though they were more useful because they were the keepers of the tender secrets of the servant girls whose declarations of love they put to paper. Theirs was no easy life. In winter they blew on their frozen fingers; in summer they sweated under their bob-wigs, and were surrounded by the evil smell and the bones of the dead. They had to provide ink, paper, wax, grammar, syntax and style, all for 5 sous. A petition to the King or the Ministers cost 12 sous, for the style had to be more distinguished than in a letter, say, to a shepherd in a distant village, who in any case would need the help of the local priest to find out what his loved one's heart was murmuring.

The public letter-writers, Mercier observed, were the Ministers' most diligent correspondents. He saw no handwriting but theirs on a Minister's writing table. At the beginning of the reign of Louis XVI, the ordinary people thought they had a king after their heart (they were not far wrong), so petitions were sent by the thousands. When the course of events estranged the King from his people, the public letter-writers of the Charniers, who during the boom had bought new bob-wigs, now found their stalls deserted by petitioners. They turned back to the love-sick servant girls whom they had neglected while the going was good.

Mercier, watching the scribes at work in the stench of the cemetery and the charnel house, was fascinated by the servant girls treading their way through putrid bones, past gaping graves with rotting bodies, to whisper to the writers their declarations of love.

The inhabitants of the Halles had clamoured for over two centuries to have the Cemetery of the Innocents closed. A decree of the Parliament of Paris, dated January 1, 1766, forbade burials inside the town, but this stopped nobody from dumping their dead in the

Cemetery of the Innocents. However, in the year 1785 a house-holder in the rue de la Lingerie went into his cellar, where he found rats devouring a corpse. He turned on his heels, wanting to get away from the stench as quickly as possible. A rat bit him as he escaped, and the unfortunate man died within two days. When the police arrived, they filled their nostrils with scented cotton wool before venturing into the cellar. The foundations of the building had given way under the impact of the loose earth of the cemetery, which, because of the continuous digging, had moved as if shifted by a minor earthquake. Among the foundation stones a number of corpses was found in the company of regiments of rats. In short, the dead had moved back with the earth into human dwellings. The Council of State condemned the church and the cemetery, and that, one might say, put the final stop to the Paris of François Villon.

In January 1786, the demolition of the church began. The bones of the dead were taken to the quarry of Montsouris beyond the Barrier of Saint-Jacques, and were inhumed on the Left Bank beside a house known as la Maison de la Tombe-Issoire. The galleries of the Charniers were turned into shops, the soil of the cemetery was carted away and the ground filled with fresh earth. It became the Market of the Innocents (of the Charniers only two arcades remain, 11-13 rue des Innocents) and to the Square des Innocents the Fountain of Pierre Lescot and Jean Goujon was transferred from the corner of the rues aux Fers (now rue Berger) and Saint-Denis.

A gentleman called John Scott, who was to write a book entitled *Picturesque Views of Paris* with drawings by Frederic Nash, visited the Market of the Innocents in 1818. "It is here that the costume and manners of the lower orders of Paris, the gaieties and gallantries of porters, footmen, cook-maids and market girls may be con-templated." He admired the fountain in the middle of the Square des Innocents because "of that want of superfluous ornament which often distinguishes the French school".

The fountain was erected in 1551 according to the designs of Pierre Lescot and Jean Goujon. It is supposed to have replaced an ancient one of the thirteenth century, mentioned in an old agreement between Philippe le Hardi and the Chapter of Saint-Merri. The fountain originally had only three arcades, but when it was moved into the Market, Augustin Pajou was employed to execute a fourth, and "its great merit is proved by the impossibility of distinguishing which of the four is the supplement." The lions and basin were added after the move, and "are not so much esteemed as the other parts of the monument; the water by which the fountain is fed, and falls finely down the slope of the steps, comes from the Canal de l'Ourcq." Goujon had placed a naiad: Pajou added three of his own. "The Lions assist the cascade by vomiting from their open mouths torrents of the foaming liquid." The fountain is still in the Square des Innocents, as also is an arch of the cemetery: the first, a comparative newcomer; the second, one that was left behind.

The Church of Saint-Merri in the rue Saint-Martin belongs also to the district of the Halles. It escaped the fate of the Church of the Innocents because its cemetery was suppressed in 1520, the parishioners being buried thereafter in the Cemetery of the Innocents.

In 1832 a barricade was erected in front of Saint-Merri, a few yards from the intersection of the rues Saint-Martin and Aubry-le-Boucher. The red flag floated on the barricade and Maréchal Soult mobilised the garrison of Paris and the Garde Nationale to restore order. The revolutionaries were not many in number, and the rising lasted only from June 5 to 6. June 5 was the day of the burial of the popular General Lamarque, who died from cholera, his last gesture being to kiss the sword given to him by the Bonapartist officers of the Hundred Days. That apparently was as good an excuse as any to rise against King Louis-Philippe. The rising was swiftly put down by the troops, and only the barricade of Saint-Merri still held out on June 6. An old hand of the July Revolution, whose surname was Jeanne, led the men and threw back ten assaults by the military. Shots were fired from windows and from behind doors. The bells of Saint-Merri tolled the whole day long. At six in the evening the troops attacked from three different directions. Jeanne and his men tried to force their way through the attackers, but most of them were bayonetted to death. For decades the district bore marks of the fighting.

The parents of Georges Cain, the curator of the Musée de Carnavalet from 1897 to 1918 who wrote delightful books on Paris, had known an old lady who lived near Saint-Merri. She trembled with fear whenever she went past the door of the tenant who lived on the ground floor of her house. Her friends could not understand her persistent fear, and Cain's parents asked for the reason. Many decades before, her husband had fought with the Garde Nationale on that famous June 6, while she, hearing the firing, was at home waiting for him in anguish. Suddenly a man on a stretcher was brought into the house. She rushed downstairs. The wounded warrior was covered with a blanket which she lifted, expecting the worst. It was the ground-floor tenant, wounded in the jaw.

"Oh, what joy," she cried, "that it's only you, Monsieur Vitry." He never forgave her.

The porters of the Halles, known as Les Forts and also as the seven hundred muscular fellows, belong to a corporation that depends directly on the Préfécture de Police. Each fort has his number and each team its chief. Their fame and the respect that their presence inspires are even greater than those of the Dames des Halles. Their number was usually seven hundred and thirty-five, a hundred and six dedicated to butcher's meat, a hundred to poultry, a hundred and ninety-one to butter, eggs and cheese, fifty-four to fruit and vegetables and a hundred and eighty to fish. The remaining hundred and four were inside the pavilions. (Average figures for the 1920s.) Every fort carries a medal on which is engraved the coat of arms of Paris.

They have always been famous for the pride they take in their work, their good humour, huge appetite and loud laughter. One is struck by their bonhomie, which does not desert them while they carry the heavy carcases. The aprons of the meat porters run with blood, their necks have the muscles of an ox, and one cannot but feel that nothing pleases them more than lifting weights from which most people would shrink. Nowadays they too turn up at the Elysée on New Year's Day, wearing their large hats.

The forts, like all other workers of the Halles, radiate gaiety, and the visitor wonders why they are so conspicuously different from other manual workers, The forts, like the fishwives, have their own —in every sense valid—explanation. They deal with reality. The carcase of a sheep or a panier groaning with turbot exists as an entity. It is not just a cog in some great wheel. It stands on its own and you know what will become of it, whereas the workman in a factory has no connection with the final result. Moreover, the forts work in the open; they are paid after every errand; tips abound, and the eating places and bistrots are at their elbows. They are not herded together, there is no workbench, and each errand is personal to the man who runs it. When he lifts meat off the hook, or has it slung over his shoulder, he expands like a virtuoso waiting for applause.

The lorries are cleared of boxes, often faster than the commission agent expects, so that the tips are generous, and the forts rush off to the bistrots for a drink of muscadet. In this age of doctored wine, the innkeepers of the Halles would not dream of serving the sort of wine that is offered by some of the bars of the boulevards. Only the best will do for the people of the Halles.

In the rue Antoine-Carême used to gather the Hommes Sauvages, who sold herbs, foliage and fern. They were called the Wild Men because their merchandise came direct from suburban gardens, picked generally while the owners were still asleep or while they were absent from home. In this age of supervision and control, the

Hommes Sauvages have mainly disappeared, though there still remain the little old men who walk round the streets, clutching a small bunch of flowers or herbs which nobody seems to buy. As the hours pass, so the flowers wilt and the herbs turn sickly, yet they go on clinging to them until the Halles become deserted under the midday sun. Their bus or métro fare from the suburbs costs more than the money they ask for their withered goods.

The Hommes Sauvages may have gone, but a new, brisker trade has sprung up in the Halles: vendre à la sauvette. This form of trade is based on running away. The vendors, usually Algerians or Tunisians, turn up in the Halles a few minutes before the vegetable stands close, when the greengrocers practically give away their left-over wares. The vendors hire a handcart which they fill with their purchases and push uphill, generally in the direction of Montmartre. They are not of a retiring disposition, but stop in some busy market street, preferably in front of a greengrocer's, shouting their cut-throat prices, pushing cabbages or lettuces under the noses of house-wives on their way into the shop. Their price is a quarter of what they would pay in the shop, so trade is brisk and profitable until the irate greengrocer telephones the police. Since the police sirens and the flashing lights of the police cars warn them in time, they bolt, leaving behind the handcart which in any case carries the owner's name who, when notified by the police, will come and fetch it, only to hire it out under the same conditions the next day. It does not amuse the Paris police to confiscate vegetables: they would prefer to catch the vendors themselves, but they are landed as a rule only with the goods, and it is a piteous sight to watch the smart, white-gloved policemen picking up cabbages and cucumbers and, with a gesture of disgust, throwing them inside their vehicle for distribution to the hospitals.

Handcarts are not strictly necessary. You can hold in your arms as many vegetables as you can carry and accost the passersby on the pavement. On Sunday mornings in the rue Montorgeuil the police suddenly appear, and the vendors dash into the rue Etienne-Marcel. A North African, with a policeman hard on his heels, will slow down as he passes a possible customer, and whisper fiercely, "4 francs the lot."

Around the turn of the century, it was the practice of the gendarmes who had caught a deserter from the army to march him through the streets of the Halles before taking him to the military prison. When they reached the rue de la Ferronerie, one of the gendarmes would take the prisoner's cap and pass it round. The tradesmen, porters and fishwives would then fill it with coins, which the gendarme would give to the deserter. Often the poor soldier would burst into tears at the sight of such kindness.

Though deserters are no longer taken through the Halles, the habit of generosity has not died out. When a man comes out of prison and finds his way to the Halles, everybody, including the prostitutes, give him food, drink and money on the understanding that tomorrow he will look for work. If he returns the following night in the hope of being helped again, he will find all hearts and purses closed to him.

In 1810 Napoleon went to the Halles and walked round, contemplating the inadequate number of pavilions, the crowds, the carts jostling each other and the horses practically unable to progress. He turned to Bélanger, the architect of the new cupola of the Halle-au-blé. "I don't like this mess. The place lacks design. There is no discipline here. This market is not worthy of the capital of an empire." In February 1811 he signed a decree concerning the embellishment of Paris. Article thirty-six mentioned the Halles. A vast covered market was to be built, extending from the Market of the Innocents to the existing pavilions, which would be demolished. Nothing came of it. Under Napoleon III were constructed the pavilions that have survived to this day, but soon there were the same crowds, the same lack of design and discipline. Traffic jams became insufferable, long before the coming of the motor lorry. Napoleon's grandiose plan was finally shelved.

Since life is one half-measure after the other, nobody has adopted the Emperor's conception of the Halles. Had his plan been followed, the Halles would not have been condemned to extinction. For the Halles are going. The days of onion soup and chips are numbered, and while the authorities and the Municipal Council debate the future of the terrain, the bulldozers are waiting to erase eight hundred years of history, habits, customs, laughter, courage and gaiety. The meat market is moving to La Villette; fish, vegetables, cheese and fruit to Rungis, near Orly; many of the old houses will come down, bistrots and restaurants will close, and even the girls of the rue de Cygne, who for generations were famous for their large breasts, for only women with voluptuous shapes were accepted in the street, will have to look for a new beat. If you go today to the Halles and speak to the people and ask them what they intend to do after their world has vanished, they change the subject, and you feel as though you are enquiring after the health of a patient in a hospital for incurables.

III

Cabarets, Restaurants, Cafés and Brasseries

Paris has always been the gastronomic centre of France. There is no special kudos in that, for throughout the ages Paris has remained the El Dorado to which all provincials flocked, a French Klondyke. Naturally, since the provincials knew only the cooking of their own regions, they still prepared regional dishes when they cooked in the capital. Hence Paris benefited from the good dishes of the provinces; and as a result, you find in Paris every possible variety of French food. "Why," asks the Parisian, "should I travel when all the fine dishes of France are on my doorstep?" To travel from, say, Nantes to Dijon is expensive and takes time, whereas in Paris you can do that with two tickets d'autobus—culinarily speaking, of course.

In the beginning there were no restaurants. Meals were eaten in the cabarets and hôtelleries, which were taverns, eating houses and inns. The guests sat at the same tables (which were not yet called tables d'hôtes, a refinement that was to come much later). There also were the rôtisseurs, the cook-shops, where food was bought to be taken home.

In the rue de la Huchette, which is still with us in that beehive of old streets between the Quai Saint-Michel and the Boulevard

Saint-Germain, the rôtisseurs were already flourishing in the fourteenth century, though strictly speaking it was the street of the
apothecaries: their sign a lamprey. The rôtisseurs were more sought
after than the apothecaries. On his return to Italy, Father Bonaven-
tura Calatagirone, General of the Franciscans who was instrumental
in the signing of the Treaty of Vervins between Henri IV and
Philip II of Spain, spoke glowingly of the cook-shops in the rue
de la Huchette, the only marvels, he affirmed, that he had found
during his long journey. The Infidel's reactions were no different.
The Turks attached to the different Ottoman ambassadors found
nothing more agreeable than to go to the rue de la Huchette and
inhale the wonderful smells. It was in a cabaret of the rue de la
Huchette that the Abbé Prévost d'Exiles wrote *Manon Lescaut*.

The oldest cabaret one knows of was La Pomme de Pin, which
opened its doors around 1400 in the Cité on the spot where nowadays one of the pavilions of the Hôtel-Dieu stands, giving on to the
rue de la Cité and the rue de Lutèce. François Villon was a client,
but Villon was no ideal customer from the cabaretier's point of
view, as these lines show:

> C'est bien disné, quand on s'échappe
> Sans débourser pas un denier,
> Et dire adieu au tavernier
> En torchant son nez dans la nappe.

Rabelais also visited it. Boileau, Molière, Racine and La Fontaine
often met there. Edmond Beaurepaire described it as a joyous
academy, where even the greatest minds could not help getting
drunk at least twice a week.

When Guillaume Colletet, academician and poet, was hard up—
a frequent occurrence—he wrote flattering poems either to Cardinal
de Richelieu or some other powerful patron. One day he asked
Desbordes-Gruyn, proprietor of the Pomme de Pin, whether he
would give him credit on a poem he intended to write to the Cardinal.

"On condition you finish it tonight," the cabaret-keeper replied.

"If that's the only condition, then serve me at once with your best burgundy."

Colletet got to work and wrote a long and pious poem, entitled *Les Couches sacrées de la Vierge*, which on second thoughts he dedicated to Jean-François de Gondi, first Archbishop of Paris. The prelate was so impressed by the poem that he presented Colletet with a silver statuette of Apollo.

"It's silver all right," Colletet said to Desbordes-Gruyn, "but how can we turn it into the silver you pay with?"

The silver Apollo remained the inn sign till Desbordes-Gruyn's death. The Pomme de Pin survived into the eighteenth century.

A cabaret-keeper needed a certificate from his guild, the municipality and the King's Attorney. The guild had five holidays a year —Easter, Whitsun, Assumption, All Saints and Christmas—when the cabaret-keepers who sold only drink could remain open, but those who served food had to close. Some of the cabarets were outside the Walls like the Hôtel de Stockolm in the rue de Buci, where one dined for 18 sous (100 sous equalled 5 francs), and next door the Hôtellerie de l'Eau in the rue de Bourbon-le-Château, where the price was 20 sous. In the Mouton Blanc near the Cité, Molière, Racine, Boileau, La Fontaine, Lully, Mignard and Dufresnois used to gather, and at 10 rue Childebert (now rue Bonaparte) a wine merchant called Chamfort cooked meals for painters. Two fried eggs there cost 3 sous.

The cabarets, as later the cafés, were generally frequented by people of the same profession or trade. Men like Racine or Boileau would not have entered a cabaret where, for example, tailors drank. In the eighteenth century in the rue de Richelieu, one Charlotte Bourette kept the Café Minerve, patronised by men of letters. She was known as the Tenth Muse because she addressed in verse her literary customers, who replied in kind. One wonders what her verses were like when a glass was smashed or some distinguished man left without settling his bill.

Also in the rue de Richelieu was to be found the Taverne Anglaise, where for the first time in Paris roast beef was served with boiled vegetables. It was very expensive, for boiled potatoes and vegetables were considered a curiosity. Nearby in the Galerie Beaujolais of the Palais Royal at the restaurant called Les Trois Frères Provençaux, General Napoleon Bonaparte and Paul Vicomte de Barras were often present in the days after the Revolution. At the time of the Directoire in the Café Hardy, rue de la Grange-Batelière, déjeuners à la fourchette (cold collations) were served.

The first café in Paris and in the world was established by Procopio dei Coltelli, a Sicilian, in the year 1686 in the rue de l'Ancienne Comédie. The Café Procope is still in the same place, though it has become a restaurant. La Fontaine, Voltaire, Benjamin Franklin, Danton, Robespierre, Bonaparte, Balzac, Victor Hugo, Gambetta, Verlaine and Anatole France were among its clients.

Yet the old cabarets were slow to die, their strength the excellent wines they served. "Mon Dieu, how witty the French are," observed the Prince de Ligne to his companion Count de Poelnitz, as one night they were leaving a Paris cabaret.

"It isn't difficult with the wines they have," the Count answered.

The table d'hôtes was the forerunner of the restaurant, its heyday the second half of the reign of Louis XV. The customers all sat at the same table, and the latecomers were put at the bottom. The meek and the modest fared badly. You needed a strong personality to make your presence felt. The table d'hôtes was the happy hunting ground of overbearing men who learnt quickly to come early and take the best seats at the top of the table. When the meal was served, they took such large helpings that little was left for the well-behaved, modest guests. The strong men knew that those at the lower end of the table would not dare to complain; and they seldom did. The servants, for there were no waiters yet, were under the influence of the bullies, whom they admired in any case, and they saw to it that they got the best morsels and that their glasses were always full. As with food, so with conversation, which mattered so much in the eighteenth century. Those at the top of the table chatted, argued and related anecdotes. Down at the bottom, conversation was carried on in whispers, and even that could meet with disapproval from the top. To broach a subject or start a discussion at the lower end was strictly frowned on. The hard core of the tables d'hôtes victimised foreign visitors who were not versed either in French or table d'hôtes habits. The Germans and the Swiss were the worst sufferers. The English found a simple way round. They sent out for their food and dined in the peace and quiet of their rooms at the inn. For the polite traveller and diner-out, the restaurant came as a gift from above.

According to Reichard's guide book, published in Weimar in 1805, a Parisian called Boulanger in 1767 conceived the new-fangled idea of serving fresh eggs and poultry on separate tables, without cloths. Over the door was written: "Venite ad me omnes qui stomaco laboratis et ego restaurabo vos." From Boulanger's offer to restore their stomachs with food, according to Reichard, the word restaurant originated: a good anecdote though shaky etymology.

The habit of eating in restaurants spread, to the detriment of the cabarets and tables d'hôtes. The food was good and varied. In 1788 an English visitor noted in his diary the bill of fare of the Restaurant Beauvilliers. There were a hundred and seventy-eight different dishes, which included soups, roasts, entrées and puddings. The favourites were fricandeau with spinach, veal en papillotte, choucroute, soused herring, partridge with cabbage, and duckling with white turnip. In short, the sun of gastronomy was already shining on the Paris whose good people were preparing themselves for the Revolution and the Terror.

Prices were similar to those before the First World War; between the reign of Louis XVI and Sarajevo, one paid roughly the same in good restaurants. At Beauvilliers a meal cost about 4 francs, a bottle of Clos-Vougeot or Chambertin or Hermitage came to 4 livres (about 4 francs), and Beauvilliers was considered an expensive restaurant; so much so that in his Guide Book Reichard recommended the traveller to avoid it and to frequent third-class restaurants, where "conversation is pleasant and often edifying."

The Revolution gave restaurants a new impetus. The great houses of the aristocracy were closed and their chefs, if they were lucky not to be despatched in the wake of their masters, found themselves out of work. The fortunate ones opened restaurants on their own which did remarkably well, since the Revolution brought into Paris, and also created, a large number of military men, deputies and officials. Thus were born some of the famous names in the history of gastronomy, like Naudet, Meot, Robert (of Sauce Robert fame) and Véry, whose famous restaurant in the Boulevard Magenta lasted long enough to suffer damage at the end of the nineteenth century from an anarchist bomb. Deharme, another chef of the old order, kept the Marmite Perpétuelle in the rue des Grands-Augustins. The Perpetual Pot simmered for eighty-five years without the fire ever going out. Day and night, juicy capons were cooked in the pot, and as one was taken out, a fresh one took its place. The capons were eaten with coarse salt.

In the rue de la Harpe, Leblanc, also a chef of the old régime, kept a cook-shop-cum-restaurant, his whole ground floor filled with Bayonne hams, even the smallest weighing no less than twenty pounds. The curtains were drawn to keep out the flies, and an enormous black and white cat presided over the hams, its task to keep away the mice. Leblanc was a modern-minded cook in the sense that he despatched his ham pâtés all over France.

However, the true moderniser was Marie-Antoine Carême, perhaps the most gifted of the chefs. He was born in a hut in the rue du Bac, one of twenty-five brothers and sisters. He was still a boy when a pastry cook took him in out of charity. Because he worked hard and seemed intelligent, Robert took him over, eventually passing him on to La Guipière, chef to Murat, King of Naples. La Guipière, to whom Carême dedicated his *Memoirs*, died in the retreat from Moscow, the poor man probably freezing to death while trying to heat a casserole. Carême became Napoleon's cook, then Talleyrand's, and was the head chef at the banquet given in 1814 on the Plain of Vetus for the Allied sovereigns. For the rest of his life he was considered the premier cook of France. For some time he acted as chef to Emperor Alexander I. He revolutionised pastry, which before his time was heavy and, therefore, expensive. By creating the thin, flaky pastry known as pâte à choux, he broke down, as it were, the social barriers, bringing cake within everybody's reach. The heavy, expensive cakes that the working-classes used to chew on Sundays in the guinguettes gave way to the light, cheap choux à la crème, thanks to Carême whose greatest pleasure, as he often declared, was to watch little urchins in the streets devouring pastry made from his recipes. He wrote *Le Patissier royal* in 1825 and *Le Cuisinier parisien* in 1833, the year of his death, when he was forty-nine years old.

For those who could afford little for food, the nineteenth century produced several interesting restaurants, two of which certainly deserve mention.

In the rue de la Gaîté in Montparnasse, the Maison des Acacias had a distinctive renown, for there the food was sold by auction. Neither the plats du jour nor the other dishes were priced; there was no bill of fare; in fact, the prices were left to the clients, the highest bidder receiving each dish. The waiter might bring in a smoking stew and shout, "How much?" Each dish had a reserve on it. "5 sous," the waiter would call, pushing the plate under a hungry customer's chin. The customer might examine it, sniff it, look at it from every angle, eventually perhaps refuse it. "6 sous," someone might call, and after brisk bidding it would be knocked down to, and put before, the most reckless guest. There was only one snag: frequently the dish became cold before the auction finished. As at a sale, the bidding often became acrimonious, in which case the dish was put up again. It was not unknown for the unadventurous to leave the restaurant with an empty stomach.

In the rue du Départ, a street created in 1849 between the Boulevard du Montparnasse and the second Montparnasse Station which was still under construction, a certain Monsieur Cadet, known to his clients as père Cadet, established another restaurant for modest purses, La Grande Californie. It was certainly big, with its four entrances, enormous hangar-like dining-hall, two inner courtyards and a garden. The clientele could not be called distinguished. It included tramps, pickpockets and beggars. Plates, cutlery and glasses were attached by chains to the long tables. The customers sat on low benches, and père Cadet, assisted by his heavily limping wife, gave them copious food inexpensively. Because it was she who collected the money, the clients nicknamed her Mother-Five-and-Three-Make-Eight. They were obliged to leave their hats, coats and parcels in one of the courtyards, for the Cadets refused to have smelly objects indoors. It was also forbidden to cut and chew tobacco in the dining-room. Cadet was a strict believer in hygiene, and La Grande Californie smelt, like a prison, of disinfectant.

It was a self-service restaurant in that the clients lined up before the kitchen, took their food and moved into the dining hangar, where they sat down if there was room, or ate standing. In one of the courtyards cigarettes made of stubs were sold. The usual meal, consisting of soup and braised beef with carrots, cost 3 sous, a sausage 2 sous, and a soup alone 1 sou. Some of the more luxurious dishes came to as much as 4 sous. A journalist asked Cadet how he managed to feed his clients so cheaply. "Quantity is my secret," he replied, and truly enough around three bullocks, ten calves, five or six sheep and thirty rabbits were slaughtered daily by his butchers on the premises. He employed fifty females just to clean the vegetables and peel the potatoes, and over three thousand casks of wine were sold in a year.

Every day Cadet distributed several hundred plates of soup to the needy. He became one of the first mayors of the fourteenth arrondissement. La Grand Californie closed its doors in 1866 to the great regret of its habitués.

In those almost pioneer days of popular restaurants around 1850, an enterprising restaurant-keeper set up his establishment in the rue de la Huchette. He had the original idea of giving free tobacco with meals. He expected thereby to attract a large number of guests. Indeed he did, and was soon ruined.

The cafés evolved too. In the seventeenth century the Parisians gathered on the Pont-Neuf; at the end of the eighteenth in the Palais-Royal; and during the Romantic Period, that is the first half of the nineteenth century, on the Boulevard des Italiens and the Boulevard Montmartre. The boulevard first called Coblenz, then de Gand or des Bains-Chinois, took the definite name of Boulevard des Italiens when the Italian Opera House established itself in the rue Favart on the site of the present Opéra-Comique; its cafés became the centre of attraction of the boulevardiers. After the Baron Haussmann all the inner boulevards became their meeting places and hunting grounds. Only near the Madeleine was there any peace and quiet.

The Café de la Régence and the Café Turc were the meeting places of domino and chess players. Farther out in the Boulevard Bonne-Nouvelle, the Grand Café de France was patronised by billiard players. It had nine tables. The Café de Mulhouse and the Café de l'Europe catered for commercial travellers and tradesmen. The literary gents still went to the Café Procope as in Molière's time, and the bohemians, needless to say, spent their evenings in the Café Momus of *La Vie de Bohème* fame in the rue Saint-Germain-l'Auxerrois.

The financiers, whose number was legion in the Second Empire, patronised the cafés of the rue de la Chaussée d'Antin. The smart set frequented such places as the Café Anglais, the Café de Paris, La Maison Dorée, and the Café Tortoni, especially Tortoni, which had seen the citoyens, the incroyables, the dandys (*sic*) and the lions: fundamentally the same noisy young men, though belonging to different decades. Tortoni had the best ices. Fashionable folk arrived in carriages and were served with ices without having to alight. Not for anything would people of fashion have been seen in the more modest cafés near the Portes Saint-Denis and Saint-Martin.

On the Left Bank the Café d'Orsay in the rue de Lille was the favourite of the officers of the Imperial Guard during the First Empire. It became a literary resort after the Restoration, Alfred de Musset being one of the regulars. He used to get drunk on absinthe. A full tumbler always stood before him. With glassy eyes he would contemplate the beverage, seemingly afraid of it. Lifting the glass to his lips, he would put it down without tasting it. After going through the motion at least five times, with sudden decision he would swallow the lot and call for another. The café owner, a retired butcher, often approached his table, begging him to drink no more, saying it would only harm him. On such an occasion Musset rose from the table, and leaning against the wall, said in a contemptuous voice:

"Back to the meat stall!"

Then he sank back on the banquette.

With the advent of gas lighting, cafés with gas lamps became the fashion, even in the outlying districts. In Batignolles, before it was attached to Paris to become part of the seventeenth arrondissement, the Café du Gaz was the most popular. Of course, smart people did not visit suburban cafés, leaving them to small rentiers, retired army officers and tradesmen.

The sedate customers took soft drinks or coffee, known as gloria if served with a drop of brandy; in such cafés wine and alcohol were not drunk except in some such form. "Family liqueurs," inoffensive sickly stuff, were also served, and bavaroise with milk was the only food available. Smoking was prohibited.

As the century approached its end, so café habits changed. By the 1890s women appeared in cafés, not only on Sundays with their families but on weekdays too and alone, though always wearing hats. In the cheaper cafés and brasseries, men did not remove their hats; they smoked cigars, which were more favoured than cigarettes. Posters covered the walls and in spite of the spirit of the Revanche, frankfurters and Munich beer were in demand. Choucroute à toutes heures came into its own. (Surely from that derives the hackneyed story of the café that advertised five o'clock tea at all hours.)

In working-class estaminets, cider was chiefly drunk; the customers kept their caps on. Vermouth, coffee, absinthe and hot wine all cost 2 sous. In short, the cabarets, whose offsprings were cafés, restaurants, estaminets and brasseries, had reverted to type. They had again become what they had been in the beginning: popular drinking places, and not as select as in the seventeenth, eighteenth and early nineteenth centuries. Where they were different was in the matter of publicity, which in the old days was unnecessary.

The Café Foy in the rue de la Chaussée d'Antin, managed by a Monsieur Nigaud before the Bignon brothers made it famous, had among its clients Bouffé, director of the Théâtre du Vaudeville. He was nicknamed "C'est pour moi" ("It's on me"), because, when it came to paying, he had his drinks chalked up. He drank large quantities of champagne. Came the day when Nigaud asked him to settle his enormous, outstanding bill, adding that he would not be asking for it if the café had been doing well, but alas that was not the case. Bouffé said that Nigaud's trouble was that he did not know how to sell himself. He needed publicity, and Bouffé offered to take charge. He would invite the best known journalists in Paris, and do all the talking. Nigaud would only have to provide adequate food and drink for the distinguished company. Deeply moved, Nigaud thanked Bouffé and put the bill back into his pocket.

Bouffé was as good as his word. A few nights later, after the show at the Vaudeville, he appeared in the café with a group of his down-at-heel actors, whom he introduced as famous journalists. Nigaud served them with an excellent meal; and champagne flowed till five in the morning, when he sent them home in fiacres, at his expense. In the morning he bought every Paris newspaper, but of course there was not one word about the Café Foy. He complained bitterly to Bouffé. Were they really such influential men?

"Didn't you recognise them?" Bouffé asked. "The tall one was Théophile Gautier, the bearded one Emile de Girardin, the one with the long moustache Alexandre Dumas, the little old man Nestor Roqueplan, the fat man who sang so lustily was, of course, Lamartine, the giant Eugène Sue himself, and the one who looked the very picture of health Dr Véron in person. What more do you want? Aren't they illustrious enough for you?"

"But they haven't written about me."

"You should invite them more often."

"Never. I'd go bankrupt if I did," said Nigaud, holding out the bill.

"C'est pour moi," said Bouffé, waving it away.

The brasseries de femmes were at their height between the Franco-Prussian and the First World Wars. They were not so much brasseries as unauthorised brothels. There were two categories, one for men, who were mostly soldiers, commercial travellers and trades- men, the other for Lesbians. The waitresses wore low-cut bodices and skirts above the knees. As a prelude, the client ordered a drink from the waitress he fancied. When she brought the drink she sat down beside him. There were no silly games or pretensions. Once the price was settled, they went either down to the basement or up to the first floor, depending on where a room was free; the more discreet rooms were reserved for the local tradesmen who did not want to be observed by anyone in the neighbourhood. The cus- tomers who had not the wherewithal for a few minutes of love stayed in the brasserie, ogling and pinching the waitresses. However, short shift was made of such unprofitable clients. In the brasseries for Lesbians, decorum was a little more observed.

In 1891 the police raided the Brasserie du Divorce in the rue Saint-Séverin, and the manageress, the cashier and the concierge were hauled before the Tribunal Correctionnel (Tenth Chamber). The prosecution used the waitresses as witnesses against them. The oldest was seventeen. They were simple, provincial girls, picked up by the concierge, who pimped for the establishment. The girls were told that they would be employed simply as waitresses, and one cannot but wonder at their lack of curiosity when on arrival in the brasserie they were dressed up immediately as Arcadian shepherdesses, to quote the manageress's words. They wore nothing under their short skirts, and, if they showed repugnance, the cashier scolded them, saying that they were not business-minded. The manageress and the cashier were sentenced to six months' imprisonment and the concierge to three.

The women who ran brasseries de femmes had a strong sense of publicity. They advertised in the newspapers and had business cards distributed in their district. "The most elegant dress is the simplest," announced the Brasserie du Sénat. "You can see our simply dressed ladies every night." The Grande Brasserie de la Seine: "All Paris throngs to see our pretty Women Doctors noted as much for their healing power as their charms." The Brasserie des Sorciers: "Here your fortune is told by famous fortune-tellers. Visit our basement where our fortune-tellers seek the Stone of Philosophy."

The great pastime in a Lesbian brasserie de femmes in the rue Grégoire de Tours was to watch the girls fighting each other with razor blades and to lay bets on them. The girl who first drew blood by cutting the other on the leg was declared the winner. The waitresses were as proud of their scars as were duelling Prussian students. Often they bled like pigs, but that only added to the gaiety of the evening. If a kind-hearted customer tried to intervene, they turned on him in fury.

The café-concerts were in the same tradition, though there were always women stupid enough to imagine that they were employed because of their singing voices.

"You sing well," the manager of a café-concert said to one of the artistes, "but you are too severe with the public."

And he cancelled her contract.

IV

Joan of Arc in Paris & the End of English Rule

At the beginning of September 1429 Joan of Arc left Rheims, where Charles VII had been anointed (sacré) King of France. Until her coming into his and France's life, he was piteously called the King of Bourges. She joined the Court at Saint-Denis, then with King and army advanced as far as La Chapelle, an ancient borough dating back to the time of Sainte-Geneviève and enclosed by high walls. Joan spent the night in an old building known as the Logis de Sainte-Geneviève, situated behind the Church of Saint-Denis-de-la-Chapelle (now 96 rue de la Chapelle), confident of taking Paris from the English.

On the morning of September 7 she rode with the King, followed by the troops, along the rue du Coq (prolongation of the rue de Clichy). They reached the windmill of the village of Batignolles, where battle was joined with the English, after which Charles VII withdrew to Saint-Denis, having again lost faith, but Joan took the army to the adjoining village of Monceaux, determined to besiege Paris the next day. (Monceaux lost its "x" as recently as the last century.)

When day broke she left part of her army in the village and

marched with the rest on Paris. They took the old Roman road which today roughly corresponds to:

rue de Lévis,

rue du Rocher,

the present corner of Boulevard Haussmann and rue de l'Arcade, where she crossed the watershed of Ménilmontant on the Bridge of Arcan. (The watershed ran from the Hill of Ménilmontant, crossed the Champs-Elysées and reached the Seine at Chaillot. Now it is the main underground collector of drainage on the Right Bank),

rue de la Ville-l'Evêque,

rue de l'Arcade and the rue des Mathurins, which cross each other, cutting across the orchard of the Monks of the Holy Trinity known as the Mathurins, whose farm was on the site of the present number 39 rue des Mathurins,

rue Vignon,

rue d'Argenteuil,

and then reaching the Enceinte of Charles V at the present Place du Théâtre Français.

According to the *Registre des délibérations du Chapitre de Notre-Dame*, her force consisted of twelve thousand men, three hundred chariots and six hundred assault ladders, as well as siege ordnance, including cannons, barrels of gunpowder and stone cannonballs. With the grinding noise of the men-drawn chariots, the army reached the Porte Saint-Honoré (161 rue Saint-Honoré). Joan chose the Porte Saint-Honoré because there the walls appeared to be more vulnerable than at the Porte Saint-Denis, which was strongly fortified. She lined up her army behind the Butte Saint-Roch, levelled down by the Baron Haussmann when the Avenue de l'Opéra was constructed, and the Butte des Moulins, also levelled down, where now rues Sainte-Anne and des Petits-Champs meet. (The Butte Saint-Roch was between the Avenue de l'Opéra and the rues Thérèse and des Pyramides.) The cannons were dragged up on the two hillocks because there they were out of reach of the English cannons at the Porte Saint-Denis.

Before the Porte Saint-Honoré, Joan of Arc was wounded in the leg by an English arrow, yet she still wanted to continue the siege, but on the King's order the army commanders forced her to abandon the battle. She returned by the same route to Monceaux, then to La Chapelle, where she rested in the Logis de Sainte-Geneviève. Deeply dejected, she contemplated the jealousies of men and the untrustworthiness of the King. Her work, she thought, lay in ruins.

Eventually she took the road to Saint-Denis. On arrival she went straight into the Abbey church and prayed "humbly and devotedly". She hung up in the church, as an ex-voto offering, the armour she had worn when she was wounded.

In those turbulent times, crime was rampant and cruelty stalked the town. On December 15, 1427, Sauvage de Fromonville, a nobleman, was brought before the English Regent because he did not belong to the English Party. The Regent summarily condemned him to death and appointed Pierre Baille, Grand Treasurer of Maine, to preside over the execution. That worthy refused to allow the condemned man to receive the Last Sacrament. He personally hurried him up the ladder and, when he was already under the rope, struck him over the head with his stick, then belaboured the hangman who had dared to enquire why his victim had been refused confession. The hangman was so frightened that he omitted to take all the necessary precautions. As a result, the rope failed to hold and de Fromonville fell to the ground, still alive. Unimpressed and unmoved, Baille ordered him to be taken up the ladder again. This time the rope held.

After Joan's unsuccessful siege of Paris, misery and hunger descended on its inhabitants. Under the pretext of taking a walk outside the Walls, many Parisians passed through the city gates; once they reached the countryside, they took to robbing and killing. Ninety-eight such strollers were caught, twelve were hanged and eleven were taken to the Halles to be beheaded. When it came the turn of the eleventh, a young man of twenty-four, a girl broke through the crowd and, calling out loudly, claimed him as the man she intended to marry. She had probably never seen him before and was acting out of pity. She was so lovely and begged for his life so touchingly that all present were moved, and he was taken back to the prison of the Grand Châtelet, where he was set free on condition that he married her. If a woman was to be executed and a man stepped out of the crowd, offering to marry her, she was set free. Thus young girls escaped death more often than their elders.

The Seigneur de la Bottière discovered that his wife had a lover who was none other than his neighbour. He invited him to dinner, then after the meal took his wife and the lover for a walk. When they reached the woods, the husband killed them both. Shortly afterwards, he was apprehended, judged and condemned to be beheaded. He declared to the judges that every one of them was a cuckold, and that because he had refused to be one of them, they, the cuckolds, had decided to get rid of him. Such, he maintained, was the only reason for the death sentence. He refused to have his eyes bandaged, but took the executioner's sword and ran his fingers along the blade. Then he turned to the executioner and said, "Dispatch me quickly, my friend. It's up to you and your skill. The blade is well sharpened."

Not all noblemen behaved as exemplarily as the Seigneur de la Bottière. Nearly two hundred years later, another nobleman, whose name is not recorded, was sentenced to death. He had committed several crimes, including robbery. When he mounted the scaffold, he grabbed the Franciscan friar who had come to confess him, and threw him into the crowd. Then he went for the hangman and bit his neck. It took some time to overpower him. As a punishment for his outrageous behaviour, the hanging was cancelled and he had to undergo the more painful ordeal of being drawn and quartered.

In 1431 the ten-year-old Henry VI of England was sent to Paris to be anointed King of France in the Church of Notre-Dame. He entered the town through the Porte Saint-Denis. The city gate was decorated with the coats of arms of England and France. The magistrates and the Provost of the Merchants, received him in their scarlet robes under a canopy of sky-blue silk sprinkled with golden fleurs-de-lys. When the cortège was formed, it was carried by four magistrates. The little monarch walked under the canopy, and the crowd thought that the procession resembled that of Corpus Christi.

Nine champions and nine damsels, accompanied by a multitude of knights, moved in front of the canopy. In their midst marched an impostor whom the English had taken in the battle of Beauvais. He pretended to be a prophet, and the people believed in him because he had stigmata on his hands and feet similar to those of St Francis. They had venerated this man like a saint. Now he was roped like a common thief.

Twenty-four heralds and twenty-five trumpeters walked before the King, who was encompassed by five ecclesiastics, a cardinal and four bishops. The procession stopped at the Fountain of Ponceau in the rue Saint-Denis. Three young girls represented sirens, and in the middle of the fountain rose a colossal artificial tiger-lily that spouted wine and milk through its petals. Whoever succeeded in pushing his way through the throng could drink as much as he wanted. A tableau represented savages dancing in a small jungle. (The same pageant was shown fifty-one years later on the occasion of Louis XI's entry into Paris.)

Beyond the Fountain of the Trinité, which was at the corner of the rues Saint-Denis and Greneta, extended a long wooden stage on which a mystery play based on the life of Our Lady was enacted. Farther on, another mystery play showed the life of St John the Baptist. In the Cemetery of the Innocents a stag hunt was improvised, the stag having been locked up there the night before.

In front of the Grand Châtelet a boy of the same age as Henry VI held a court of justice. He wore two crowns and was flanked by other boys dressed as princes of England and France. This pageant was much applauded, though some of the more patriotic spectators complained that the "king" more often consulted the English "princes" than the French ones.

The procession passed in front of the Hôtel de Saint-Paul, where

Isabeau of Bavaria, widow of Charles VI and grandmother of Henry stood in a window. The little king doffed his hat to her. She bowed, then turned away and cried; and well she might for all the calamities she brought on France.

Next Sunday the King was anointed in Notre-Dame by the Cardinal of Winchester. Then he returned to the Palace of the Louvre, where he dined at the round marble table at the end of the banqueting hall. The royal suite and the guests dined in the same hall. So dense was the crowd on the staircase that neither the representatives of the University and of Parliament, nor the Provost of Paris himself, could force their way up. They had to wait until a passage was opened for them, but by then their seats had been taken by cobblers, mustard-makers and their like. A useless tussle ensued. If a guest was strong enough to remove one of the interlopers from his own seat, the man immediately pushed another guest off his chair and took his place. Thieves had also managed to find their way into the hall, where they reaped a fair harvest. The entertainment that followed the banquet was on a mean scale, and the consensus of opinion was that Parisian burghers and merchants treated their guests more lavishly when their children married.

When on April 3, 1436, the troops of Charles VII appeared at the Porte Saint-Jacques, the defenders were so impressed by the size of the French King's army that they decided to open the gate. However, the key was in the keeping of the Bishop of Thérouanne who, with the Bishops of Lisieux and Paris, was a staunch supporter of the English. The problem was solved by lowering a long ladder. The first to climb it was the Seigneur de l'Isle-Adam who planted the King's banner on top of the gate with the cry, "Town conquered!"

The Parisians sided with Charles VII; the three Bishops, the Provost and the Captain of Paris with the English. About four thousand Parisians collected beside the Porte Saint-Denis; with three divisions, the English advanced along the rue Saint-Martin, shouting, "St George! St George! Death to the French traitors!" The

Bishop of Thérouanne commanded one of the English divisions. Another division, led by the Provost, marched towards the Halles. The Parisians threw chains across the streets to impede their progress, and, from the windows, the women and children threw tables, logs, stones and boiling water on them. Surprised to find the Porte Saint-Denis so well guarded, the English retreated into the Bastille. Meanwhile the royal troops infiltrated into the town, and once they were inside, the Parisians in their zeal pulled down the Porte Saint-Jacques, shouting, "Saint-Denis! Saint-Denis! Long live the noble King of France!"

The Parisians were pleasantly surprised by the royal troops' agreeable behaviour. They had feared the worst, yet the King's men neither looted nor molested them. They considered it a miracle for which they thanked St Denis. (The troops had strict orders to behave well, and any of them found pillaging, or even entering a burgher's house, were hanged on the spot.)

The English were in such vast numbers behind the walls of the Bastille that their food soon ran out. Paying an enormous ransom, they were allowed to leave Paris. They did not want to be seen in the town, so they left across the fields on the other side of the enceinte. The Parisians gathered on the walls to watch them go. The Bishop of Thérouanne, who departed with the English, was loudly jeered by the populace.

The King of Bourges was now truly King of France, and she who had been the mover of it all was burnt at the stake in Rouen less than two months later.

V

For l'Evêque

At 19 rue Saint-Germain-l'Auxerrois stood the prison of For l'Evêque, the building taking up the space between the street and the Quai de la Mégisserie. It had earlier been the ecclesiastical court of the Bishops of Paris, Forum Episcopi, hence For l'Evêque. It was a cosy sort of prison, as prisons go, and the defenders and admirers of the old régime like to harp on the easy life prisoners led there.

If a book or pamphlet were published without royal permission (privilège du Roi) and the author happened to be a distinguished man like Voltaire, Diderot or Mirabeau, he was sent to the Bastille or to Vincennes; the bookseller and printer went to For l'Evêque, and the colporteur, who was hardly more than a newsvendor, to Bicêtre. A writer could gauge his importance both in society and literature by the prison to which he was sent. Many must have sobbed in deep disappointment when they discovered that the Bastille was not their destination. Generally, the prisoners in For l'Evêque were a miscellaneous lot in so far as there were among them debtors, hoodlums, actors and actresses, noblemen, forgers and pimps. No dangerous criminals were sent there.

Lack of room was the most disagreeable feature. The four-storey house, with its slate roof and two turrets was approximately thirty feet wide and a hundred and fifteen feet long. Around two hundred and fifty people were usually crowded into it. The cells were less than six feet square, which makes it difficult to visualise how the prisoners managed to throw large dinner parties and entertain lavishly. That they did so is clear from the records, however. Mlle Clairon (Claire-Josèphe-Hypolitte Legris de la Tude), the famous actress, seemed to receive the whole of Paris society at her princely table at For l'Evêque, to which actors and actresses were specially privileged to be sent since they belonged to the Royal Household (Chambre du Roi). They went there without police escort to purge their contempt for whatever they had done; they never stayed long and were occasionally allowed out to perform.

For l'Evêque had no governor: the man in charge of the prison was the Concierge, who writers on French prisons, like the late Frantz Funck-Brentano, have compared to the master of a family boarding-house. Except for the chaplain and the clerk, he paid every member of the staff, and kept his staff as small and as cheap as possible. He employed only two warders, whose duties included guarding the gates. Rules of 1690 and 1717 obliged him to pay them 100 livres a year each, and since dogs cost less than men, he kept an imposing number of large dogs, which mounted guard at the gates when the warders were busy elsewhere, and acted as bodyguards to the Concierge when he made the rounds of cells and dungeons. They jumped at the throats of prisoners who made threatening gestures.

The Concierge had no true authority. In eighteenth-century Paris there were several houses of detention run by private individuals, the best known at Picpus, presided over by Mme Marie de Sainte-Colombe, where Louis de Saint-Juste was once locked up for petty theft. The position of the Concierge of For l'Evêque was no higher then hers. Prisoners who had enough money were looked after and served by their own servants; the rest by old women who lived on tips.

The Lieutenant of Police strictly forbade gaming in prisons, especially the game of faro. He had For l'Evêque in mind when he issued the order, for the prison was famous for the faro parties given by the inmates. On January 14, 1724, two lieutenants of the Constabulary and two clerks of Parliament accompanied Police Commandants Divot and Delafosse to For l'Evêque. They climbed to the third floor, where in the cell of three detained officers, Chapelain, Dumontois and Delalande, they found an elegant company of sixteen playing faro for high stakes. Dressed in an expensive linen dress, Mme de Coade, herself in prison for illegal gaming, ran the party. Among the gamesters from outside the gaol were Mme de la Marre, wife of the Procurator of Parliament, Causanel, a lieutenant in the Régiment de la Ferre-Infanterie, and the Chevalier de Sauvegrain. Consternation was mutual. The guests, however, recovered quicker than the police, burst out of the cell and made good their escape before the police could catch them. The inmates could not be arrested because they were already detained, so the six officers withdrew empty-handed.

Jean Noiseux was a violent man who loved fighting. When arrested, he drew his knife on the police, who managed to disarm him only after a fierce fight. The police had arrived to take him to For l'Evêque on his parents' demand, because they feared that "he might disgrace the family". Prison life did not change his habits. The Concierge at the time was called Chevallier. On November 5, 1728, he wrote to the Lieutenant of Police: "This man is drunk every night and spends his time inciting prisoners to sedition. At ten o'clock last night when the cells were already locked, he kicked up such a row in his cell that his cellmates had to call for help." Chevallier had gone upstairs to stop the noise, Noiseux had grabbed him by the collar, and if the two warders and the dogs had not followed, the Concierge would surely have been injured, for the dogs had had to bite hard before the prisoner let him go. Therefore,

Chevallier earnestly begged the Lieutenant to have Noiseux transferred to another prison, preferably the Châtelet. The Lieutenant
wrote in turn to Cardinal de Fleury, the King's Minister, pointing
out that the Concierge and his warders would not feel safe until
Noiseux were removed from For l'Evêque. So small was the power
of the Concierge that if he, his two men and many dogs were
unable to master a prisoner, all he could do was to implore the
Lieutenant to have the man removed. Noiseux was in fact transferred to Bicêtre.

A certain Chevallier (no relation of the Concierge) was put into
For l'Evêque for forging lottery tickets. He continued his work in
prison. A man called Luron came regularly to fetch the fresh tickets
and put them into circulation. In his cell Chevallier had all the
apparatus he needed, and fellow prisoners came to watch him at
his work, which they found most instructive.

Prisoners received anyone they wanted. In the seventeenth
century serious efforts were made to exclude mistresses; by the
eighteenth they were abandoned: the mistress reigned supreme.

In the 1720s a fellow called Saint-Louis, known also as Louis
Legrand or La Planche, was brought to For l'Evêque. He specialised
in letter-writing, his letters being addressed usually to rich foreigners.
Prison dampened neither his ardour nor his industry. He wrote,
for instance, in these terms to the Ambassador of Modena:

"Monsieur, One of your friends has described you as a most
amiable person in whom I can have enough confidence to introduce
a young lady, fifteen years old. You are only asked to be
discreet because of her parents. I do not sign this in fear that it
might fall into wrong hands. Be good enough to let me know
through the emissary whether you are interested in the little
lady."

Here is a reply from a rich Englishman:

"I am sensibly grateful for your offer. It is not my habit to meet
young ladies; however, if the young person of whom you give such

a favourable account would like to come around at five o'clock after dinner, I would receive her with pleasure. . . ."

In another letter written to Mme Berrichon, who kept a shop at the corner of the rue de Grenelle and the Barrière de Grenelle, he proffered the name of a gentleman interested in her daughter, a Monsieur de Bontemps who, being a nobleman, could be of practical help to mother and daughter. There was no cause to worry about the daughter's honour and reputation, for the nobleman would personally defend them.

Saint-Louis plied his trade, which also included finding women from outside for his fellow prisoners, until the Concierge secured his transfer to Bicêtre.

A young lady, Anne Thiebaut, complained to the Lieutenant of Police that on a visit to another young lady held in For l'Evêque for debt, she had stopped for a meal with her friend, and that while they were dining merrily, another detainee, the Chevalier de Faiol, had burst in and insulted them. The nasty old man had shouted as if they were deaf, and would have beaten them had not other prisoners restrained him. Since Mlle Thiebaut was obliged to visit her friend regularly, she begged the Lieutenant to impose silence on the Chevalier, so that she should not have to listen to insults and coarse language unfit for the ears of a young lady of her station. The Lieutenant was in a dilemma. How could he impose silence on a prisoner in For l'Evêque? What would be the point of issuing an order that the Concierge would be unable to carry out? After due reflection the Lieutenant found the sensible solution: the Chevalier de Faiol was set free.

Ladies visiting friends in prison had to put up with a lot of unpleasantness because of the Concierge's lack of authority. At the time of Mlle Thiebaut's complaint, the Concierge also appealed to the Lieutenant. A man called Garnet, famous for the scandal he created in cabarets, was now a prisoner in For l'Evêque. "He causes constant trouble," wrote the Concierge. "He fouls the beds of other prisoners, incites them to revolt, ill-treats the warders. . . ." The Lieutenant took a less lenient view of Garnet: he was transferred to the Châtelet.

Into the interesting world of For l'Evêque entered in 1770 Clotworthy Skeffington, second Earl and sixth Viscount Massereene in the Peerage of Ireland. He was then twenty-seven years old. In his early days he had been a man of fashion: "The most superlative coxcomb Ireland ever bred" (Thicknesse, 1770). He "spent an ample fortune in the most wretched dissipation" (Croft, 1780). In a suit as to the validity of his will, the jury at Carrickfergus found that he had been insane at the time he made it. One witness said that "on the death of his favourite dog he had given positive orders that fifty dogs should attend the funeral in white scarves, and that all dogs in the parish should also be present."

He arrived in Paris in 1770 in the hope of curing his spleen, the English ailment much admired in France. It was known too as melancholia. Within a few weeks he was in debt to Parisian tradesmen to the tune of 376,732 livres. His own version was that he had been cheated at cards, but it is most unlikely that he would have sat down to play with tradespeople, or that they would have pursued him for card losses. In any case Lord Massereene refused to pay his creditors, saying that they had robbed him and that he would not give them a sol. Aware that he had a large income and vast estates in Ireland, the tradesmen assumed, quite erroneously, that a little coercion would bring results. They had him arrested and put into For l'Evêque, believing that the overcrowded prison into which the sun never penetrated would do the trick. They did not know their man.

Lord Massereene quickly settled down. With a large income one could do well for oneself in For l'Evêque, as he proceeded to demonstrate. The best cook-shops sent in food and wine, and since he could afford to entertain lavishly, his cell was full of visitors, mostly English. Since the prisoners had the run of the entire building from morning to evening, he took plenty of exercise in the court-yard and up and down the stairs. When he felt in need of women, his friends and servants provided him with as many as he wanted. He kept open cell, sent carriages to fetch his women, and paid their jewellers' and dressmakers' bills and for their boxes at the Opéra. He indulged in every pleasure and lived without a single worry, which was more than could be said for his creditors who, in accordance with the law, were responsible for his basic keep; he had only to pay for the extras. The tradesmen appealed to the Procurator General, begging him "not to permit any visitor to see milord except for those who attend to his business affairs, especially no member of the opposite sex, for as long as milord has company that amuses him he will not attend to his debts." The Procurator General replied that the Concierge was the sole master at For l'Evêque and that it would be impossible to impose a measure that went against all the traditions of the prison.

Another solution had to be found, The creditors' expenses rose steeply. Seven years after the arrest, the debt stood at nearly 1,000,000 livres, so they conspired together in sending to Lord Massereene two ruffians, Verdier and Jullot, to persuade him that with 1,000 écus they could bribe both warders. All he needed was a disguise, which they would provide for him. Lord Massereene fell into the trap. It was decided that the escape should take place at seven in the evening, when it was already dark, on March 17.

He was dressed in a grey suit, his face half hidden by a vast cravat and high collar; he wore false whiskers and a hat with a large brim. What he did not know was that Verdier and Jullot had sent an anonymous letter to Dinant du Verger, the Concierge, informing him about the plot. The Concierge hardly knew how to act; he was not used to prisoners escaping. He appealed for help to the Lieutenant of Police, who sent a police inspector with a handful of men. They hid between the prison gates, and when milord appeared they jumped on him, threw him down, tied him, and dragged him into one of the rat-infested, underground dungeons. The creditors congratulated themselves. Everything had gone as planned. Milord would certainly capitulate and settle his debts.

Once again they misjudged their man. Lord Massereene shouted from the dungeon to all who were willing to listen that he was ready to stay there until he reached the ripe age of ninety, but that on no condition would he pay his debts.

The British Ambassador protested at Court, and Massereene was released from the dungeon and sent back to his cell, where the gay life recommenced. By 1780 the creditors' expenses had risen to nearly 2,000,000 livres. However, another danger was in the offing for milord. Louis XVI, in the days of his reforming zeal, sought to improve the lot of prisoners, and since For l'Evêque was badly overcrowded he decided to have it razed to the ground. By a royal decree of August 30, 1780, criminals were to be transferred to the Châtelet and debtors to the Hôtel de la Force, a spacious prison at the corner of the rues Pavée and du Roi-de-Sicile. On the day of moving the creditors waited in the street in the hope of catching Massereene. It is not known what they intended to do if they caught him, but by then they were unhappy, disillusioned men. Accompanied and surrounded by friends, he ran the whole way from For l'Evêque to the Hôtel de la Force. The creditors had failed again. Life in the new prison was as pleasant as in the old; and the debt rose to 3,000,000 livres.

Lord Massereene married in prison Marie-Anne Barcier, the sister of another detainee. She came every morning to spend the day with her husband.

On July 14, 1789, the debtors in the Hôtel de la Force heard the boom of the cannon in the Place de la Bastille. Massereene grasped the situation better than the other prisoners and incited them to break out collectively. Some protested that, being unarmed, their task would be hopeless. Massereene brushed aside the objection. He led them up the stairs, where they tore down the iron banisters and, now well armed, they marched to the gates. Because of the troubles in Paris a detachment of infantry had been sent to the Hôtel de la Force. The officer in charge called to the advancing prisoners: "One step more and my soldiers will fire!" Massereene stepped forward. "If you kill me, you will, according to law, be responsible for my debts." Everybody in Paris knew about the colossal sum he owed, and the officer let the prisoners go. Thus ended nineteen years of incarceration of a man who had been imprisoned because of his debts and let free also because of them.

The party reached the British Embassy. The first thing Lord Massereene did was to offer his companions a copious meal with excellent wines. A few days later he was smuggled out of France, and before the end of the month he landed in Dover with his wife. He died in 1806 without having evinced any desire to see France again. The Hôtel de la Force was demolished in 1850.

VI

From the Cours des Miracles to the Procession of the Fat Ox

The first cour des miracles, or courtyard of miracles, was established in the rue de la Grande-Truanderie, which took its name from the truands (beggars, vagrants) who infested the street and the neighbourhood, which was known as la Truanderie. The street was also called Via Mendicatrix. The name cour des miracles was a mocking reference to the fact that these people who limped round the neighbourhood, their arms or legs in bandages, shouting from pain, fainting, often blind, were miraculously as hale and hearty as the next man when they returned to the yards in which they lived.

Around 1350 another group of beggars and thieves was set up in two adjacent houses, the larger containing twenty-four rooms, in the rue des Francs-Bourgeois. The wretches who lived there paid no duties or taxes whatsoever, and were referred to as free citizens; hence the name of the street. The houses were known as the Little Houses of the Temple or the Almshouses of the Francs-Bourgeois. A burgher, le Masurier, had given them to the Grand Prior of France for the purpose of accommodating forty-eight poor.

Henri Sauval, author of the truly monumental *Histoire et Recherches des Antiquités de la Ville de Paris*, which was published in

1724, forty-eight years after his death, by Claude-Bernard Rousseau, called them the wicked poor, for they were neither impressed by, nor grateful for, the charity they received. They stood in the doorways, insulting the pedestrians, kept the neighbours awake at night with their awful din, and stole anything on which they could lay their hands. The almshouses became refuges of debauch and prostitution. When, however, the big private mansions began to rise in the rue des Francs-Bourgeois in the seventeenth century, the inmates were forced to leave. They dispersed in groups all over the city. Their number had considerably increased since the fourteenth century. The cour des miracles of the rue de la Grande-Truanderie being full, they created new crumbling, filthy thieves' kitchens for themselves. Some went to the Cour de Roi-François in the rue du Ponceau, some to the Cour Sainte-Catherine nearby or to the Cour Brisset and the Cour Gentien in the rue de la Mortellerie (now rue de l'Hôtel-de-Ville); others to the Cour de la Jussienne in the rue de la Jussienne, near the Chapel of Sainte-Marie-l'Egyptienne (demolished in 1792)—crumbling, filthy thieves' kitchens all of them, with yards that had always been inhabited by thieves, beggars, rogues and the wicked poor.

The cours des miracles multiplied rapidly. They spread as far as the rue Saint-Honoré, Bourg Saint-Germain, Faubourg Saint-Marceau and the Butte Saint-Roch. The most populated was between the rues Montorgeuil and Neuve-Saint-Sauveur (rue du Nil). This was a foul conglomeration of narrow alleyways and horrible shacks, built of mud, each housing about fifty families with their children—legitimate, bastard and stolen. In 1630 the Town of Paris decided to cut a street through the neighbourhood between the Impasse Saint-Sauveur and the rue Neuve-Saint-Sauveur (now part of rue du Louvre), but nothing came of it, for the masons who began work on the new street were soon manhandled by the rogues.

One of the rules of the inmates of the cours des miracles was never to keep anything for the morrow, so whatever they earned by begging or thieving was spent the same evening. Their days invariably ended in drunkenness. The women prostituted themselves for a sol or just for pleasure. They went to church only to steal, to cut purses or to pick pockets (most people carried their purses attached by a string or a ribbon to their belts) yet they had some form of faith. At the bottom of one of their yards was a painting of God the Father which they had stolen from a church and took to worshipping. Men who had given women of the yard handsome children were paid by other women to lie down with them so that they too should have good-looking babies to take out when begging. A pretty babe in arms was a handy asset.

Each yard had a school for thieving. A rope, to which were attached a purse and small bells, was stretched across one of the mean rooms, used specially for the purpose. The apprentice had to be able to cut the purse string without the bells tinkling and without moving his body. If he failed he was beaten; if he succeeded he was declared a master, yet was still beaten. It formed part of his schooling to become immune to beatings, which were a hazard of life once he started to exercise his skill. The new master would be taken to some crowded place like the Cemetery of the Innocents, and would be ordered to try out his art in his teachers' presence, perhaps on a woman praying on her knees before the Virgin, her purse hanging loosely from her belt, or on someone else whose purse seemed easy to cut. As he approached the prospective victim, the teachers' trick was to shout to all and sundry, pointing at the new master, "Look, this fellow is a real purse-cutter! He's going for that poor creature there!" Everybody's attention was of course drawn to the young thief, and the teachers joined with the crowd in pouncing on him, kicking and beating him. It was part of his training not even to glance at his companions who, while he was being belaboured, reaped an excellent harvest of purses and the contents of pockets. His own colleagues denounced him more loudly than the rest, calling him by every vile name of which they could think. Then in the noise and the pushing they and the new master vanished one by one. After that final test, the new master joined one of the groups, and from then on he was considered a fully-fledged purse-cutter and pickpocket.

No one was allowed to operate alone because in a group it was more difficult to be caught. If one gang saw another in a church or a street, they went elsewhere; it was not in their interest that too many thieves should congregate in one spot. They arrived for work, however, individually. Each night the head of the yard designated the different places to be visited the following day. An intelligent system was evolved. In each district there was a hiding place, which might be behind a doorway, in a stable, or anywhere that the uninitiated would not notice. Groups consisted of either six or twelve men, but because they were not allowed to arrive together, and because no man could know how many intended to go to any one place, each went on his own in the morning to the hiding place in the district he had in mind, where only a dice was hidden. The first arrival turned the dice from square one to square two, then went off to the appointed place. The next man turned it to square three, and so on until square six was reached. If there were a seventh arrival, he would see that the group was complete, and know that he must go elsewhere. If the group was to consist of twelve men, two dices were left in the hiding place.

An Academician, who was a friend of Sauval who relates the story, in his young days discovered such a lair of dice in the Halles. He rose at dawn and hurried to the hiding place, where he turned the dice to square six even if it were on square one. He was proud of having reduced the number of those who went to the Halles to cut purses or pick pockets.

The ruffians of the cours des miracles were known as the Argotiers, and their thieves' language as argot. It was said that the language had been invented by debauched scholars. Their world was the Royaume argotique.

In 1255, the Hospital of Quinze-Vingt was founded, beyond the Porte Saint-Honoré, by St Louis. It was for the blind, who took to begging in the rue Saint-Honoré, which was conveniently sited near the hospital and on the route taken by the maraîchers to the

Halles. The blind often begged at night, when the market gardeners passed with their carts, because they knew them to be generous men. However, because they could not be seen in the dark, or easily identified, they always had with them a boy who was supposed to hold a lighted lantern to his face when he heard the trundle of a cart. In their unlit darkness the blind beggars fretted about whether they could trust the boys, who might be indolent or simply forgetful, and they were known to ask passersby whether the light was shining strongly enough. Street-women were among their most constant benefactors, and to show their gratitude the beggars recommended them to any men who gave them alms.

In the Hôtel d'Armagnac at 1-33 rue des Bons-Enfants, there took place on the blind peoples' feast days a thrilling game, which invariably attracted a large audience. Four blind men and a pig were let into an enclosure in the courtyard. Each blind man was armed with a big stick, and the pig was promised to the one who succeeded in killing it. There ensued the spectacle of the blind hurling themselves at the spot where they heard the pig grunting, while the pig ran round in circles, trying to escape them. "There he is, the dirty pig!" one of them would cry, but as the pig was by then at the other end of the pit, the blind man would find himself, in the general excitement, belabouring one of his mates. The audience rocked with laughter at such fun.

After a while the blind were disentangled and allowed to rest. Then they were at it again. Rarely did one of them manage to hit the pig, let alone kill it. Often they gave up, not because of the blows they had received, but because of the laughter of the onlookers.

When St Vincent de Paul was the priest of the parishes of Clichy, du Roule, de la Madeleine and d'Antin, he heard of a market in infants near Notre-Dame, where foundlings were sold to beggars.

One could buy a baby for 8 sols. The beggar took away his purchase, and broke its arms and legs so as to arouse more compassion in the hearts of those whom he would accost with the poor, unfortunate child. St Vincent persuaded the authorities to abolish that infamous practice, and prompted by the misery and suffering of foundlings, he created the Oeuvre des Enfants Trouvés, the foundling hospital of Paris.

To his Sisters of Charity he gave a recipe for a soup for a hundred needy:

"Fill a large pot with five buckets of water, put into it twenty-five pounds of bread, seven quarters of fat, four pints of peas, white turnips, leaks and onions, and salt, for 14 sols. The lot will not cost more than 100 sols for a hundred people. It should be distributed in bowls."

On the feast days of SS Leu and Giles, the inhabitants of the rue aux Ours raised a high pole in their street and tied to the top a basket containing a fat goose and 6 écus. They smeared the pole with grease and promised the goose, the money and the basket to whoever could reach them. In spite of the grease there were plenty of competitors, but as with the blind and the pigs in the Hôtel d'Armagnac, it was rare that anyone succeeded. There was a difference, however; if no one reached the basket, the person who climbed nearest to it was at least given the goose, the basket and the money being kept for the next holiday.

Each district, each profession and each guild had their own patron saint or saints. The Town of Paris celebrated the feasts of SS Denis, Marcel and Geneviève; the University, SS Nicolas and Catherine; the Sorbonne, St Ursula, and the six guilds of the tradespeople had a patron saint each. Drunks fervently celebrated the feast of St Martin. Loose women celebrated the feast of St Mary Magdalene. In the fifteenth and sixteenth centuries to ask for medlars in a church was considered proof of enormous stupidity, and it was the custom on the feasts of SS Simon and Jude to send simple people to

F   81

the Temple for this very purpose. They were assured that the saints would see to it that they received the fruit. What actually happened, however, was that their faces were blackened with soot by lackeys hired for the purpose, and a good time was had by the onlookers. In Mid-Lent, the apprentices in the Halles were sent to kiss the bas-relief of a sow on the wall of a house; as they leaned forward to do so, their noses were banged into the wall. For the rest of the day they over-ate and got riotously drunk.

On the feast of St John footmen and maidservants danced through the streets, often behaving scandalously. In contrast, at the Hôtel de Ville, the aldermen and the Provost of the Merchants gave a magnificent supper followed by a ball for their families and friends at which they danced respectably to the music of violins. On Christmas Eve the common people were so intoxicated that Notre-Dame was guarded by the Watch. It was said in the seventeenth century that those who went to Midnight Mass did not seek God but groped for Him. On Easter Sunday, when canary-bread was distributed in the almshouses, there was again a great deal of drunkenness among spectators and recipients. However, the populace behaved at its worst on the feast of Epiphany; and respectable people in the reign of Louis XIII deeply regretted the passing of the good old days of Charles V, when the masses were still decent and behaved respectfully.

At 54 rue Quincampoix there was a famous cabaret called l'Epée de Bois, where the Dancing Masters and Violin Masters met. In 1658, Cardinal Mazarin, by letters patent, instituted the Community of Dancing Masters and Violin Masters, who continued to meet at the Epée de Bois until 1661, when it was incorporated into the Royal Academy of Dance, merging eight years later with the Royal Academy of Music to form what became known as the Opéra.

The cabaret remained a meeting place of musicians and dancers until 1719 when John Law of Lauriston, the monetary reformer and originator of the Mississippi Bubble, set up his bank in the street. The Epée de Bois turned into a rowdy tavern, where those who wanted to make quick money spent what they hoped to make. John Law believed in credit as a universal remedy and in paper money equalling the value of gold. He advocated a central bank that would have the monopoly of collecting taxes and issuing public loans. The bank's capital would be provided by selling shares to the public.

He offered his plan to Scotland, England and Savoy; all three rejected it. Then he thought of France, which was on the verge of bankruptcy following the death of Louis XIV. Philippe d'Orléans, the Regent, jumped at the plan, and Law founded his bank, which did well at first. Almost everybody who could afford to do so bought shares in the bank. Flushed with success, Law created the Compagnie des Indes, which received the monopoly of external trade, and as a result of the fever of speculation, shares originally valued at 200 livres rose to 20,000. An unlimited number of bank notes was printed and put into circulation. The shakier the enterprise became, the faster the printing machines worked.

Then came the collapse. Law could not pay dividends, and the frightened shareholders turned their shares into banknotes, and their banknotes into gold and silver—until the supply of gold and silver ran out. Law and his bank, which had amalgamated with the Compagnie des Indes, went bankrupt. Only banknotes under 10 livres were honoured. The bank closed its doors and there followed a riot. Law had lost his own fortune too in the course of his grand design. He left France and, in 1729, at the age of fifty-eight, he died a pauper in Venice.

Indirectly, a broker named Lacroix was one of his victims. Lacroix had made a vast sum of money while the going was still good. A German, Count Antoine de Horn, assisted by de Miles, a Piedmontese nobleman, and de Tournai, the son of a French banker, decided to bag the broker's fortune. They chose the simplest method. On Good Friday, 1720, they met him at the Epée de Bois on the pretext of selling him an estate. The French accomplice stayed in the street as a look-out while in a private room upstairs his colleagues murdered Lacroix in cold blood. A waiter, hearing strange noises, opened the door, saw the corpse, locked the door and rushed out to give the alarm. The Piedmontese climbed out through the window, slid down a drainpipe, and got away before the police arrived, but was caught shortly afterwards in the Cemetery of the Innocents. The German followed him out through the window, sprained his ankle as he landed on the ground, and was arrested on the spot. In spite of de Horn's excellent connections (he was distantly related to the Regent, and his brother was a ruling prince in Germany) six days after the murder he and the Piedmontese were broken on the wheel in the Place de Grève.

It was the habit of beggars to carry sticks. Sticks and canes made no special impression in a world where men of quality carried a more dangerous weapon, the sword. Disbanded soldiers, ruffians and rogues all begged in the daytime. To beg was a recognised way of earning a living, there being no stigma attached to it as long as the beggar stuck to asking for alms. It often happened, however, that when a humble beggar found himself alone in an alley with a charitable person who had stopped to give him a coin or two, the beggar's stick turned swiftly into an arm. Down it came on the victim's head, and by the time he had recovered, his possessions and the beggar were gone. Now and again these rogues operated in bands. Then there was no question of begging: they attacked like a pack of wolves, though usually only after dusk. Thus the system of gangs evolved.

The gangs approached a house at night and threw pebbles at the windows. If no irate householder leaned out, they knew that the house was uninhabited. One gang leader, Raffia, collected around him youths between the ages of fifteen and eighteen. He and his mob specialised in robbing goldsmiths and silversmiths, who at night hung in front of their shops large glass cases, each one lit by two candles, which contained their finest jewels. Raffia was sixteen years old. Dressed as a peasant, his technique was to stand open-mouthed in front of a glass case, staring at the jewels with the admiration one expected from a stupid peasant who had never before seen anything so fine. The people who passed probably smiled in pity mingled with condescension at the simple fellow wearing a cotton cap. However, Raffia excelled at cutting glass. His associates boasted of his having extracted jewels unnoticed from practically every jeweller's case in Paris. Eventually he was caught, and confessed to all his thefts. When he was taken to the scaffold in the Place de Grève, he loudly proclaimed that his mother was an honest woman who knew nothing of his misdeeds; he offered his life to God, being unafraid of death, but feared that his mother would die of shame. He burst into tears.

"Set your mind at rest," said the Clerk of the Court. Again Raffia recommended his mother to him as he mounted the ladder.

It was the custom for a condemned man to be taken to the main door of Notre-Dame, where the Clerk of the Court read out his sentence, a taper was given him and he made amende honorable. Then he was lifted into a cart, and in the company of the hangman and the priest who would confess him, he rode to the Place de Grève, where the gibbet awaited him. The magistrates who had sentenced him held themselves in readiness at the Hôtel de Ville, which overlooked the place of execution, in case he wanted to reveal something of importance before he died. Many condemned men took advantage of this possibility of delaying death. They entered the building and spent as much time as they could in spinning yarns, adding details that were untrue, inventing crimes they had never committed. A clerk took down all they said. When they could think up nothing more, they were led back to the hangman. There were several who then asked to be taken back to the magistrates because they had forgotten to confess to some of their worst crimes. Some thus succeeded in keeping death at bay for many hours.

In 1764 a certain Pierre Padoix had the capital idea of denouncing as accomplices a number of decent residents of Saint-Germain-en-

Laye. He was kept the whole night in the town hall, waiting for the arrival of the good people who in the morning were brought in in chains, among them a surgeon and his wife. Padoix accused the woman of complicity in his crimes, and she was taken to the Châtelet, where she died of shame the same day. When Padoix was taken to the gallows he confided in the Lieutenant of Police that the folk of Saint-Germain-en-Laye were innocent, that he had invented the whole story, and would he thank the magistrates for the excellent supper and comfortable night at the Hôtel de Ville? There is a record of a condemned man who was given there a meal consisting of an omelette, a chicken, a salad, a pound of bread, a bottle of wine and three coffees.

It was the custom in Paris, originating in the Middle Ages, for the crowd in the square, and the people in the windows and on the roofs, to intone the Salve Regina when a condemned man appeared on top of the ladder. After the last verse the executioner did his job. Now and then the chant was interrupted by a loud shout of "Vive le Roi!" as a messenger arrived on horseback at full gallop from Versailles, waving a letter of pardon.

In 1731 the King's pardon saved the life of one, Boulleteix, who had killed a companion in an affray. His head was already in the noose when the messenger arrived. He was untied and taken to the Café Marchand in the Quai Le Pelletier (now Quai de Gesvres), where he was given several glasses of wine while the Clerk of the Court passed round his own hat, collecting money for him. On the next Sunday Boulleteix went to the Place de Grève and begged from the crowd. The nearness of death "had turned his blood," his face was the colour of saffron and "a number of decent people gave him money."

A citizen discovered one day that his silver forks were missing. He accused his servant girl of stealing them. Though she protested her innocence, he brought his complaint before the Courts. The girl was sentenced to death, then hanged. Six months later the forks were found in the nest of a magpie. In the Church of Saint-Jean-en-Grève (demolished before the Revolution), at the corner of the Place de Grève and the rue de Lobeau, the repentant citizen had a daily Mass offered up for the poor servant girl. It came to be known as the Mass of the Magpie.

In 1830 a murderer called Verdure was executed. His brother, who was among the spectators, afterwards went to a low cabaret, where he laughingly showed his friends four watches he had stolen from onlookers while the guillotine did its work.

At around the same time, a criminal called Lacenaire, who had served several sentences, used to dine in a small and cheap restaurant frequented by artists and men of letters. Lacenaire had a remarkably fine handwriting and took temporary employment with a firm of letter copyists. He begged all and sundry in the restaurant to give him work. He had fallen on hard days and would copy anything at a very modest rate. Out of sheer kindness two young playwrights gave him their play to copy. The next day he brought back the manuscript, declaring that he would not do the work.

"I read the play," he said. "I find it stupid."

With all the thrills and spectacles that Paris offered, the Parisian was loath to undertake journeys. He was convinced in any case that dangers of many sorts lurked beyond the city walls. In the 1760s an anonymous writer wrote a little leaflet on the Parisian's reactions if he ventured out of the town. It was entitled *Le voyage de Paris à Saint-Cloud par mer, et le retour de Saint-Cloud à Paris par terre*. The distance between Paris and Saint-Cloud was under ten miles.

The Parisian who undertook the journey took his food with him, lest the food of that distant world might be poisonous. He took leave of family and friends, offered up prayers to all the saints, and went on board the small galleon that plied between Paris and Saint-Cloud. Impressed by the vessel and the large expanse of water, he enquired when he could expect to sight East Indiamen. Passing Chaillot, he already imagined himself in the Levant, far from his own people. He shed a tear, thinking of his street. He caught sight of a fish: it must be a dried cod. The Cape of Good Hope would shortly heave into view. When he saw the smoke from the glass-works of Sèvres, he became convinced that it was from Mount Vesuvius.

On arrival in Saint-Cloud he went straight into the first church to thank the Lord for having reached his destination safe and sound; then he wrote a long letter to his dear mother, describing the dangers of the voyage. He looked less elegant than at his departure, for having sat on a coil of ropes, the seat of his velvet breeches was covered in tar. He strolled round Saint-Cloud, meditating on the mysteries of Nature and on the existence of life beyond the gates of Paris.

The return journey by land filled him with awe. He discovered to his disappointment that neither cod nor herring were caught in the Seine. When he saw the Bois de Boulogne he felt sure that ancient Druids dwelt there. The hillock Mont-Valérien was the true Calvary, which cheered him up as proof of his being still among Christians, and when he caught a glimpse of a stag, then of a peacock, he congratulated himself on having seen all God's wonders. When the coach halted at the Château de Madrid, he knew that he was in Spain. Throughout the journey he remained a true patriot, never for a moment denying his origins. Yes, he was a born native of Paris, his mother sold cloth at the Barbe d'Or and his cousin was a notary.

On reaching his home he was received with acclamation, and his aunts, who had not been near the Tuileries for twenty years, the Tuileries being in another neighbourhood, congratulated him on his courage and spirit of adventure.

Of the different hearty amusements of previous ages, the nine-teenth century retained the Procession of the Fat Ox. Learned men of the century thought that it derived from the festival of Isis and

Osiris; butchers thought that it was to advertise their trade and have fun at the same time.

The procession took place during the three days preceding Ash Wednesday, and set off each day from a different point, perambulating the principal streets of the Right Bank, then repairing to the Hôtel de Ville, the Préfecture de Police and the Tuileries, where King Louis-Philippe beamed at the ox. The procession ended at the Porte Saint-Antoine. It was escorted at front and rear by two detachments of mounted gendarmes. After the first piquet of gendarmes came a military band, followed by twenty butchers on horseback, dressed as armed Mamelukes. Behind them came the Boeuf Gras, moving at a slow pace, its horns gilded and decorated with festoons, its body covered with a white blanket with embroidered gold fleurs-de-lys. On its back was a small gilt saddle in which sat a child, winged and armed like Cupid. Four ropes, concealed under garlands of flowers, were fastened to the animal's neck, held at equal distance by four strong men accoutred like savages— covered from head to foot with flesh-coloured silk, and wearing short petticoats of tiger skin. They carried clubs decked with flowers.

The procession stopped before every cabaret, and drinks were served in profusion. With the crowd mingled butchers dressed in white, each carrying a bottle and glass for those who were either not permitted to leave the ranks or who could not reach the inns.

At the end of the third day the much acclaimed beast was slaughtered.

VII

In the Marais

The pride of the old district of the Marais is the Place des Vosges. The square has preserved its seventeenth-century elegance and dignity. If Henri IV returned—he was assassinated before it was finished—he would recognise it as the square designed under his supervision by the architects Androuet du Cerceau and Claude Chastillon. He might regret the trees in the garden because they interfere with the splendour of the view; however, the good and kind King would admit that in the Marais, where trees do not abound, the children who play in the square need the trees' shade in summer.

Officially declared a square in 1605, it was called Place Royale, a name it kept until the Revolution. In 1792 it was changed to Place des Fédérés, the following year to du Parc-d'Artillerie, then de la Fabrication-des-Armes, des Vosges in 1800 because Vosges was the first among the departments to pay the new, heavy taxes, once more Royale in 1814, de la République in 1830, des Vosges from 1831 to 1852 when it reverted to Royale, and from 1870 onward des Vosges again.

In 1338 Pierre d'Orgement, Chancellor of France, built a large turreted house, surrounded by a high wall, on the north side of what is the present square. His son Pierre, Bishop of Paris, sold the house in 1402 to the Duc de Berry, brother of Charles V who two years later exchanged it for a house owned by Louis d'Orléans, situated between the rues Saint-Antoine and de Jouy of today. Following the assassination of the Duc d'Orléans by the partisans of Jean-sans-Peur in 1407, the house was bought by the French Crown and became known as la Maison royale des Tournelles. Charles VI often visited it from his palace of Saint-Pol. After him the Duke of Bedford, English Regent of France, resided there and embellished it. His wife died in the same house in 1432. Kings Charles VII, Louis XI and Charles VIII lived in it, and Louis XII died there on January 1, 1515. François I summoned the burghers of Paris to Tournelles when he needed money.

Henri II found Tournelles "mean, insalubrious and nauseating", and used it for short stays only, generally during journeys. On July 1, 1559, between the present rues de Sévigné and Birague, the King, wearing the colours of Diane de Poitiers, jousted with Gabriel de Lorge de Montgomery, Captain of his Scots Guards. Montgomery's lance lifted the King's vizor and penetrated into the brain through the eye. Henri was carried to Tournelles where he died after ten days of awful agony.

The dying King forgave Montgomery, who left for England and became a Protestant. A Valois can forgive, but not a Medici, and Catherine de Medici, Henry II's widow, bided her time, waiting to avenge herself on the man who had accidentally killed her husband. Montgomery returned to France, and was eventually captured after desperate resistance in Domfront (Orne). On Catherine de Medici's insistence, he was sentenced to death, tortured, and dragged in a tumbril to the Place de Grève, where he was executed on June 26, 1574.

Catherine de Medici persuaded her son Charles IX to have Tournelles pulled down, and, when royalty left the district, the deserted gardens became a horse market, the horse-copers bringing beggars, thieves and tramps in their wake. The once-royal neighbourhood virtually turned into a cour des miracles. The area served another purpose too, for men of rank and fashion found it an ideal place for duelling.

The most famous duel of all concerned the Mignons, Henri III's pretty boys. On April 27, 1578, at five in the morning, three Mignons, Quélus, Maugiron and Livarot, met Balzac d'Entragues, Ribérac and Schomberg, partisans of the House of Guise, in truly mortal combat. Balzac d'Entragues was the only one unscathed. Livarot's wounds kept him in bed for seven weeks. Maugiron and Schomberg died on the spot, Ribérac the next day. As for Quélus from whom the whole idea had emanated, he languished for thirty days in the Hôtel de Boissy in the rue Saint-Antoine, where he was visited every day by the King, who offered 100,000 francs to surgeons if they saved him, and gave a similar sum to Quélus, who was the best loved of his Mignons, to encourage him to fight death and make survival worthwhile. When he died Henri broke down and cried for days. The people of Paris were amused and thought it was a huge joke.

Another famous duel took place on the night of January 26-27, 1614, between Philippe Hurault du Marais and the Marquis de Rouillac. Each had his second fighting with him. They fought with sword in one hand, holding a burning torch in the other. The Marquis de Rouillac was the sole survivor.

Cardinal de Richelieu wanted to extirpate duelling. Notwithstanding a royal edict, on May 12, 1627, a savage duel was fought between Messieurs de Montmorency-Bouteville, de Chapelles and La Berthe on one side, and Messieurs de Beuvron, Bussy d'Amboise and Buquet on the other. Bussy was killed and La Berthe wounded. Beuvron and Buquet fled to England, and Montmorency-Bouteville and Chapelles, who made good their escape on horses lent by Baron de Chantel, were captured in Vitry-le-Brûlé, now a parish of Vitry-le-François (Marne), and brought back to Paris. In spite of the influence at Court of their friends and relations, they were beheaded in the Place de Grève thirty-five days after the duel.

The last notorious duel in the Place Royale was fought on December 12, 1643, between the grandsons of Henri de Guise and

Admiral de Coligny. It was not a case of family feud, nor intended as revenge for the Massacre of St Bartholomew: it was because of a row over two women. Coligny lightly wounded Guise, who grabbed his adversary's rapier with one hand and ran him through with the other. Thus died the last of the Colignys. Guise's friends regarded it as a most chivalrous duel.

By that time the Place Royale had reverted nearer to its origins, and was inhabited by quality, though women of easy virtue roamed beneath the arcades at night. In his *Historiettes*, Gédéon Tallemant des Réaux relates that the Duc de Candalle, son of the Duc de l'Espernon, offered a soldier a piece of gold if he would have intercourse with one of those women in the full sunlight of noon in the middle of the square. The soldier was as good as his word, and when the performance began all the great ladies appeared at their windows to watch the spectacle.

When Louis XIII died, Richelieu had a statue erected to him in the middle of the square. The Cardinal found a bronze horse which Catherine de Medici had in her time ordered from Daniel de Volterre, a pupil of Michelangelo. She wanted a statue of Henri II, but nothing came of it. Briard fils now sculpted a larger-than-life-size statue of Louis XIII which he mounted on the bronze horse that now looked no bigger than a pony. On the marble plinth was inscribed:

"To the glorious and immortal memory of the most high and most invincible Louis the Just, XIII of the name, King of France and Navarre. Armand Cardinal and Duc de Richelieu, his principal minister in all his illustrious and generous schemes, heaped with honours and gifts by so good a master and generous monarch, had this statue raised as an eternal mark of his zeal, loyalty and gratitude."

A wag coined a less fulsome inscription: "He had the hundred virtues of a lackey and none of a master." And for the tomb of the King this epitaph was suggested:

> Ci-gît le Roi, notre bon maître
> Qui fut vingt ans valet d'un prêtre

The eternal mark of Richelieu's zeal was melted down during the Revolution; in 1819 a white marble statue of the King by Cortot and Dupaty was erected in its place and is still constantly visited by the pigeons.

In the Hôtel d'Aubray, 12 rue Charles-V, built in 1620, resided Marie-Madeleine d'Aubray, Marquise de Brinvilliers, born in Paris in 1630, who both by birth and marriage had the world at her feet. Her social position was such that she could have had everything anyone could normally want. Yet she wanted a little more: in fact to watch others die a horrible death.

She was a small, round-faced woman whose blue eyes radiated kindness, and whose skin was praised by her contemporaries for its whiteness. Her father, Dreux d'Aubray, was civil governor of the Grand Châtelet, where the Paris parliament, a judiciary body, met. Her husband, Antoine Gobelin, Marquis de Brinvilliers, was the last of the Gobelins. They were originally dyers from Rheims who settled on the Left Bank, and made a vast fortune. The village of Les Gobelins was called after them. Antoine de Gobelin was too rich to have anything to do with business. Marie-Madeleine and her husband lived in fine style. She took the Chevalier Godin de Sainte-Croix as her lover, and under his great influence, together they concocted potions consisting of vitriol, poison of adder and arsenic. Police Lieutenant Nicolas-Gabriel de La Reynie, who under Louis XIV organised the Paris police, wrote of her, "Who would have believed that a woman brought up in an honest family, and whose figure was so fragile, could go to hospitals for the fun of poisoning the sick to observe the effects of her poison?"

She gave François Roussel, one of her lackeys, a slice of ham which made him feel "as if his heart were stung". Her father, shocked by the way she carried on with her lover, had Sainte-Croix put into the Bastille, but he did not remain there long. The Marquise decided to punish her father, but succeeded in killing him off only after the tenth dose. Then, with the connivance of a servant, she poisoned her two brothers.

She remained a quiet little woman with a sweet smile and the patients in the hospitals looked forward to her visits. In 1670 Sainte-Croix died of natural causes, and not of poison as was later suggested. When an inventory was taken, bottles and powders were found in the turret of 5 rue de Hautefeuille where he had mostly lived. The contents of the bottles and the powders were tried on animals, which died in terrible pain. The Marquise fled to England, later moved to the Low Countries, and was supposedly arrested in a convent in Liège by Desgrez, an agent of de La Reynie, who had come to the convent disguised as a priest. However, the truth was that a French spy, Descarrières, had found out where she was, arrested her and brought her back to Paris. A full, written confession of her misdeeds was found on her. She had poisoned more people than the authorities suspected.

She was executed in the Place de Grève on July 16, 1676, after having made amends and due apology in Notre-Dame. (During her incarceration she behaved with decorum, and her piety was sincere.) She wore only a shift, and a rope tied round her neck. The large crowd included ladies of fashion, the Marquise de Sévigné among them. "It is, is it not, a beautiful spectacle?" she called to them from the tumbril. Bare-footed she mounted the scaffold. The executioner took a leisurely quarter of an hour in preparing her for death; he shaved her hair, set the trap, turned her head towards the gibbet, then turned it away, almost more of an agony than the hanging itself. After she was hanged, her body was burnt and her ashes scattered. "The next day," wrote Madame de Sévigné, "the people came to look for her bones because they thought her a saint."

Today the Hôtel d'Aubray is occupied by the Sisters of Bon-Secours-de-Troyes, and in the court of honour, where Sainte-Croix used to throw his weight about, an old nun stands, waiting to give an injection to a patient, for injections are given free to the poor of the neighbourhood. If you enter the house and look up at the

winding staircase with its wrought-iron rails you may see another
nun coming down to minister to the sick. The past has truly been
scattered to the wind.

By the second half of the eighteenth century, the Marais had lost
much of its elegance. Its new inhabitants were the poorer, but very
conservative, small nobility. Bigoted, and bemoaning the awful
morals of their day, despising its worldliness and the wickedness of
the fashionable Faubourg Saint-Germain, they hated the philoso-
phers, and read only novels of chivalry and the *Mercure de France*.
They spent their time playing cards for small stakes and abhorring
the mutinous poor of the Faubourg Saint-Marcel who filled the
cabarets of Vaugirard on Sundays.

During the Empire, the Marais continued to decline, yet it was
in the Marais, in the cul-de-sac Saint-Pierre (now rue Villehardouin)
where history was nearly changed. The year was 1812.

On October 22 a sergeant of the Paris garrison arrived in Dr
Dubuisson's mental home at the Barrière du Trône (now Place de
la Nation). He came to deliver a message to General Malet, who
was detained there by the Emperor's orders. "Compiègne", the
sergeant whispered. That was the code word of the conspirators.
The general nodded: he had been waiting to hear it for a long time.

Claude-François de Malet, born at Dole (Jura) in 1754, had been
a musketeer under the old order, but rallied to the Revolution
and fought with the Army of the Rhine, then with the Army of
Italy; he was made a general of brigade in 1799. He became hostile
to the Consulate, then to the Empire. In vain Napoleon tried to win
him over to his cause, but Malet conspired against him, and in 1808
was put into the prison of La Force in the Marais, where he continued
to plot the downfall of the Emperor. In time he got himself transferred to Dr Dubuisson's mental home.

After the sergeant's departure the general sat down to dine with
the other inmates. Someone observed that surely tomorrow news
would arrive of a victory in Russia: Paris had been without news

for some time. After dinner Malet played his usual game of whist, and retired towards ten. He waited until eleven, then tiptoed out into the garden. It was pouring with rain. He let himself out of the grounds, using a stolen key, and vanished into the night in the company of the Abbé Lafon, a fervid royalist who was also a detainee. The Abbé carried a leather box crammed with papers, the proclamations of the Provisional Government. The two men hurried along the rue Saint-Antoine, crossed the Place des Vosges, took the rue des Minimes, reached the rue Neuve-Saint-Gilles (now part of the rue de Turenne), then turned into the rue Villehardouin, where they entered a hovel. The Abbé Caamano, a pock-marked Spaniard, was waiting for them. The hovel was in ideal surroundings for conspirators, being close only to large gardens, convents and monasteries. Malet donned the general's uniform that the Abbé Caamano had laid out for him, signed the proclamations and orders, then had a quick meal accompanied by a glass of claret.

At eleven-thirty a naked man stepped out of a fiacre and burst into the house. This was Rateau, a corporal of the Guard of Paris, who, in his excitement to put on the elegant uniform of an adjutant which Malet had promised him, had discarded his corporal's uniform in the cab. Rateau was twenty-eight years old.

At dawn Malet was ready to leave. The Abbé Lafon had in the meantime had second thoughts and did not want to follow him. "Too late," said Malet, "the guillotine is at the door." At half past four, followed by faithful Rateau, he arrived at the barracks of Popincourt, where he announced to Colonels Rabbe and Soulier that Napoleon had been killed on the ramparts of Moscow and that the Provisional Government had made him military governor of Paris. On his orders Generals Guidal and Lahorie were released from La Force, Guidal designated as Minister of Police and Lahorie as Prefect of Police.

Malet hurried on to General Hulin, the military governor of Paris, whose residence was in the Place Vendôme.

"You are under arrest," Malet informed him.

"Show me your orders," Hulin replied.

"Here they are," said Malet, breaking his jaw with a pistol shot.

Hulin's wife appeared, wakened by the bang; Malet told her to look after her wounded husband. Then, still accompanied by Rateau, he crossed the square to the office of the staff of the Paris garrison. Commander Doucet, Chief of Staff, and his adjutant, Laborde, hesitated to accept orders from Malet, who immediately drew his pistol. They had, however, noticed his movement in the looking-glass, and sensing that something was wrong, managed to over-power both him and Rateau. By then messengers had arrived from General Hulin.

Tied with ropes, Malet was dragged to the balcony and shown to the troops in the square. Guidal and Lahorie were arrested.

The conspirators were tried at once. No lawyer dared defend them, and with dignity Malet conducted his own defence.

"Who are your accomplices?" the President of the Tribunal asked.

"The whole of France, including you had I succeeded."

All the conspirators—fourteen in number—were sentenced to death, and on October 29, in six fiacres, escorted by gendarmes, they were taken to the Plaine de Grenelle, the usual place for military executions. When Malet faced the firing squad he called to the soldiers: "It is my privilege here to give you orders. Aim! Fire!" He shouted, "Long live liberty!" as he fell.

One of the fourteen was an old captain called Borderieux who had seen many campaigns. He had followed Malet because it was a captain's duty to take orders from a general. He did not quite under-stand what it was all about.

"Long live the Emperor!" was his last cry.

VIII

The Bastille

The Bastille (see Illustration 30) was built to form part of the
Enceinte of Charles V at the end of the rue Saint-Antoine. Hughes
Aubriot, Provost of Paris, was charged by the King with the supervision of the new fortifications, and it was he who laid the foundation stone of the Bastille on April 22, 1369. The fortified Castle of
Bastille-Saint-Antoine was finished in 1383 in the reign of Charles
VI. The rue Saint-Antoine became a cul-de-sac with the Castle at
the end, and to leave Paris one had to take the rue de la Bastille to
the new Porte Saint-Antoine. The Bastille had two towers at the
start, constructed with the object of strengthening the defence of
Paris against the English. In time two further towers were erected,
parallel with the first two. Eventually their number increased to
eight. At first they were connected by drawbridges only. The walls
came later. The whole was surrounded by a moat.

A guard was always mounted at the entrance gate facing the rue
Saint-Antoine. The gate opened on the Courtyard of the Governor,
whose mansion was later built in the sixteenth century, and a moat
separated the courtyard from the Castle proper, to reach which one
had first to cross a drawbridge guarded by a sentry. Past the guardhouse was a high gate, beyond it the Great Courtyard, to enter

which five more gates, each with a sentry, had to be passed, and two drawbridges crossed. The Great Courtyard was a hundred and twenty feet long and eighty feet wide. The windows of the prison officials and clerks gave on to the Great Courtyard and when there were too many prisoners some of the privileged ones were transferred to rooms adjoining those of the clerks. Strictly speaking, there were no cells in the Bastille. It was no ordinary prison.

Alongside the building that housed the officials and clerks rose the Tour de la Comté, next came the Tour du Trésor, so named because in that tower was guarded the treasure the Duc de Sully had collected for Henri IV. An arcade followed which in the days of Charles VI was still the city gate. Inside the walls lodged the prison staff. The old chapel beyond the arcade had been turned into prisoners' quarters. At the corner stood the Tour de la Chapelle, one of the two original towers, the other being the Tour du Trésor. A wall ten feet thick, raised to the height of the towers, contained the prisoners' rooms.

On the other side of the wall was the Courtyard du Puits, where a new building was erected in the seventeenth century. Five steps led to the entrance door, beyond it a staircase to the suites upstairs. To the right of the staircase was the entrance hall to the stately room where the Ministers and the Lieutenant of Police or the higher officials interrogated the prisoners. The room was known as the Chambre du Conseil. In an adjacent room were kept the prisoners' papers and belongings. Behind the Salle du Conseil lodged some of the high officials, their deputies and some of the turnkeys.

On the left of the entrance door downstairs were located the kitchens, pantries and the laundry. Their doors gave on the Courtyard du Puits. Above the kitchens were three rooms on each of the three floors in which were kept privileged prisoners and the sick. The King's Lieutenant had his suite above the Salle du Conseil, the Major (Deputy-Governor) on the second floor, and the surgeon on the third.

On the other side of the Great Courtyard near the Tour de la Liberté, so called because of the dungeons in its cellar, lived the bulk of the prisoners. Each had one large and one small room, their windows overlooking Paris.

The chapel was on the ground floor. In the walls were three heavily barred recesses, and against the walls were two similarly barred wooden closets, from within which, one at a time in each closet or recess, the prisoners heard Mass. They pulled the curtains aside at the Sanctus and drew them at the Postcommunion. There were two Masses daily for prisoners, and since only five could be present at a time, if there were more than ten prisoners in the Bastille they were unable to go to Mass every day, unless there were those who refused or did not feel like going. In matters of conscience there was no compulsion.

Beyond the chapel rose the Tour de la Bertaudière, followed by the apartments of the Assistant-Major, the Captain of the Gate, some servants and turnkeys. Nearby stood the Tour de la Bazinière, but to reach it one had to pass a guardhouse and go through a heavy gate. If one followed the alley one reached the Tour du Coin at the angle of the Courtyard du Puits. In the building beside the tower lodged the cooks, the scullions and lackeys. The rooms above theirs were rarely used. The Courtyard du Puits was only twenty-five feet long and fifty wide, with a well in the middle into which the cooks threw all the garbage, and, since they kept chickens in that small enclosed space, the well was filthy and the water undrinkable. The Tour du Puits faced the rue des Tournelles, and the entrance to the Castle was between the Tours de la Bazinière and de la Comté.

The towers were about seventy-two feet high. Four of them faced Paris, four the Faubourg Saint-Antoine. They were connected by high walls, along the tops of which the prisoners were allowed to stroll by permission of the Lieutenant, though invariably accompanied by a guard. The thirteen pieces of ordnance atop the walls were fired on feast days and occasions of national rejoicing.

Though from time to time prisoners were held in the Bastille, it remained a military fortress until Cardinal de Richelieu turned it exclusively into a place of detention. His first prisoner was Charles Leclerc du Tremblay, brother of Father Joseph, the Grey Eminence.

It was not defamatory to be locked up in the Bastille, for all prisoners were detained under a "lettre de cachet", which was really a letter of introduction from the King. However, such a letter was not something that one sought. It was short:

"Monsieur le Gouverneur, Sending to my Castle of the Bastille Sieur (name followed) I write this letter to tell you that it is my intention that he should be received by you and kept in safety until my new order. The present having no other purpose I pray to God to keep you, Monsieur le Gouverneur, in good health."

Beneath the King's signature was that of the Minister.

The prisoners' rooms were cold and humid in winter, hot in summer. The furniture in the reigns of Louis XIV, XV, and XVI consisted of an iron bedstead with mattress and green curtains, two tables, two jugs, one fork, one spoon, a tin goblet, brass candlestick, a pair of snuffers, chamber-pot, two or three chairs and now and then a rickety armchair. The prisoners received a provision of matches, one tinderbox, flint and one candle each day. The rooms were swept weekly and the sheets changed fortnightly. Each room had treble doors, all locked.

The price of food was according to a tariff from 50 livres down to 2 livres and 10 sous a day. Laundry and candles were included in the price. The lowest rate permitted no more than the tipping of the turnkeys and servants, so that those who could afford only that lowly sum were really fed by the prison. The food was prepared by a chef who was the Governor's steward. He had a cook, a scullion and a sawyer of wood under him. The food was cooked with little care and the rations were meagre, providing the Governor with his goldmine, according to the prisoners. On meat-days, the midday meal included soup, boiled beef and a vegetable; on fast-days, soup, fish and two vegetables: in the evenings on meat-days, a slice of roast meat, a stew and a salad. The prisoner who paid the highest tariff received half a chicken extra for his dinner, or a pigeon or a rabbit, all of them smelling of cabbage; on fast-days, a dish of eggs, a vegetable, and a pudding which was hardly worth 2 sous. Sunday's dinner consisted of soup, boiled cow, which the steward had the cheek to call beef, and four small pies; for supper, there was a slice of roast veal or mutton, a small plate of beans, full of bones and turnips, and a salad. The cooking oil, just good enough for street lamps, was nauseating. Now and then the prisoners were given mutton chops or tripe and spinach, and on fast-days carp, either fried or poached. On the feast days of SS Louis, Martin and Epiphany, even the non-paying prisoners received half a roast chicken or a pigeon.

Daily all prisoners were supplied with a pound of bread and a bottle of wine which tasted like vinegar. The cutlery was poor, one needed influence to be allowed silver knives and forks. Worst of all was the tasteless, badly cooked food. The prison officials had no supervision whatever over the kitchen, as it was directly under the control of the Governor. A few rich prisoners were occasionally allowed to have food sent in from eating-houses. It cost three times as much as could ever be paid for prison food, however. The ordinary, non-paying, prisoners received five logs a day in winter; the privileged ones had as many as they wanted.

(Thus groused the Sieur Brossays Du Perray who was long detained in the Bastille in the reign of Louis XV.)

Day and night, the sentry inside the Bastille rang a handbell every hour to show that he was awake. The night patrol rang a handbell every quarter of an hour. The bridges were drawn between ten and eleven at night; if a King's Messenger arrived, a bridge was let down whatever the time.

On arrival in the Bastille the ordinary prisoner was searched, and his clothes, luggage and linen carefully examined to see whether there were hidden papers concerning the reason for his arrest. Men of rank usually escaped such close scrutiny, but were asked to hand over their knives, razors, scissors, watches, canes, jewels and money. Then the prisoner was taken to an apartment and locked behind three doors. If he had no servant of his own, he had to make his own bed and fire. Dinner was brought at eleven in the morning and supper at six in the evening.

At the beginning of his detention, books, paper, and ink were withheld from him, and he was not permitted to go to Mass or for a walk, nor to write letters, not even to the Lieutenant of Police on whom his fate in the Bastille depended. Permission to write to the Lieutenant was normally given when the prisoner petitioned the Major, and, once this privilege was granted, he was then allowed to Mass, though only every second Sunday. In his letter to the Lieutenant the prisoner might ask for authority to write to his family, to receive their reply and to keep his own servant in the Castle. One had to apply to the Lieutenant for the smallest trifle, and his decisions depended on the detainee's case.

The Bastille possessed a library founded by a foreigner who was a prisoner there in the first decade of the eighteenth century and who died within the walls. Some of the prisoners had the privilege of visiting the library; others had the books brought to their rooms.

The fate of the prisoners was in the hands of the Lieutenant and the Ministers. They were not discouraged to write to the King. Many did so: none received a reply.

During his detention Brossays Du Perray spoke to old prisoners who had been, or had known those who had been, contemporaries of the Man in the Iron Mask. All they could tell him was that the Governor always stood in his presence, which seemed to confirm that he was of royal blood. However, this was only hearsay since none of them could have been present. The mask was not of iron but of black velvet.

When Louis XVI came to the throne, many prisoners were released, among them an old man who had been detained for forty-seven years. The old man thought he was dreaming. His legs had become so weak, and his eyes were so unaccustomed to the harsh light of liberty, that he had to be helped into the carriage that was to take him home. The shaking of the carriage exhausted him, and on arrival he had to be lifted out. There he was in his street, but his house had long been pulled down, and a public building stood on the site. The whole neighbourhood looked different and he saw no familiar face.

He plied the other old men of the district with questions about his family. They could not help him. He went to see the man he had worked for before his detention but did not recognise him. Slowly it transpired that his wife had died thirty years before and that his children had left Paris long ago. Shattered, the old man waited on the Minister and begged him to be allowed back to the Bastille. The Minister took pity on him, and the retired porter of the house that had been pulled down was attached to him, so that he should have near him someone to whom he could speak of his wife and children. The old man turned the bedroom he was given into a replica of his room in the Bastille. It was not the same thing, and he died soon after.

On July 2, 1789, the Marquis de Launay, Governor of the Bastille, reported to Monsieur de Villedeuil, Minister of State, that the Marquis de Sade, who was then a prisoner in the Bastille, had been shouting through his window to the people in the rue Saint-Antoine that the prisoners were to be butchered and murdered and that the people should come at once to their help. The Governor, therefore, felt compelled to withdraw all de Sade's privileges, including that of walking along the walls. Undismayed, de Sade constructed a sort of loudspeaker from a tin pipe used for emptying water, and continued vociferating through his casement window. People assembled in the street, and he abused the Governor and urged them to come to his help, otherwise he would be massacred.

He gave his version in a letter, complaining that, because of a little trouble he had caused, the Governor had seen fit to denounce him. According to the Governor he had harangued the populace, shouting that preparations were in progress to butcher the prisoners, and exhorting them to pull down that monument of horror. "It's all true," he added.

On July 4, the Marquis de Sade was sent to the madhouse of Charenton, and the one to be massacred was the Governor when the Bastille was taken ten days later.

Vast crowds visited the Bastille from July 15 onwards, and their number was so large and their behaviour so unruly that Soulès, a moderate, who was appointed Governor by La Fayette, stopped further visits and wrote to the Municipal Council explaining his reasons: "such damage has already been done by them to the fortress that it will cost at least 200,000 livres to have it repaired." Danton, who the night before had been made Captain of the National Guard, was so incensed by Soulès's letter, and convinced also that a moderate like him would let the enemy back into the Bastille, that he went to the Bastille at the head of a shouting mob, where he collared the new Governor and dragged him to the Hôtel de Ville. Soulès's order was rescinded and visitors flocked again to the Bastille. Later, public dances were held there, wine flowed to the sound of fiddles, and the printed patterns on chintzes of the epoch showed the ruins of the Bastille with the inscription: "Ici l'on danse!"

IX

Fiacre, Coachman and Omnibus

Already in the eighteenth century traffic had become a problem. In vain did the exasperated passenger shout, "Whip them, coachman!" The fiacre remained stuck to the spot, since the coachman had enough sense to appreciate that horses could not fly. In time the expression "fouette, cocher!" came to mean that the passenger hailed from the provinces, for only provincials still had faith that the whip would open a passage through the congestion. This is not to imply that Paris coachmen were more reluctant to use their whips than were their counterparts in the country. They used them on their own horses, other coachmen's horses, on fellow coachmen, indeed on pedestrians. In brief, the whips were always at the ready, yet their use did not hasten the flow of traffic. Then, as now, the streets of Paris were often invincible.

Here dustmen barred progress with their carts and bins; yonder a wagon laden with heavy stones was waiting beside a construction site to be discharged, or a shaft-horse might have fallen. As one lot of chaos sorted itself out, water carts appeared, moving in slow procession and stopping in front of every house. Then the heavy wagons from the country, laden with fruit or vegetables, got in everybody's way; their drivers appeared frequently to be asleep, but as their seats were practically on the shaft, they could hardly see in any case where their horses were taking them. The horses knew the way, but theirs was a ponderous progress. Washerwomen were among the worst traffic offenders, their vehicles staying for three to four hours outside a house while inside they made out the laundry list. (A laundress's cart, it is recorded, once kept as many as four hundred carriages waiting.) The never-too-patient coachmen would suddenly succumb to their passengers' entreaties or their own fury, and try to whip their way through the pedestrians, who might not find time to run for safety.

There was little respect for the pedestrian. The running footman pushed him out of the way, the dogs cavorting beside their master's carriage caused him to trip, and if a coachman or a gentleman driving his own equipage felt that the pedestrian was somehow to be blamed for the delay, the poor fellow received the full impact of the driver's anger, generally imparted by the whip.

One day in the year 1776, as Jean-Jacques Rousseau was taking a stroll in Ménilmontant, a Great Dane, running in front of a berline, charged straight into him and bowled him over. The dog's master did not bother to stop, but next day, discovering who the victim was, sent a servant to him.

"My master would like to do something for you, sir," the servant said. "He charged me to find out what you want."

"I want him to keep his dog on a lead," replied Rousseau, dismissing the man.

Coachmen, like the carriages and horses, were the reflection of their masters' rank and station. One saw at a glance whether the turn-out belonged to a courtesan or a duke, a President of Parliament or a financier. Even the words used to instruct a coachman differed from class to class. On leaving the theatre, the inhabitants of the Marais ordered their coachmen to take them to their lodging; those of the Ile-Saint-Louis to their house; and those of the Faubourg

Saint-Germain to their mansion. The élite of the Faubourg Saint-Honoré simply said, "Go!"

Outside the theatres lounged the aboyeurs, the barkers, who sprang to life when the show was over. In booming voices they shouted, "The coach of Monsieur le Marquis!. . . . The coach of Madame la Comtesse! . . . The coach of Monsieur le Président! . . .", their voices reaching the cabaret where the lackeys were drinking and the billiard saloon where the coachmen were arguing.

In 1640 Nicolas Sauvage of Amiens had the original notion of putting at the public's disposal, at certain points of the town, carriages with coachmen and harnessed horses. He brought his idea to Paris. The first such point, or cab rank, was outside an inn in the rue Saint-Martin called Au grand Saint-Fiacre. Hence the fiacre. Apart from sedan chairs, which could be hired from 1617, the only other vehicles for hire before the fiacres were the carosses à 5 sols, but they had no ranks, and one had to search for them or go direct to the coach-house. They were a haphazard enterprise. An order of Parliament promulgated in 1622 forbade their use to soldiers, pages, workmen, lackeys and all other liveried persons, so as to safeguard the comfort of the citizens.

In the eighteenth century, the fiacre was no elegant turn-out. The coachmen were proud that the horses came from the royal stables, albeit only after the animals had become too old or afflicted for further work. The miserable beasts had to work eighteen hours a day, constantly under the lash of the whip. They were seldom rubbed down, and pulled their cabs emaciated and dirty. Their happiest moment was when some lover took the cab and sat in it behind drawn curtains with his mistress, because then the fiacre pulled into a side street and remained stationary while the tryst lasted.

Foreigners were revolted by the shabby cabs and skinny horses, comparing them with the cleaner and smarter cabs of London, Brussels and Amsterdam. The fiacre owners themselves were dissatisfied with the irksome police regulations. One day they drove in procession to Choisy to petition Louis XVI. The Court was unpleasantly surprised to observe the arrival of eighteen hundred empty fiacres: not a reassuring sight. The petition was not accepted, the fiacres were ordered back to Paris, the four leaders were imprisoned and their leader sent to Bicêtre, which was both gaol and lunatic asylum.

The fiacres often broke down; none the less one had to pay the fare. They were not allowed to ply outside Paris without paying special dues. The fiacre owners continued bitterly to complain of their daily tax of 20 sous, and their vehicles remained dirty and rickety well into the nineteenth century.

Between 1830 and 1855 new fiacre models appeared: citadines, urbaines, deltas, cabriolets compteurs, lutéciennes, cabriolets milords, thérèses and les cabs. The old, yellow cabriolet gave way to the coupé, a small carriage that became the most popular, much to the regret of the old coachmen. "All these coupés, all these modern carriages," they said, "will never last. You take a good old cabriolet not because you want to reach your destination quickly but because you want to chat to the coachman." Yet the coupé won.

In the middle of the century the Compagnie Générale was formed. It came to own most of the fiacres in Paris. They had a hundred and sixty employees in their office, a hundred and sixty inspectors to check on the coachmen, nine hundred workmen in their coach-building yard, a hundred and eighty blacksmiths, nine hundred cleaners and nine hundred grooms and stable boys. The company was run by efficient men who brought order and system into the world of fiacres. They chose their horses with care and trained them scientifically, starting with three hours of work a day, because they appreciated that if a horse was overworked at the beginning, it might die before it reached the target of staying out, say, from seven in the morning until midnight. The horses were well fed and kept clean, since that too was in the interest of business. "In Paris," one of the managers observed, "you need powerful horses accustomed to privation and misery." The company succeeded in controlling all their interests with the irritating exception of the coachmen themselves.

The fiacre coachmen were born rebels, always ready to fight and, when possible, to cheat boss and passenger. They hated the entire world, including the Préfecture de Police, though when summoned there—a frequent occurrence—they grovelled abjectly. That did not stop them cursing the authorities the moment they were allowed to go. They came to the capital from Lorraine, Normandy, Auvergne and Savoy. There were hardly any Parisians among them. Some of them came because they loved horses. They were the good and decent coachmen with whom owners and police had little trouble. They had but one aim, namely to put aside enough money to buy their own turn-out, an object achieved by quite a few of them. However, they were not the typical Paris coachmen.

The drunks formed a large proportion. Between fares, they rushed into the nearest cabaret to swallow a "canon" of wine. Yet they drove well and seldom had accidents, driving being second nature to them. They were not disliked by passengers and did not ill-treat their horses. "A drunkard's horse is never skinny," says an old French proverb. The drunk chose the life of a coachman because it gave him a sense of freedom and independence. He was the master and the ruler while he sat on the box and held in his hand the badge of his importance, the whip.

A third category, known as the bohemians, consisted of a recalcitrant group who took to the trade thinking that it entailed little work and even less control. The bohemians were in constant trouble with their employers and the police, and frequently ended up either in the gutter of unemployment (during the last century the workless were still free to starve to death) or in prison. They were disappointed men, for a coachman's life was not as easy as they had hoped. They were not wine drinkers like the friendly drunkards. Absinthe was their beverage and in their language strangling a parrot meant swallowing a glass of absinthe. The horses could fall down dead as far as they were concerned. In the days of the Second Empire a fiacre of the Compagnie Générale failed to return to the coach-house one night. In the morning an inspector was sent out to look for it. He found it at a street corner, minus coachman and horse. On the previous evening, the coachman had taken the horse out of the shafts, sold it in the street, then gone off on a huge drunken spree. On being arrested in a tavern near the Fortifications and hauled before a magistrate, his defence consisted of but one sentence, "I felt like having a night out."

The career of a coachman fascinated men in different walks of life. Even those in whose lives the horse as such played no part hankered after the whip and the box. Among coachmen, many oddities were to be found, such as waiters, barbers, wigmakers, water-carriers, dismissed schoolmasters, clerks, bankrupt photographers, unfrocked priests, and in the 1860s there was an ambassador's son who preferred the life of a fiacre coachman to that provided by his station.

In Alphonse Daudet's *Sapho*, the heroine's father was an old, drunken fiacre coachman, and one night, as she and her lover left the theatre, they ran into him. His list of woes was long. The woman he had married, after deserting his daughter and her mother, had been taken to hospital, business was bad, and money increasingly scarce. However, he still held the whip firmly in his hand. Since his daughter had had several influential lovers, he wondered whether she needed a coachman. He would not mind driving her horses. She explained that she had no carriage. "Tant pis alors," he said and swaggered off.

On September 16, 1855, Monsieur Juge, Director of the Ecole Normale of Douai, was on a visit to Paris with his wife. They took a fiacre in the Place de la Concorde and drove to the Bois de Boulogne. The coachman, whose name was Collignon, overcharged them, and M Juge, who disliked being done, went to complain at the Préfecture de Police. On September 22, Collignon was ordered to call on him to refund the excess charge. It was a matter of only a few francs. Collignon bought two pistols. Two days later he sold all his chattels and went to 83 rue d'Enfer (now rue des Ursins), where M Juge was lodging. The two men spoke calmly, without raising their voices. Collignon paid, but as M Juge bent over the table to sign the receipt, Collignon whipped out a pistol and shot him through the head. As Mme Juge threw herself on her dying husband, Collignon fired at her also, but missed. He raced down the stairs and out into the street, where he was caught by a policeman who had heard the shots.

On November 12 he appeared at the Assizes, and neither there nor in prison showed the slightest regret or remorse; not even when led to the gallows.

Towards the end of last century, a certain lady retired from brothel keeping. She had done remarkably well, though she had started on the lowest rung of the ladder, in a provincial establishment near the military barracks. With industry and acumen she had worked her way to the top. She had had the advantage of a clever ponce, whom she married in the course of her career, and he advised her on business matters, looked after her interests, pimped assiduously, and in short was her right arm in every sense. Now all that was over. Their fortune was big enough to enable them to turn their backs on the past, and they bought a private mansion in the centre of the capital. Yet both she and her husband felt rather isolated in fashionable Paris. (Fashionable in those days was used as a French word.) She tried everything she could think of to make herself noticed by the quality. She bought good furniture and pictures by winners of the Prix de Rome, took the best box in the theatre and left nothing to chance. Nevertheless her isolation continued. Then one day she heard that a famous private coachman, who had been in the service of a distinguished nobleman, was looking for a job. She promptly sent for him.

The coachman, of course, knew about her. He asked for double the wages that he would have accepted elsewhere. She agreed. He was willing to drive only every other day. She agreed to that too. He needed a stable boy who would also fetch his meals from the house and not the sort of food with which servants were satisfied. Again she nodded her consent.

"There is one more condition," the coachman said. "I am not driving your husband."

In the 1860s a story circulated in Paris which was probably true. It serves to reveal the coachman's mentality. A gentleman won a large sum of money at his club. He left after midnight and took the coupé that he hired by the month. When he reached his house he found that his wallet was missing. It must have dropped out in the carriage. He hurried to the coach-house, where he found the coachman feeding the horse, not yet having looked inside the cab. The gentleman opened the door, saw the wallet lying on the seat, and said to the coachman, "Thank God I found my wallet. It contains all this. I won it at cards tonight." He showed the coachman the imposing bank roll and gave him a good tip. After he had left the coachman went to the back of the coach-house and, in his despair at having missed the chance of a lifetime, hanged himself from a rafter.

The Compagnie Générale also hired out carriages for private use. A barouche with two horses cost 1,200 francs a month in the second half of last century, plus 150 francs for the coachman, and, if one wanted a footman on the box, that was 6 francs a day extra. A page cost more because of the epaulettes, and the company even provided powdered personnel on demand. They had a beauty parlour on the premises. If required, they provided bells for the horses. At weddings, there was no extra charge for the flowers worn by the coachman in their buttonholes and those which decorated their whips.

The smart young set liked hiring pony-chaises, which had a rather dashing appearance. They drove the chaises themselves, usually to show off in the Bois de Boulogne. The bloods had to pay in advance, whereas for a family barouche the paterfamilias was not required to settle before the end of the month.

Public transport was one of Blaise Pascal's ideas. The name omnibus orginated from him too. He spoke of it to the Duc de Roannez who in 1661 obtained a concession from Louis XIV. The first omnibuses appeared in the streets of Paris eleven years later. The itineraries were fixed by the King. The coachmen wore the livery of the Town of Paris, and the fleur-de-lys was painted on the doors of the coaches. There were three lines, each served by seven carriages. The first plied between the Porte Saint-Antoine and the Luxembourg; the second between the Place Royale (Place des Vosges) and the Church of Saint-Roch; the third between the Luxembourg and the Church of Saint-Eustache. The coaches had to ply between the different districts at regular intervals, and it was laid down that the passengers be charged for their seats only, and at a moderate price.

The first omnibuses had room for six passengers; later, two more seats were added. The coaches were strictly reserved for the members of the middle classes. Now and then a nobleman might ride in one, but that was such a rare and untoward event that it was likely to be reported in the gazettes. The lower orders were not permitted to use the coaches, which lasted for fifteen years, then vanished from the streets.

Pascal's idea was not resurrected until 1826, and not in Paris but in Nantes, where it had such a signal success that Monsieur Baudry, who was responsible for the venture, wanted to start a similar enterprise in the capital. Baudry, however, had a revolutionary past (he was mixed up with the Carbonari) and Delavau, the Prefect of Police, eyed him with suspicion. The Prefect also saw political dangers in a venture that sought indiscriminately to cater for all classes. Instead of Paris, therefore, Bordeaux became the next city to have omnibuses. They were again so successful that Debelleyme, the new Prefect of Police, gave his fiat to the venture, and the Enterprise Générale des Omnibus was founded in Paris.

The first omnibuses had fourteen seats. A ticket cost 5 sous, the same sum as in the time of Louis XIV. The heavy coaches, shaped not unlike a gondola, were drawn by three horses. Each coach had three trumpets worked by a foot pedal which called the passengers in lugubrious tones. In 1853 appeared the impériales (top-decks), where smokers, students, and workmen preferred to travel. One paid only half price on the top deck.

In time, only two horses were used to draw an omnibus; but at every incline—there were thirty-one on the company's itinerary—an extra horse was harnessed to the omnibus to help it up the hill. The heavy horses were brought from Normandy, Perche, Ardennes and Brittany. Geldings were preferred. The same pair of horses always worked together and had the same coachman. Each omnibus had ten horses attached to it which worked in five relays, a relay extending no longer than sixteen kilometres. In this way the horses endured, some remaining at work at the age of fifteen in spite of having been every day in harness.

Pickpockets reaped an agreeable harvest on the omnibuses. The women specialised in slitting pockets. The men preferred purses, using a string with a tiny piece of lead on the end. The technique was to allow the weighted string to drop into a purse when a passenger opened it to pay the fare, and later to whisk away the closed purse while the victim was staring through the window, otherwise distracted. If the purse resisted, the pickpocket waited for a sudden stop, when he fell over his victim and, apologising profusely, grabbed it. At the next stop he lifted his hat to the passengers and stepped off the omnibus.

The omnibuses and the army of horses they required made traffic even more difficult in Paris. What, people moaned, would it be like in a hundred years time? There would be so many horses that traffic would come to a complete standstill.

X

Belleville & Ménilmontant

The villages of Belleville and Ménilmontant were inhabited by market gardeners, vine growers and farm labourers. Theirs remained a completely rustic world until the villages were attached to Paris in 1860 by the Baron Haussmann as the nineteenth and twentieth arrondissements (now separated by the rue de Belleville). In one sense the two villages had always been a part of Paris, for they were the Sunday resort of the Parisian working class, who brought their wives and sweethearts to fill the guinguettes and cabarets, spending the day in eating, drinking and dancing. It was a day in the country away from their narrow streets and cobbles. Their wedding feasts, too, were celebrated in the guinguettes of Belleville and Ménilmontant, which formed the same parish, cut across by the rue de Ménilmontant, the high street of the commune. The guinguettes of Ménilmontant were less noisy and rowdy than those of Belleville. The villagers were inordinately proud of the fine view they had of Paris from their hillock. Between 1836 and 1868, the rue de Belleville was in fact called the rue de Paris.

The heights of Belleville were known as the Haute-Courtille, courtille in old French meaning a house with a garden. The lower part of the Grand' Rue de Belleville (now rue de Belleville) was forbidden to traffic on Sundays. The famous guinguettes in the street were Boeuf-Rouge, Coq-Hardi, Sauvage, Gallant Jardinier, Carotte Filandreuse and the cabaret of Papa Dénoyez, who inherited the popularity of Ramponeau, a cabaret-keeper of legendary fame who has a street called after him. The Basse-Courtille was the rue du Faubourg-du-Temple. There was a saying in the eighteenth and early nineteenth centuries that "To see Paris without visiting the Courtilles is like going to Rome without seeing the Pope."

Around 1780 a captain of artillery named Detienne retired to Ménilmontant, where he bought a house. He laid out a vegetable garden on the flat roof, where he grew melons, celery and cabbage. This was considered so surprising and out of the ordinary that provincials went to stare at it as part of their sightseeing tour of Paris.

The rue de Ménilmontant rises from the boulevard of the same name. Number 4 was a dance hall, Aux Armes de France, which in 1856 changed its name to Salle Giffard and became a political café where local enemies of the Second Empire plotted. In the early days of the Third Republic the Salle Giffard was still used by those who regretted the fall of the Commune. Number 27 was also a dance hall, le Bal des Grands Pavillons, as was number 40, le Bal des Barreaux Verts, which was renowned for the good manners of its customers. In dance halls and guinguettes behaviour was usually rough. If you wanted to dance with a girl, you approached her, or even took her from her partner if you thought you could win the ensuing fight. In the refined atmosphere of the Bal des Barreaux Verts, however, a man who wished to dance with a girl first presented her with a rose, which he sent by a waitress. If the recipient were willing, she pinned the flower to her bodice.

For centuries the village of Ménilmontant depended on the parish of Saint-Jean-Baptiste-de-Belleville. As the population of Ménilmontant grew, and it grew fast since the population of Paris spilt out into it, the priest of Saint-Jean-Baptiste had a modest

chapel built at 69 bis rue de Ménilmontant, in 1823. When Ménilmontant became a parish on its own in 1847, the chapel became the
Church of Notre-Dame-de-la-Croix, in honour of a statue of Our
Lady who was invoked under that name as the patron saint of the
oratory of the country retreat of the Monks of Sainte-Croix-de-la-
Bretonnerie at Ménilmontant. The oratory and the country retreat
were destroyed during the Revolution, but the statue was saved,
having been hidden at Bagnolet in the Department of Seine-Saint-
Denis. The small Church was enlarged between 1863 and 1869,
aesthetically speaking not a happy period in French church archi-
tecture. During the Commune, the Church of Notre-Dame-de-la-
Croix was turned into a club, where on May 6, 1871, the murder
of the Archbishop of Paris and the massacre of the hostages was
decided on by public acclamation.

The rue de Belleville rises from the Boulevard de Belleville.
Towards the end of last century it boasted a funicular railway notorious for its technical troubles. On Sundays and Mondays, the street
was probably busier than any inside the capital. At number 8 stood
the Bal de la Folie-Dénoyez, the annexe of the tavern, which at
weekends was crowded well before noon by Parisians in search of
fresh air and a garden, which however would have had little meaning for them were not food and drink also provided. Next door to
the tavern was the Follies-Belleville, a music hall. Shops remained
open on Sunday and Monday because of the large influx of visitors.
At number 17, a hat shop, the Halle aux Chapeaux, gave away a
free beret with every hat bought. This was to attract the custom
of workmen, whose usual headgear was the beret. At number 18 a
cabaret called Grand Condé changed its name to Grand Mirabeau
in 1792. Its attractions consisted of four cellars, nearly a hundred
feet long, two saloons, an orchard and a yard with a well, giving it
an irresistible country air and appeal. The Théâtre de Belleville was
at number 46, and at number 94 was found the farm of the Priory
of Saint-Martin-des-Champs, known as la Ferme de Savy.

Around 1764, Marshal of France Maurice of Saxony fell in love with Mme Favart, wife of Charles-Simon Favart, the playwright, who had married her in 1745 when he was thirty-five years old and she eighteen. Favart survived both the love affair and his wife. She remained with him until her death at the age of fifty-five. He lived to the great age of eighty-two and was buried in his garden at number 112.

At 139, at the corner of rue Lassus, stands the Church of Saint-Jean-Baptiste-de-Belleville which with the cemetery was considered the heart of the parish when Belleville was still a far-away village. The original church was built in 1635 on the site of a chapel that had been erected in 1548. In time it was pulled down, and the present church was not completed until 1859. It received several hits in May 1871 when the Government troops fought their way into Paris. The terminus of the funicular railway was in front of the church. There was one more music hall, the Lac Saint-Fargeau, before one reached the Haute-Courtille.

The guinguettes of the Haute-Courtille stood side by side, their gardens separated only by hedges. Wine flowed and the kitchen ranges, usually in the gardens, looked more like forges. Meat roasted on the spit was the customers' favourite. Each guinguette had its orchestra. Noise never ceased from Sunday morning to Monday night, when silence fell on the Haute-Courtille. Paul de Kock, the French writer of the last century, often went to the Haute-Courtille. "The gardens of the wine merchants," he wrote, "are lit up only on Sundays and Mondays." For him the Haute-Courtille was a place of drunkenness and nothing else. He described in his novels scenes of violence among drunken groups of workmen which ended with knifing and killing. "One is so accustomed to their shouting that one no longer pays attention."

The most famous feature of the rue de Belleville and the Haute-Courtille was the Descent from the Haute-Courtille which used to take place on Ash Wednesday. Early in the morning, every available fiacre, cabriolet, char à banc and barouche was hired by Parisians to go to the Haute-Courtille. Then, in a fine state of intoxication, they swept down in their vehicles along the length of the rues de Belleville and du Faubourg-du-Temple, not stopping until they reached the boulevards. They went armed with sugared almonds, flowers, eggs and flour, which they threw at the watching multitude. It was necessary to be in good voice, for vociferation was part and parcel of the entertainment. Over a thousand carriages took part in the procession, and the onlookers were estimated at tens of thousands. All windows on the route were let for the occasion, the taverns had already filled the night before, and excitement was intense.

"In 1803," wrote Lord Redesdale in his *Memories*, "Lord and Lady Yarmouth were detained in France—he interned at Verdun—when war was declared after the rupture of the Peace of Amiens, and their second son, Lord Henry Seymour, was born in Paris in 1805. . . . The Lord Henry was a very eccentric personage. Unlike his brother, Richard Lord Hertford, who was a handsome man and in his youth a dandy of the 10th Hussars, Lord Henry was singularly ugly, even grotesque. . . . He was a hero of the various Salles d'Armes, a famous fencer and athlete, and the founder, or at any rate, one of the founders of the French Jockey Club."

A French nobleman was supposedly the real father of the Lord Henry, who was rich and enjoyed practical jokes. He offered a friend a cigar into which he had put a few grains of gunpowder. The cigar exploded after a few puffs, burning the friend's face and hand. Lord Henry laughed loudly. The incident nearly caused a duel. Lord Henry was not keen on duelling. Once a French army officer boasted of his duels to him, observing, "I'm a very unfortunate man. I have fought ten duels and killed all my adversaries."

"I am more unfortunate than you," Lord Henry replied. "I have fought only one and the first shot killed me."

He also was the founder of the Société d'Encouragement et Amélioration de Chevaux en France. He owned a famous racing-stable and was immensely popular in Paris, particularly among the ordinary people, who much admired the eccentricities of the

Englishman who had been born in Paris and spent most of his life there. He had moments of great generosity, and when he died he left the bulk of his fortune to the Paris hospitals. The Parisians nicknamed him Milord l'Arsouille (blackguard, debauchee, also used as term of endearment), and wherever he appeared crowds gathered, shouting "Vive Milord l'Arsouille!"

In the days of Lord Henry's fame there came to Paris a strange personage, Charles de La Battut, son of an English apothecary and a French emigrée. He was born in 1806. The apothecary, being married to another woman, could not recognise him as his son, but succeeded in persuading an impoverished Breton nobleman to adopt him. Hence the name of de La Battut. On the death of the chemist, the illegitimate son inherited 100,000 livres and went to Paris to make a name for himself. He strove hard to be recognised as an eccentric, hoping to emulate Lord Henry, but as he was noisy and vulgar, he made little headway, though he tried everything, including the Descent from the Haute-Courtille on Ash Wednesday, driving a char à banc drawn by six horses with piqueurs blowing hunting horns. His huge carriage led the procession downhill. He showered sugared almonds and money on the crowd, and all he got in return was the shout, "Vive Seymour! Vive Milord l'Arsouille!", for anything so spectacular, the people believed, could only have been conceived by Lord Henry.

Charles de La Battut used to arrive on the heights of Belleville on the night of Shrove Tuesday, bringing a party of the prettiest Parisian actresses to the Bal de Saint-Martin, a cabaret and dance hall of repute, and while supping and drinking and making a lot of noise, he waited for his hour of glory, the Descent from the Haute-Courtille. He drove the char à banc down the rue de Belleville year after year, yet to his chagrin the people still acclaimed him with the heartbreaking shout, "Vive Seymour! Vive Milord l'Arsouille!" He did what he could to disabuse them, leaving the char à banc outside his house in the Boulevard des Capucines the whole day long, but people merely thought that Lord Henry had changed domicile.

In 1835 de La Battut's money ran out, and still unrecognised by the Parisians, he left for Naples, where he soon died. Many decades later the theory was evolved that Charles de La Battut had never existed and that the name was a pseudonym of Lord Henry who on such vulgar excursions did not wish to appear under his own name. Lord Henry, however, hardly had the temperament to appear under a name other than his own. Still, one wonders how an English apothecary in the early part of the last century could have left so much money to an illegitimate son.

When the ruined de La Battut ceased appearing on Ash Wednesdays at the Haute-Courtille, people lost interest in the Descent, for without Milord l'Arsouille it had lost its meaning and lustre. The last procession took place in 1836.

As far back as 1852 the Municipal Council of the two villages protested against the invasion of workmen who, instead of coming only on Sundays, bringing their hard-earned money to spend in guinguettes, began to infiltrate the rustic scene, taking lodgings and settling with their families. The natives did not want their villages to become working-class districts. However, with the "Haussmannisation" of Paris in full swing, thousands of workmen's lodgings and huts were pulled down to make way for the new boulevards, squares and wide streets, and the workmen moved in large numbers into the two villages. Rural Belleville and Ménilmontant became in fact working-class districts, and a hotbed of those who plotted against Napoleon III. In May 1871 Belleville was one of the last strongholds of the Commune, ferociously resisting the troops of the legal Government of Versailles.

The last of the combatants of the already almost defeated Commune were entrenched in Belleville in the rue Haxo. On May 26, 1871, Emile Gois, Colonel of the Commune, went in the company of a brother officer to the Prison of La Roquette in the rue de la Roquette, leading a firing squad consisting of as many as thirty men.

In the prison were detained the hostages of the Commune. Gois asked for fifty to be delivered up to him. They were assembled in the prison courtyard, where the roll was called. Some of the prisoners brought their luggage, believing that they were being transferred elsewhere. There were among them priests, gendarmes and four civilians suspected of treason, by which was meant supporting the legal Government. Emile Gois first wanted to have them shot on the spot, but was persuaded by his men to take them to Belleville.

As the hostages were marched out of the prison, a vast crowd awaited them in the street, hurling invectives at them and throwing filth in their faces. The women especially excelled with their curses and the choice ordures they flung at them. At the corner of the Boulevard de Ménilmontant an even more hostile crowd was waiting. Onlookers stepped into the road and, with the encouragement of their escorts, hit the hostages. At the Carrefour Oberkampf there was a violent scuffle.

The cortège reached the rue Haxo and stopped before the villa at number 85. At the window were two members of the Commune; on the other side of the Fortifications, only a few hundred yards away, German soldiers were playing waltzes on their accordions. An eighteen-year-old girl, dressed as a zouave, had followed the procession from the prison, showing great zeal in insulting the hostages and spitting at them. In a loud voice she had promised to kill them all. She now grabbed a rifle from one of the soldiers and shot dead the Abbé Planchat, founder of a charitable institution. The two members of the Commune leaned out of the window and gave the sign. The remaining hostages were pushed into the garden and the fusillade became general. When the corpses were counted, there were fifty-two and not just fifty: the wardens of La Roquette had delivered two too many. Among those who perished in the massacre were eleven priests and Jesuit Fathers and thirty-six gendarmes. The corpses were thrown into a trench in the grounds.

In 1872 the Jesuits bought the Villa of the Hostages and put a railing round the trench. The names of the victims were inscribed on a tablet, and a memorial chapel was erected in 1936.

By the end of the last century Belleville and Ménilmontant had lost the last vestiges of their rural past. They acquired a far from savoury reputation. The taverns were no longer filled by artisans relaxing after their work: local hooligans had taken over. To hail from Belleville or to speak with a Belleville accent was no recommendation. The same went for Ménilmontant. The criminals of the neighbourhood were young, as too were the ponces and streetwalkers. The district had become one in which crime and prostitution were the privilege of youth. The young hunted in packs and lorded it in the taverns with their aggressive behaviour. Their crimes had the impetuosity of their age.

One afternoon in 1913 a youth named Lucien Picard went to a tavern in Ménilmontant at 107 rue des Haies. He stopped in the doorway and fired two shots. One bullet killed a girl of eighteen, Amélie Van der Heyden, known as Mélie, the other lodged in the shoulder of Alexis Lecca, known as Cricri. Attracted by the shots, a posse of police arrived on the scene with swords drawn. Mélie's corpse was carried to the local police station, and while Picard was being escorted to the central police station, a crowd of about twenty young men followed, led by the wounded Cricri, who asked a friend in the crowd, one Ernest Renard, to avenge Mélie's death, which he could not do himself because of the bullet in his shoulder. Calmly, Renard approached Picard, whom he stabbed with a long stiletto, the blade penetrating deep into the right lung. Picard was taken to hospital. Both Cricri and Renard were arrested and taken before Police Commissioner Deslandes, but as Cricri was wounded, he too was escorted to hospital.

From questioning the witnesses, Deslandes discovered that Mélie was the daughter of an honest artisan of Belgian origin. They lived in Montreuil-sous-Bois (arrondissement de Sceaux), where she had met Picard and left the parental home to become Picard's mistress.

She had remained faithful to him, in the underworld meaning of the word, until she met Cricri, whose brother was the lover of Casque d'Or. Casque d'Or was a prostitute of repute. She had started her career by picking up men in the Bois de Boulogne who were then robbed by her male accomplices. She had caught the public imagination, and had been much publicised, even making appearances in music halls until the police intervened. It had been a feather in Mélie's cap to become, as it were, Casque d'Or's sister-in-law. Moreover, Picard was only a burglar whereas Cricri was a fully fledged apache who had an exalted position among the young criminals of Ménilmuche (Ménilmontant in their language).

Commissioner Deslandes went to see Picard in hospital. Picard looked enormously proud of himself.

"I am a killer from Montreuil," he boasted. "I won't have a little apache from Ménilmuche take my girl. That was why I killed her."

XI

Monceau & Batignolles

In the seventh century the Merovingians, who had made Paris their capital, hunted in the thick forest that spread from Montmartre to Saint-Cloud, taking in the hamlets of Passy, Chaillot, Roule, des Ternes, Monceau and Batignolles. Though farmers slowly established themselves on the edge of the forest, the game reserves remained, and deer, stag, hare and rabbit caused much damage to the cultivated land. The Revolution did away with the reserves. Because of its sandy soil Batignolles was covered with vineyards. By the eighteenth century Monceaux (as it was then spelt) had become a flourishing agricultural community. The dairy farmers were known as nourrisseurs, and their farms provided Paris with milk. Streets like Cardinet, des Moines and Jouffroy were dairy farms before Monceau was urbanised. After the Revolution one of its first paved streets took the name of rue des Fermiers (now 16 rue Jouffroy— 91 rue de Saussure). When Baron Haussmann attached the outlying villages to Paris, Monceau and Batignolles were engulfed in the new seventeenth arrondissement, which also took in des Ternes and Epinette. The limits of Monceau are rue Des Renaudes, Boulevard de Courcelles and rues Lévis and de Tocqueville; of

Batignolles, Boulevard des Batignolles, Avenue de Clichy and rues
La Condamine and Lemercier.

In 1753 Laurent Grimod de la Reynière, a fermier général, bought
the château of the village of Monceaux (22 rue Legendre). He had
waxed scandalously rich on the salted meat he supplied to the army
of the Prince de Soubise during the Seven Years War. But he made
good use of his fortune. He built a mansion at the corner of the rue
de Bonne-Morue (now Boissy-d'Anglas) and Avenue de l'Elysée
(now Avenue Gabriel), and fed extremely well. He was a glutton
of the first order, and gave dinner and supper parties the excellence
of which still echoes down the centuries. Gluttony in fact killed him.
He died in harness with a napkin round his neck and foie gras on
his plate.

His son Alexandre-Balthazar-Laurent not only followed in his
father's footsteps but took the art of gastronomy so seriously that
at one time his parents had him locked up by lettre de cachet in
the monastery of the Canons of Domèvre. His parents were enraged
by the "philosophical breakfasts" he gave and also because of the
fortune he spent on food. He was a lawyer by profession, but
gastronomy and literature remained his chief interests. His main
works were: *Reflexions philosophiques sur le plaisir, par un célibataire*
(1783), *La Lorguette philosophique* (1785) and *Almanach des gourmands
ou Calendrier nutritif* which he published from 1803 until 1812. An
anonymous versifier wrote:

> Grimod, tes vers valent moins que ta prose,
> Et cependant ta prose ne vaut rien . . .

Grimod was born with deformed fingers. A Swiss, to whom he
paid a life pension, made him artificial fingers which he used with
great dexterity when eating, writing and drawing.

During the carnival of 1783 he gave a "funereal and lugubrious"
feast that ended with a supper of seven courses, each consisting of a

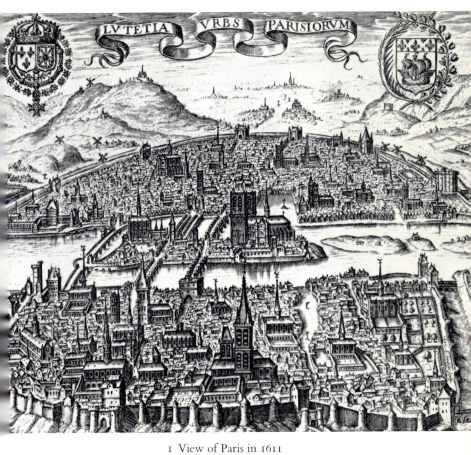

LVTETIA VRBS PARISIORVM

1 View of Paris in 1611

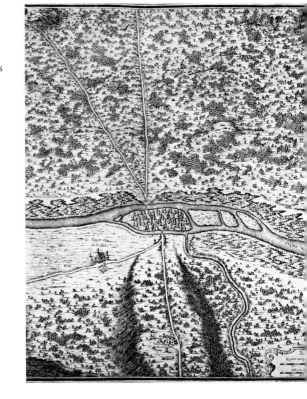

2 Map of Lutetia (known as
the map of Strabon)
(*INTRODUCTION*)

3 Queen Isabelle of Englar
(Isabeau d'Angoulême), 2r
wife of King John, receiv
at the Enceinte of Philipp
Auguste by the aldermo
(échevins) and the Prove
of Paris
(*INTRODUCTION*)

4 The actor Jean du Pourtalais and the Priest of Saint-Eustache (*CH. I*)

A thief making amende honorable before entering the pillory (*CH. I*)

6 Cemetery of the Innocents (*CH. II*)

7 Procession of the Fat Ox (*CH. VI*)

PROMENADE DU BŒUF GRAS.

Dedié au Commerce de la Boucherie de Paris.

8 Entry of Charles VII into Paris in 1436 (*CH. IV*)

9 Illustration from *Le Troisième Livre des Proverbes contenant la vie des Geux* by Lagniet, 1660 (*CH. VI*)

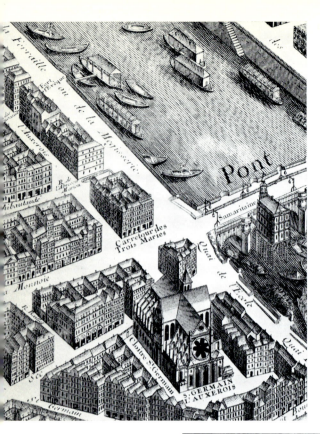

10 For l'Evêque on the map of Turgot (1734) (CH. V)

11 Tournament in the Place Royale (Place des Vosges), on April 5, 6, 7, 1612 (CH. VII)

12 Ramponeau's cabaret in the Basse-Courtille, around 1775 (*CH. III*)

13 Restaurant of Les Trois Frères Provençaux, around 1840 (*CH. III*)

14 Fiacres (*CH. IX*)

15 The Passy terminus of the Passy-Bourse Omnibus Line, around 1900 (*CH. IX*)

16 Descent from the Haute-Courtille, February 17, 1839 (*CH. X*)

17 Parc Monceau, when still known as Folie de Chartres (*CH. XI*)

18 View of the Château de Madrid and Bagatelle (*CH. XII*)

19 Harlots taken to the Hospital (*CH. XIII*)

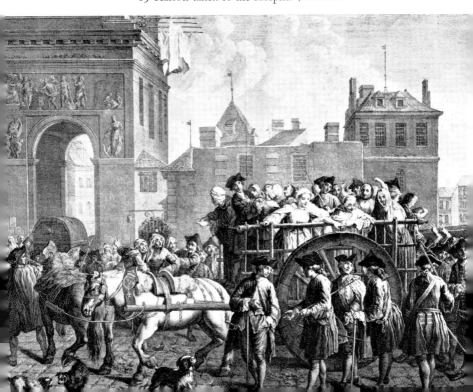

20 A seraglio in the Palais Royal (*CH. XIII*

21 Contemporary photograph of Courbet's effort in May 1871 (*CH. XIV*)

22 View of the Abbey of Saint-Germain-des-Prés (*CH. XV*)

23 Construction of Boulevard Saint-Germain around 1860 (*CH. XV*)

24 Place Maubert around 1746 (*CH. XVI*)

25 Church of Saint-Julien-le-Pauvre (*CH. XVI*)

26 La Grande-Chaumière, Montparnasse, around 1835 (*CH. XVII*)

27 The concert in the Catacombes (*CH. XVII*)

28 Anglais! voilà les Français!
The accident on the frozen Canal de l'Ourcq, on November 24, 1815 (CH. XVIII)

29 The Comte de Paris and the Prince of Wales during Queen Victoria's visit
to France in September 1843 (CH. XVIII)

Vue de la Bastille de la Cour du Passage (Première enceinte)

30 The Bastille (CH. VIII)

A Tour du Coin	*F* Tour de la Liberté	*L* Chapel
B Tour de la Chapelle	*G* Tour de la Bertaudière	*R* Great Courtyard
C Tour du Trésor	*H* Tour de la Bazinière	*S* Courtyard du Puits
D Tour de la Comté	*I* Salle du Conseil	*T* Kitchens
E Tour du Puits	*K* Library	*V* Governor's mansion

meat dish prepared in twenty-two fashions. The number of guests was twenty-two. They were forbidden to speak. The dining-room, hung with black drapery, was heavy with incense. The footmen, dressed as choir boys, sang dirges, and a coffin stood behind the table. When at seven in the morning his wife looked in, on the arms of her lover the Baron de Breteuil, Grimod received them with a quotation from a poem by the Abbé Delille: "And these two great débris console each other."

His prodigality forced him to sell the Château de Monceau to one, Juvet, a Paris apothecary. The château changed hands several times before Haussmannisation destroyed it.

The parkland beside the village of Monceau belonged to the royal family. Henri IV used often to stroll through it; Louis XIV came there to hunt. In the reign of Louis XVI the land became the property of Louis-Philippe-Joseph, Duc d'Orléans, known to history as Philippe Egalité. He was Duc de Montpensier until the death of his grandfather, Louis Duc d'Orléans, and Duc de Chartres until the death of his father, Louis Philippe, Duc d'Orléans. Philippe Egalité was the richest landowner in France. Struck by the prevailing Anglomania, he introduced into France horse-racing in the English style; he also wanted an English park, and appointed Carmontelle, a pupil of Le Nôtre, to turn the unkempt parkland into an English garden. "I want a picturesque garden," he said, "a land of illusions," adding that "Only illusions can amuse one." (One wonders whether he remembered those words as the tumbril took him to the guillotine on November 6, 1793, only nine and a half months after his cousin Louis XVI, for whose death he had voted.) When the English garden was completed the natives named it la Folie de Chartres.

Ruins, pagodas, empty tombs and pyramids were built. Water was brought to the park and cascaded from artificial rocks, the sheep pen was copied from Marie-Antoinette's at the Petit-Trianon and the cowshed was in white marble. The botanical garden was filled with exotic plants. The park contained a white pavilion, a blue pavilion, a temple of Mars, a temple of Love, and baths. In a deep artificial grotto the Duc d'Orléans gave supper parties, and his orgies reminded old people of those of his forebear, the Regent; also in the grotto he held evenings of evocation directed by Cagliostro, an Italian charlatan, at which the guests evoked the dead, though only distinguished dead like Diane de Poitiers, Mary Stuart, Ninon de Lenclos and Mlle de la Vallière. Under Cagliostro's guidance they appeared and gave satisfactory answers to the questions put to them.

Now and then Marie-Antoinette visited the park. On her last appearance, on the eve of the fateful departure for Varennes, she picked a large bunch of roses.

Attached to the land and their customs, the peasants of the village of Monceau frowned at progress, and were incensed when the Duc d'Orléans wanted to drain a smelly marsh. Their cattle had always gone there to drink and from time immemorial they had washed their linen in the filthy yellow water. Soldiers had to protect the workmen.

During the Revolution the park became the property of the nation. The nation neglected it. Napoleon gave it to his High-Chancellor, Jean-Jacques, Duc de Cambacérès, in the hope that he would look after it, but the expenses being too heavy, Cambacérès swiftly returned it to the state. In 1805 Pope Pius VII visited it while in Paris for the coronation of Napoleon. Marie-Louise used to take the little King of Rome there. Her imperial husband, who had little love for the English, referred to the park as the Chinese garden. In 1811 he thought of turning it into a zoological garden, but the Russian campaign made him abandon the plan.

In 1830 the property was restored to Louis-Philippe, Duc d'Orléans, who had become King of the French. When the Boulevard Malesherbes was built, a large part of the estate was expropriated and the park ceded to the Town of Paris. It is now but one-third of its former size. The sites beside the park were sold to private individuals on condition that they built their mansions with gardens and with the same wrought-iron railings in front. They remind one, wrote a contemporary, of Piccadilly in London. Somehow the spirit of England lingered on. The owners of these English-looking houses sent their babes into the park with uniformed nurses, who pushed them in English perambulators, while their English dogs dragged their footmen from tree to tree.

Batignolles developed differently. No rich people lived there and prices were low, for no toll gate existed between the village and Paris. The district became the haven of retired tradesmen and officials. "To spend sixteen hours a day for thirty years in a shop," wrote Alexis Martin, "and live above it in a narrow room, and put aside with great difficulty a sum large enough to bring in 3,000 to 4,000 francs a year to enable you to retire to Batignolles, was in the last century the dream of most Parisian shopkeepers." Batignolles was a quiet little backwater, the Siege and the Commune its only upheavals. The rentier of Batignolles was described as a man who liked his soup hot, wore thick felt slippers, plugged his ears with cotton wool, and, leaning on his cane, floated gently down the stream of life. He lived in a small flat, with small rooms; the walls were papered and looking-glasses abounded. If there were an alcove, he pushed his bed into it; if not, then the bed was curtained. Pious pictures hung on the bedroom walls even if the householder was an agnostic. The parquet floors were waxed.

The little rentier of Batignolles went twice a week to the café to play a game of dominoes, though only with his equals. His favourite café was either A la Grande Marquise at 113 rue d'Orléans or Au Moka at 5 rue de Lévis. When he dined out he chose a cheap restaurant. He passed the ambulant soup vendors with his nose in the air: their soup was good enough for workmen but not for a retired shopkeeper. He loathed new ideas, used snuff, abhorred tobacco, never missed the Sunday family dinner, rose early, retired early, and was willing to discuss politics provided one agreed with him. He died between seventy and eighty. Eugène Scribe and Eugène Labiche made fun of him in their plays.

Civil servants were also plentiful in Batignolles, though even Batignolles was often not cheap enough for them. In 1860 the Deputy of Batignolles, Paul Dupont, a printer, read out in the Chamber of Deputies the daily budget of a civil servant earning 2,200 francs a year:

One loaf of bread	francs 0·75
One litre of wine (watered)	0·40
Meat, vegetables	3·00
Heating	0·06
Laundry	0·25
Lighting	0·03
Coal for kitchen	0·20
Schooling for two children	0·50
Clothing for family	0·80
Unforeseen	0·05

To that had to be added 400 francs a year for rent if the two children were of different sex (300 if of the same, and therefore in a smaller flat), so that the total annual outgoings came to nearly 2,600 francs. Paul Dupont's speech brought no result, yet somehow or other the poor civil servant managed to bring up his children on the yearly deficit.

Batignolles suffered from lack of water. In 1837 when the rentiers began to take up residence, a limited company was formed to supply water to the expanding village. A twenty-horsepower steam engine was installed in the village of Clichy beside the Seine. The water was pumped into a reservoir in the rue Capron, from where it was distributed by water carriers. They trudged along the streets with buckets on their backs, shouting "A l'eau-eau! Porteurs d'eau!" There was a surcharge of 1 sou a floor. Thus those who lived, say, on the fifth floor paid heavily for the commodity. The water carrier stopped in the courtyard, called "A l'eau-eau!", and the tenants shouted down. Then he climbed the stairs, if necessary to the top, even if only to deliver a litre or so for one person. If there was water left in the bucket he tried all other doors on the floor in the hope of not having to descend with unsold water. He fared worst in the houses where there were servants, for servants were a cruel lot. They waited until he reappeared in the street and only then called out their requirements, so that he had again to climb the stairs. In Batignolles as elsewhere, the water carriers were mostly Auvergnats or Savoyards. They belonged to the poorest section of the population, and if a father caught his daughter speaking to a water carrier, she was severely punished.

Next to water carriers, and in competition with them, were the well cleaners, who earned almost less. There was a well in practically every second courtyard.

A curer les puits
C'est peu de pratique
La gaigne est petite
Plus gagner ne puis

So they sang, as with their hooks, buckets and ropes they arrived to make the wells as clear as fountains.

During the Siege of 1870-71 the water carriers had to fill their buckets in the evening, carry them to spots chosen by the authorities and leave them there until the morning, so that water was at hand if a fire broke out. They received practically nothing for the work.

Street lighting came to Monceau and Batignolles in 1776. The lamps were filled with thick oil made of animal fat; the wicks were of cotton wool. The lamp-posts were sixteen feet high and just over sixty yards apart. They were lit between November 1 and April 1. Pickpockets and housebreakers, therefore, operated mostly in summer. The lamps were taken down during funeral processions so that the wreaths piled on top of the high hearses should not brush them. In 1855 the first gas lamps appeared in Batignolles. House-holders installed gas in their kitchens and on the staircase, but not in the apartments because they feared that gaslight would make curtains and upholstery fade. By 1873 the oil lamps had disappeared and gas alone reigned, apart from a few lanterns that remained until the First World War in the Passage Geofroy-Didelot, and rues Lebouteux and Cardinet. To be able to read his newspaper in the light of street lamps was a new and inexpensive pleasure for the little rentier of Batignolles who liked to relate the story of the Arab who, when asked what he admired most in Paris, replied, "The stars you put at night into your lanterns."

XII

The Bois de Boulogne

To the north-east of mediaeval Paris spread the vast forest of Rouvray. The thick and dark forest harboured bandits, outlaws and other criminals. The inhabitants of the surrounding hamlets kept well away.

Arnaud Catelan, a troubadour from the South who, like the trouvères of the North, sang his ballads "se baladant" from château to château, acquired such a reputation that his fame reached King Philippe le Bel in his Château de Passy, not far from the forest of Rouvray. The King asked the Countess of Provence, whose protégé Catelan was, to send him to Passy for a season. The Countess wrote back to say that Catelan would be bringing gifts of sweet wine and fragrant herbs of the Midi. When Philippe was notified that the troubadour had reached the edge of the forest, he sent the captain and men of his guard to escort him safely to Passy.

The captain and his men, who very likely had not had their pay for some time, took immediate advantage of the situation and the darkness of the forest. They killed Catelan in the belief that he was bringing valuable presents to their master. All they found in his baggage were sweet-smelling herbs and wine. On their return to Passy, they told the King that they had not found him, though they had searched the entire forest. The King assumed that Catelan must have decided to take a roundabout route to avoid travelling through the forest.

Days passed, but no troubadour turned up. The captain, however, began to exude sweet-smelling scent, and his men, unaccustomed to the wines of Provence, lolled about in drunken stupor. Philippe became suspicious and decided to get at the truth, using the method of his time—torture. Captain and men confessed to their crime, the corpse was found in a meadow, and the murderers were hanged. Philippe had a stone cross put up where Catelan was killed. The meadow still bears the name of Pré Catelan.

Jacques Hillairet, probably the most thorough and accurate historian of Paris, discounts the story of the troubadour and attributes the name of the meadow to Théophile Catelan or Catalan, who was Captain of the Royal Hunt towards the end of the reign of Louis XIV. The cross might have been erected in memory of Pierre Belon, a distinguished herbalist, who was assassinated in the forest in 1564. With other artists and savants, Belon had been quartered by Henri II in the Château de Madrid.

Still, the legend of the troubadour has retained its fragrance whereas the herbalist and the Captain of the Royal Hunt are rarely remembered.

Whatever the truth, banditry remained the order of the day.

Du Guesclin, Constable of France, returning to Paris, took a short cut across the forest. He had a heavy escort and got safely through. His baggage, less carefully guarded, fell into the hands of brigands. He told his King, Charles V: "Sire, it is a shame that only two leagues from your capital one cannot travel in safety." In spite of his remonstration, the forest remained the hideout of bandits.

When the English were chased out of Paris, the routiers—disbanded English soldiers who had no desire to leave the fair land of France after the Hundred Years War—took over from the bandits. One such, Robert Knolles, set himself up in the Château de Saint-Germain and pillaged the neighbourhood, coming as far as the

Seine, burning, looting, killing, setting fire to the abbey of the village of Auteuil.

The man who eventually pacified the forest was Olivier le Daim, Surgeon Barber to Louis XI. The King gave him the hunting rights of the Preserve of Rouvray. In order to protect his game, le Daim cleared the forest of marauders and put an end to brigandage. After all, it was more worthwhile to preserve a fine stag or a wild boar than some poor traveller.

His successor was Jacques Coictier, appointed personal physician to Louis XI in 1470. Coictier acquired great influence over his suspicious, superstitious master, and knew how to take advantage of him.

One day Louis XI said: "Coictier, you who seem to know such a lot, tell me how long you will live."

"Sire, I will die a week before you."

After that no medical man was better looked after by his patient than Coictier by his King.

The King often came to see him in the Preserve of Rouvray. He inaugurated in person the church that Coictier had built, and signed a royal edict giving the new parish the name of Boulogne (now Boulogne-sur-Seine), by which name also the forest was to be called.

Towards 1530 after returning from his captivity in Madrid, François I entrusted Girolamo Della Robbia with the construction of a château in the Bois de Boulogne. The château brought him no luck: he died of loving too vehemently the pretty Ferronnière whom he had installed there. The ordinary people called it the Château de Faïence; the King, the Château de Boulogne; and the courtiers, disgruntled by its distance from Paris and its lack of the facilities for spending the night offered by Saint-Germain-en-Laye and Fontainebleau, spoke of it as the Château de Madrid, to remind their sovereign lord of his enforced stay in that town.

Henri II kept Diane de Poitiers in the château, and Charles IX had children there by Marie Touchet and Mlle de la Béraudière.

Henri III, the King of the Mignons, had a bull ring constructed in the grounds. Henri IV closed it and restored the château to its original use by installing Gabrielle d'Estrées, and other royal mistresses after her departure.

In his delight when Queen Margot agreed to a separation, he gave her the château for life. She had a road cut through the forest, still known as Allée de la Reine-Marguerite, to facilitate her visits to the Abbey of Longchamps. After her death the château lost its importance. Louis XIII came to it but seldom. It is recorded that on December 15, 1610, he killed two wolves in the forest, and seven years later he bathed at Auteuil, catching a chill. In 1656 Mazarin turned it into a workshop for weaving stockings. In 1793 it was declared national property, then was sold for 648,000 francs to a citizen, most inappropriately named Leroy, who razed it to the ground. Now only the name remains.

The Château de Bagatelle was built for Jean d'Estrées, Marshal and Vice-Admiral of France, the nephew of Gabrielle d'Estrées. Later it belonged to Mademoiselle de Charolais, granddaughter of the Great Condé, whose whim was to have herself painted in the garb of a Franciscan monk. Voltaire wrote a quatrain:

> Frère Ange de Charolais
> Dis-nous par quelle aventure
> Le cordon de saint François
> Sert à Vénus de ceinture?

In 1777 the Comte d'Artois, the future Charles X, bought Bagatelle from the Prince de Chimay, and made a bet with his sister-in-law, Queen Marie-Antoinette, that he would not only have the house pulled down but have a new one erected while she was away in Choisy. The Queen stayed for sixty-four days in Choisy, and on her return indeed found that a new pavilion had been built and that the gardens had been turned into an English park watered by the Seine. There was, however, one trifle about which Artois did not care to boast. Bélanger, the architect, who had orginally estimated the cost at 600,000 livres, spent more than double to get the work finished in time. The pavilion came to be known as the Folie d'Artois.

The Revolution declared it national property. The Directory sold it to one, Lhéritier, who turned it into "a branch of Mohammed's Paradise", though even under this guise it failed to prosper. In 1806 Napoleon bought it, and now and then he lunched there; his son, the King of Rome, was often taken to the gardens; and to Bagatelle came Josephine to make the child's acquaintance.

After the Restoration, the future Charles X named it Babiole and gave it to his son, the Duc de Bercy, after whose assassination it became the property of his widow, Marie-Caroline, until the Revolution of 1830. In 1835 it was sold to Lord Yarmouth, later the fourth Marquis of Hertford, brother of Milord l'Arsouille. He bought it for 313,000 francs, less than a quarter of the sum that Artois had spent on it. From Lord Hertford, Bagatelle was to pass to Sir Richard Wallace of Wallace Collection fame.

Lord Redesdale has refuted in his *Memories* the generally accepted belief that Sir Richard was the brother of Lord Hertford. It would certainly have been strange for Lady Hertford (the fourth Marquis's mother) to have named both her sons Richard, even if one of them was illegitimate. The truth is that Richard Lord Hertford, when a mere boy, had an affair with a Scottish girl called Agnes Wallace. Richard Wallace was their son. Lord Hertford made a home for his mistress in Paris, and, when he parted from her, the child was placed with a concierge in the rue de Clichy, where he ran wild in the street until he was about six years old. The child was shown to his grandmother, Lady Hertford, who took to the clever little boy and decided to bring him up. This was much against the inclinations of her son, though in time Lord Hertford became so fond of him that he made him his agent and representative at auctions and sales of works of art.

When Lord Yarmouth bought Bagatelle, it was rumoured to be the scene of orgies. "Many of the stories," wrote Lord Redesdale, "were started by the rather second-class English Society. These stories lost nothing in the telling and so Bagatelle came to be looked upon as a sort of Parc aux Cerfs." On the other hand, J. Laffitte, a French contemporary who wrote a book called *Un Coin de Paris* about the sixteenth arrondissement, which includes the Bois de Boulogne, described Lord Hertford as a misanthropist.

Lord Hertford was a fervent art collector. When two acquaintances asked leave to fight a duel in the grounds, he politely replied that he had not the slightest objection to their shooting each other, but could not trust their skill so far as to risk his statues. He had in his park statues by Pigalle, Lemoyne and Houdon.

Lord Hertford died in 1870, leaving the residue of his large estate to Wallace "for all his care and attention to my dear mother and likewise for his devotedness to me during a long and painful illness I had in Paris in 1840 and on all other occasions."

Wallace was created a baronet in 1871 in recognition of the great services he had rendered the English colony in Paris during the Siege. He married Mlle Castelnau, by whom he had one son, who was an officer in the French army. Sir Richard died in Paris in 1890, Lady Wallace seven years later.

She left Bagatelle to her secretary, Sir Henry Murray Scott, who sold it to the Town of Paris in 1904, the building to be used for temporary exhibitions of works of art, and the grounds for collections of trees, shrubs and ornamental plants. Lady Wallace of course left the contents of Hertford House to the nation: hence the Wallace Collection.

Sir Richard left his mark on Paris too. In 1871 he gave eighty fountains to the Town of Paris. Sculptured by Lebourg, melted down by Barbizat, each cost 675 francs. The first was put up in the Boulevard de la Villette. When he made his generous present of the fountains, he thought more of the thirst of horses than of pedestrians. He probably knew the old Parisian saying: "Paris is a Paradise for women, a Purgatory for husbands and an Inferno for horses."

XIII

The Oldest Profession

Prostitution had its ups and downs throughout the history of Paris. There was never a dull moment. The Kings of France, often from a sense of morality or deep piety, would suddenly decide to extirpate it. They regarded the prostitutes as members of a corporation. If you disband a corporation, it ceases to have members; if the corporation resists, then violence must be used. On that principle the existence of loose women was frequently in danger. Charles VIII ordered them to be burnt; Marshal of France, Pierre Strozzi, had eight hundred thrown into the river; and in 1635 the Civil Lieutenant of the office of the Provost of Paris warned them "to leave the town and the faubourgs or to be shaved and banished for life without any redress." They remained.

Prostitutes had a comparatively quiet time under Henri III, the King of the Mignons, who was indifferent to women whatever their profession. St Louis, the first King to bring some order into prostitution, was also the first to forbid them to dress like decent women. This was because, at a Mass, his wife, Marguerite de Provence, had given the kiss of peace to a richly clad lady standing next to her; then to her horror the Queen discovered that the woman was a common prostitute.

In 1367 the Provost of Paris designated special districts for prostitutes. The one called Glatigny was situated on the north side of the Cité beside the Seine, and faced the Place de Grève. It formed a sort of quadrilateral based on the rue de Glatigny (absorbed in part by the Hôtel-Dieu), the rue des Marmousets (rue Chanoinesse and part of the Place du Parvis-Notre-Dame), rue de Saint-Pierre-aux-Boeufs (part of the rue de la Cité), rue d'Arcole, rue aux Fèves (part of the rue de la Cité), rue de la Licorne (part of the rue de la Cité), and rue des Deux-Ermites (part of the Place du Parvis-Notre-Dame). That warren of hovels and mean streets became the bastion of vice, the realm of bawds, whores and ponces. Since in outlook malefactors and their like were not far removed from them, they too flocked to Glatigny. It became dangerous to hazard into that busy world next door to Notre-Dame. The police of Paris, still insignificant in number, hardly dared to enter it. The good burghers of the town protested in vain. The priests of Notre-Dame fared no better, although occasionally the Provost issued an ordinance which was not however enforced. Eventually, in 1518, Queen Claude, touched by the laments of the clergy, raised the matter with her husband François I, who ordered the destruction of Glatigny. François was known to his subjects as a man whose firmness could easily change to complacency, so before he could rescind the decree, the burghers of the Cité, armed with spades, pickaxes, hammers and mattocks, moved into Glatigny, and within twenty-four hours had destroyed all the hovels. Next day the Bishop came in procession to exorcise the evil that had resided there so long.

An even worse district was Hueleu, the other neighbourhood set aside for harlots. The name Hueleu derived from Hurleur, which originated from Hue Leu or Hugues Loup, who lived in the twelfth century and gave his name to the district that was outside the Enceinte of Philippe-Auguste. The streets of the Grand-Hueleu and Petit-Hueleu did not disappear until the Boulevard Sébastopol was constructed a hundred years ago. The Hueleu district took in parts of the rues Saint-Martin, Saint-Denis, Greneta, aux Ours and du Bourg-l'Abbé.

The same François I who had Glatigny demolished apparently favoured Hueleu, for in 1532 a prostitute of that district, known as Jeanne Belle-Fille, who had been insulted by other harlots who had called her a sorceress and accused her of "having commerce with the Devil", was taken under his august protection. On pain of death and a large fine, the inhabitants of Hueleu were forbidden to molest her. She waxed rich, acquired houses, farms, woods and fields, and the royal arms of her protector were displayed on all her possessions. Charles IX made the Provost of Paris personally responsible for the closing of Hueleu, which was effected on March 27, 1565.

With the two districts closed, the prostitutes invaded practically the whole town, but they soon found a district of their own again in the rues des Gravilliers, Pastourelle, des Vertus, Phélipeaux (swallowed by the rue Réaumur), Froimantaux (Place du Carrousel) and Quincampoix. As the song had it:

> Dans la rue des Gravilliers
> Elles y sont par milliers.
>
> Dans la rue Pastourelle
> Autant de putains que de maquerelles.*
>
> Dans la rue des Vertus
> Autant de coupeaux que de cocus.
>
> Dans la rue de Phélipeaux
> Ce n'est rien que ribaux.
>
> C'est la rue Froimantaux
> Petit rue, grands bordeaux.*

Prostitutes were not allowed to exercise their profession in their lodgings; nor were they permitted to hawk their bodies after

* Maquerelle: bawd, hence maquereau: ponce; bordeaux: houses of prostitution in old French.

nightfall. When the couvre-feu (curfew) was rung they had to leave the inns, where in the fifteenth and sixteenth centuries they plied their joyless task, and return to their lodgings. They were enjoined by the police to go home quietly, to make no noise, not to upset the neighbours, to sneer at nobody, to keep their doors closed and to receive no visitors. On the Day of Assumption in 1417, Margot la Bourgeoise, Catherine du Soleil and Marguerite de Lestre, all three of them prostitutes, were caught in their rooms with clients. The Provost fined the women 40 sols each, half of which went to the King, half to the poor.

The harlots took picturesque names, and because they often got into trouble with the authorities, their names survive, whereas the names of many honest burghers and their sober wives go unrecorded. Prostitutes at the end of the Middle Ages had names like Thomase la Courtoise, Jehanette la Commune, Perette la Vilaine, Catherine aux Lardons, Etiennette la Chèvre. Somehow those names convey the flavour of the period better than those of respectable citizens.

In 1393 a harlot gave birth to a daughter. An accomplice took the child to the Porte Saint-Martin and left her outside the Walls. He had pushed a piece of linen down the child's throat so that she would be unable to cry and attract attention, but an hour later the dog of a passing hunter discovered the baby, who appeared to be dead. A large number of peasants joined the hunter, who carried the child to the Priory of Saint-Martin-des-Champs (now Conservatoire National des Arts et Métiers, 292 rue Saint-Martin) and placed her on the altar of Our Lady. By then the crowd numbered over four hundred. Joined by the monks, the people prayed to the Virgin, begging her to intercede for the poor little thing who had died unbaptised, and lo! the child moved, opened her eyes, dislodged from her throat the linen, and cried out. She was baptised in the Priory because the crowd was so dense that she could not be carried to the parish church. She was christened Marie. The Priory bells were rung, a Te Deum was sung, and little Marie died three hours later. The monks kept vigil over her corpse until the next day when she was buried with great pomp beside the altar of Our Lady. That was the origin of the veneration of Notre-Dame-de-la-Carole at Saint-Martin-des-Champs where a confraternity was formed in memory of little Marie. (Carole derives from Carolus, as Charles VI was King of France at the time.)

Until the end of the sixteenth century it was the custom to inflict punishment on harlots caught in streets where decent people resided. First a straw hat was pushed down over the harlot's forehead, who was then lifted on a donkey, but facing the tail, onto which she had to hold. To the sounds of drum and fife, she was paraded round the town. Jeering crowds and laughing children accompanied her, and when almost the whole populace had insulted her, she was returned to Hueleu. After the practice had ceased in Paris, it was im-planted into Brussels by the Ducs de Bourgogne of the House of France.

In the reign of Henri IV prostitutes moved into the rue de la Perle, which in those days was still at the very extremity of Paris. A crucifix had been erected there and was known as the Crucifix-Marque-Eau because it marked the height of an inundation of the Seine. Following the arrival of the whores, the people called it Crucifix-Maquereau. The prostitutes used to complain bitterly of decent women who, by their competition, were spoiling the trade. Nowadays, they said, a woman kept by a courtier or a Superinten-dent of Finance earned greater respect than an ordinary prostitute, though her profession was the same. When a prostitute died she was buried like a dog, whereas a kept woman received a funeral of such pomp that one wondered whether debauch were the greatest virtue.

The complaints were not unfounded. The fees of prostitutes rose, along with other prices, in the reign of Henri II. Five sols became the price, rather a tempting sum, which induced three ladies of the Court to go to a place of debauch to discover whether they were considered worth that sum. They wore masks while giving themselves to all and sundry. One of them was recognised however by her cobbler who, even in the heat of love, remained true to his last. He remembered the shoes she was wearing, for it was he who had made them. He had no opportunity to give her away since the ladies themselves boasted of their escapade and showed the 5 sol pieces to their acquaintance.

The Order of the Filles-Pénitentes was established in the parish of Saint-Eustache, and in 1572 the convent was transferred to buildings next to the Monastery of Saint-Magloire in the rue Saint-Denis. When in 1497 Simon, Bishop of Paris, drew up the rules of the Filles-Pénitentes, he intended that only fallen women and girls should be received in the convent, but before being admitted they had to swear on the Gospels that they had not prostituted themselves with the aim of finding shelter there. The Filles-Pénitentes looked after their charges so well that it seemed an easy way out of abject poverty and misery to prostitute oneself for a while in order to find a peaceful life and regular meals in the convent. If it was discovered that a woman had lied, that she had not been a bona fide prostitute, she was chased from Saint-Magloire. The Parliament of Paris regularly sent the harlots condemned for life to take up their abode within the convent.

It also happened that girls who led a decent life were sent to the convent. Their parents wanted to get rid of them, perhaps because they were ugly and had no dowry. Swearing that they had led a life of debauch, they were admitted though untouched virgins. This became so much the practice that in the end all newcomers were examined, and the virgins rejected.

Condemned men on their way from the Châtelet to the gibbet at Montfaucon stopped with their escorts in the courtyard of Saint-Magloire, where the nuns prayed for their intentions, then gave each of them three slices of bread and a glass of wine. Thus fortified, they continued on their last journey.

The Order of the Filles de la Madeleine, known as the Madelon-nettes, received in their convent in the rue Fontaines-du-Temple not only dissolute women sent by the Parliament, whom they lodged in cells with barred windows, but also adulterous women who remained in the convent until their husbands were ready to forgive them. Another function of the nuns was to educate young girls and widows whose virtue was not too steady, and look after then until they found husbands. Unlike other Orders, the Madelon-nettes put no obstacles in the way of repentant women and girls who wanted to join their congregation. The nuns lived by charity; they had no other income. Their convent was closed in 1790 and turned into a prison in 1793.

Louis XIV tried to solve the problem of prostitution by creating the Hôpital Général, but this helped so little that he issued orders, countersigned by Colbert and registered by the Parliament of Paris on April 29, 1684, to control "women of public and scandalous debauch".

In the eighteenth century, as the New World was still conveniently distant, a number of women were transported to Louisiana, like the Abbé Prévost d'Exiles's Manon Lescaut. Enlightened men of the time were, however, concerned to find a better answer. Nicolas Restif de La Bretonne, who still remains the bugbear of French literary men, rushed straight into the fray with what he considered to be a final solution. He thought himself far greater than Jean-Jacques Rousseau, and his writings of more lasting value. He gave his views in Le Pornographe, published in London in 1770.

All streetwalkers and other prostitutes were to be assembled in spacious, comfortable houses on the outskirts of the town, to which they would be taken in a friendly manner, and without compulsion. The houses would be called the Parthénions. Kept women could join them, but if they misbehaved their lovers were to be punished.

Each Parthénion would have a council of administrators chosen from among men who had been municipal councillors (échevins). Under them would serve the governesses, superannuated prostitutes chosen for their kindness and "douceur". None of the administrators, whose tenure of office would last six years, could enter the house as a client.

Women would not have to reveal their names when entering a Parthénion; governesses would be forbidden to enquire. Only the state of their health would be examined scrupulously. If ill, they would be cured. No newcomer over twenty-five would be admitted. The Parthénion being a refuge and an asylum, no father could remove his daughter, who could refuse to see her parents if they called.

A Parthénion would have two gardens, one through which the clients could sneak in, the other in which the girls could promenade. There would also be a number of wide passages. The first would be for the oldest women, none of whom however would be over thirty-six. The second would be for those between twenty-five and thirty, the third for women between twenty and twenty-five, the fourth for the eighteen to twenty age group, the fifth for the sixteen to eighteens, and the sixth for girls between fourteen and sixteen, of whom only those would be allowed to have clients who temperamentally were ripe enough to receive them. Virgins below fourteen, whether brought in by their parents or arrived on their own, were to be brought up by decent women and to choose whoredom only if they felt suited for it.

The prettier girls would be on one side of the passage, the rest on the other. If a man wanted the same girl regularly and paid for a daily ticket, the girl would be set aside for him. Such girls would live separately, but could communicate with others who were not on duty in their passage or in the communal room. If a regular lover ceased to come for a week, in other words bought no ticket for seven days, he would lose his mistress.

However much in love, a young man might not contemplate marriage to an inmate of a Parthénion, even if he were thirty, though a man of mature years who was completely master of himself would be heard by the administrators, and permission to marry might be granted to him if such a marriage were not too harmful to his interests.

The governesses would be forbidden to admonish girls; only the administrators could do so. Two sentries would be posted at the entrance of the first garden, which would be full of trees and shrubs, so that the client could flit unobserved from tree to tree until he reached the house. Once inside, he would present himself at the box office, and remove the mask that a customer would have to wear to enter a Parthénion, so that the governess could have a good look at him. Having bought a ticket, he would then be ushered into a dark room, from which he could see the communal room belonging to the corridor of his choice. His arms, cane and mask would already have been left in a locker. The girls would be visible to him, but not he to them. Having pointed out the girl of his choice, he would be taken to her room. The governess would then call the girl, who would peep through a spyhole at her admirer, and she would tell the governess if she did not fancy him, and then withdraw. She would not, however, return at once to the communal room so that the other girls should not know that one of their number had already found the man repugnant. The man would then return to the dark room, and the process would begin again. Old and deformed men would leave it to the governesses to find them women, and there would be special guards along the passages to deal severely with troublemakers who tried to upset the dignified peace of the Parthénion.

Children born in a Parthénion would be sent to wet nurses. Later they would be brought back to be educated in an annexe, where the mothers could visit them once a week. The women were to be present in the communal assembly room from eleven to one, four to seven, and from eight-thirty to eleven-thirty when they supped. When not sleeping or giving themselves to clients, they were to sit quietly in their rooms, reading or doing needlework. They would have daily dancing, singing and music lessons, attendance at which would not be obligatory, but if a girl absented herself too often, the governess in charge would sweetly and gently remonstrate with her, explaining what fun she was missing. Baths were to be taken every second day; no woman would be allowed to smell. Men who arrived drunk would be kept apart until they sobered up, when they could choose between going or staying. If they preferred to go, the price of the ticket would be refunded.

Boys born in a Parthénion would be brought up to be soldiers, thus repaying the mother's debt to the state. Girls would be taught dressmaking, hairdressing and other trades fit for women. If they wanted to marry, even a dowry would be provided.

The women of a Parthénion, other than those born there, would not be allowed to leave unless they inherited, and if an heiress preferred to remain she would be allowed to enjoy her inheritance inside the Parthénion. On feast days the girls might go to the theatre accompanied by a governess; and since Restif de La Bretonne thought of everything, he prescribed a gauze curtain to be hung in front of their box so that they could see without being stared at.

In his personal life he held prostitutes in horror and denounced them to the police whenever he could.

In the 1780s and for four decades after the Revolution, the Palais Royal was the new Hueleu of Paris, except that the refinement and elegance of the girls who plied their trade in the gardens raised them in status far above the prostitutes of previous generations. They dressed well and with taste. In the afternoon, their promenading time, they strolled decorously, often in pairs. It was in the Grande Allée on September 22, 1787, that Lieutenant Napoleon Bonaparte made his first conquest.

However, the fame of the Palais Royal rested on the shops beneath the arcades. They were mostly milliners' shops, usually with a long counter, behind which stood the saleswomen whose goods were usually themselves. But the pretence was kept up. The customer entered, saluted the milliner, and asked for a hat with a blue, yellow or red ribbon. The answer was, "Go behind into the workroom, or if you prefer it can be delivered to your address."

The establishment of Mlle Brion, who liked to be addressed as Comtesse de Launai, was known to the uninitiated as a furniture shop. She had cards printed which advertised furniture of the latest style. Each piece could be hired for 6 livres a time.

In the gallery of the Café de Foy, directly above a restaurant, was a select brothel on five floors whose inmates were advertised on embossed paper. On the first floor hung out la Lamberti, five years in the trade, small, dark haired, piquante, price 5 livres. On the second floor was fat Adèle, only six months in Paris, price 2 livres, 10 sols. (Newcomers from the provinces were not appreciated by men of taste.) Rose, an interesting blonde, 1 livre, 10 sols, received on the third floor, and on the fourth Hortense, not pretty but intellectual; with twenty years' experience of whoring in Paris, she cost more than fresh Adèle. The most expensive was Saint-Julien on the fifth floor. She fetched 6 livres a time. She was described as twenty-eight, dark haired, thin, vivacious, vicious and frequently nasty.

Such brothels abounded in the Palais Royal, and were ably supported by the gambling dens, which sent them clients; in return the bawds sent their customers to the gaming rooms. Many found the Palais Royal irresistible, and it became the rallying point of foreigners, who named Paris the cloaca maxima of the world, though it was the foreigners who took greatest advantage of the facilities offered. The staunch burghers of the town avoided the area.

When the Allies entered Paris in 1815, they saw Divine chastisement in the French defeats, as though the Emperor had lost at Waterloo because of the Adèles and Roses of the Palais Royal. The Duke of Wellington declared that Paris deserved to be taught a moral lesson. His brothers in arms set a poor example to the Parisians. The Grand Duke Constantine spent 4,000,000 francs in a month on amusements connected with the Palais Royal, and Blucher lost 1,500,000 francs in one night at the gambling den at 113 Palais Royal, which he practically never left during his stay in

Paris. He had to mortgage all his property in Prussia. The presence of the Allies made the fortune of brothels, cafés, theatres and gaming rooms; in short, Paris waxed fat on the moralisers. The Palais Royal went out of fashion around 1830, and the boulevards took over.

From the nineteenth century onwards the prostitutes had to put up with the effects of bureaucracy. Their lives were no longer in danger, the curfew had long ceased to ring, and for those who preferred the rough and tumble of streets to the peace of the disorderly house, few streets were barred. They just had to keep away from the vicinity of churches and schools. However, there were in their view too many nagging regulations, such as those concerning medical visits and decorous behaviour. Until 1914, for example, no woman was allowed to solicit if she did not wear a hat, and one could not open a brothel without the Prefect's permission. In January 1832, a lady applied to the Prefect of the Seine department.

"Monsieur le Préfet, As I am responsible for my old and sick parents I am forced to look for an honest occupation so as to be able to make their old age happy. You are aware, Monsieur le Préfet, that it is the duty of children to give comfort in their decrepitude to those who have brought them into the world, and to repay them for all they have done for them when still of a tender age. Therefore, I hope that you will not refuse me permission to open a brothel. . . ."

One sincerely hopes that the Prefect appreciated her noble sentiments.

In the middle of the last century appeared the lorettes, so called because their favourite district was Notre-Dame-de-Lorette, named after its parish church. They were not prostitutes in the ordinary sense. They were recruited among women separated from their husbands, daughters of concierges who studied at the Conservatoire, and tradesmen's daughters who dreamed of freedom. They shunned work. They never made the first advances in their love affairs, and did not go out of their way to find the loves of their lives. Everything had to fall into their laps. A lorette merely permitted a man to give her presents. She did not refuse money; she accepted bank notes, without, as it were, provoking them. Generally, these women were stupid, which did not stop them from considering themselves witty and cultured. They were keen theatregoers, though they went not to watch the play but to have all opera-glasses fixed on them. If the males were too interested in the play, "There's not a soul in this theatre," they would say, "let's go." Lorettes moved in pairs.

In the days when Paris was not yet overpopulated, it was easy to find accommodation, particularly for the lorettes, who had one advantage over the bourgeois: they were ready to live in a newly constructed house without bothering if the paint were still wet. It became a custom, almost a right, for them to move into new houses and live there until plaster and paint had dried and the proprietors had found proper tenants. To keep up the pretence of culture, the lorette might hire a piano. There would always be one or two daguerrotypes on the wall to show her interest in the arts. She sang too: generally out of tune. She believed that she was the mistress of an ambassador or a minister. She thought that her father was an officer in the army or a diplomatist, whereas he was probably a baker or a greengrocer. She did not care for intrigue: if she tired of a lover, she found another.

On November 21, 1844, three months after he went to live at 58 rue Notre-Dame-de-Lorette, Eugène Delacroix, the painter, wrote to his friend George Sand, the writer, "This new district has arisen to make ardent men like me dizzy. On my arrival here the first object that struck the eyes of my virtue was a magnificent lorette dressed in black satin and velvet, who, getting out of a cabriolet, with the unconcern of a goddess let me see her leg up to her navel. . . ."

During the Second Empire, high police officials acted as welfare officers whose job was to dissuade young women from embarking on the career of prostitute. To such an official was taken an orphan of twenty who had applied for a prostitute's card. He tried to dissuade her. "Here," he said, "we are in communication with charitable ladies who have a deep understanding of all human frailties. You can read and write, which is a big advantage. Give us a little time and I promise we will find work for you either in a shop or as a housemaid in a decent family."

The girl looked disdainfully at him. "We don't touch that sort of bread in my family," she said.

In 1632 St Vincent de Paul installed in Saint-Lazare, in the Cour de la Ferme-Saint-Lazare, the Lazarists. Their function was to look after foolish persons and their kind whom their families had put into the care of "Monsieur Vincent". During the Revolution the house was turned into a prison, and it was there in 1793 that André Chénier wrote his last poems before being taken to the guillotine. In 1834 it became a prison and detention centre for prostitutes.

When they were arrested for soliciting without a police card, or infringing police regulations, they were taken to the dépôt of the Préfecture de Police. A police magistrate decided their fate. Once they understood that they would be sent to Saint-Lazare, they would often burst into tears and beg to be allowed to go to their lodgings to arrange food during their absence for their dog or cat or birds. (Most prostitutes, in common with other lonely people, are animal lovers. Before the Second Empire, they were permitted to take their pets with them, with the result that the prison became a menagerie and the privilege was stopped.) More often than not, they were allowed home to arrange with neighbours for the care of their animals, but they first had faithfully to promise to return next day. They did not always keep their promise.

Magistrates used to tell them how long they would be detained, until one day a prostitute threw a paper weight at the head of a police officer. Thereafter they were told only when they arrived in the panier à salade (Black Maria) at the prison, where their dresses were taken from them and they had to change into prison garb, black and blue striped dress and a black bonnet. They were not allowed the use of handkerchiefs. Those who were not ill were kept for about a fortnight. Nothing prevented them on their release from starting all over again, and they were often back in prison a month later.

Some of them led such a wretched existence in the outside world that prison was a kind of rest cure. Quite a few cried their eyes out when the day of release arrived. In 1869 the doyenne of Paris prostitutes was kept in Saint-Lazare purely as a guest. She was born in 1780. She no longer left her bed, and the other women, if in the mood to tease her, called her the mistress of Marat. She energetically denied that, and spoke of handsome Barras who had fancied her, adding, "Those were the days of the great wars."

In 1932 Saint-Lazare ceased to be a prison. It became a hospital for venereal diseases.

The maisons de rendez-vous were also on the list of houses tolerated by the police. In fact, they were tolerated more readily than ordinary brothels, for no one lived in them, and the women who ran them were sensible enough to choose their customers carefully and to hold scandal at arm's length. Moreover, they conducted their business in the afternoon only, from five to seven, as a result of which they were known also as maisons de cinq à sept. They were usually large flats or private houses, and the women were recruited among shopgirls, midinettes and their kind. Married women who were unsatisfied with their pin-money looked in occasionally to earn a little extra. The keepers of these establishments encouraged the rumour that society women were often to be encountered on their premises, but that can be taken with a pinch of salt since theirs was a world of false pretence or make-believe, according to how one looks at it. One house purported to provide only schoolmistresses, but a client recognised there a woman who two years previously had frequented a similar house where every woman was an officer's widow. (In the First World War when women bus conductresses appeared for the first time in Paris, it was claimed for a particular maison de rendez-vous that all its girls were conductresses.) The maisons de rendez-vous had their heyday during the Third Republic.

In the rue de la Victoire a Mme Gautier kept such a house. Hers was truly the realm of make-believe, and her audacity was unparalleled. There appeared in Paris a publication, *The American Register*, each number of which gave the names and the hotel addresses of Americans who arrived in the capital. The proprietor was Dr Evans, the American dentist who was instrumental in helping the Empress Eugénie to reach Sir John Burgoyne's yacht and escape to England on the fall of the Second Empire. Mme Gautier wrote to every American man whose name figured in *The American Register*. Even her girls warned her not to do so, but she was not the woman to listen to advice; she usually managed to land on her feet. She sent a letter to each new arrival, inviting him to her house between five and seven, saying that she had an important communication to make. It happened now and again that an entire American family arrived, father, mother and children. Mme Gautier was equal to the situation, explaining that she ran a theatrical agency—hence the presence of the young women—and that on reading the name in *The American Register* she had thought that the father was an actor whose fame had reached Europe. This approach was not unpleasing. Mme Gautier was so sorry for the misunderstanding, and would the family take refreshment?

Among her clients was a silly man eaten with snobbism. To please him, most of the girls were turned into marquises, but none the less his social appetite remained boundless. One day he confessed to Mme Gautier that his true ambition was to go to bed with the daughter of the President of the Republic. The snob certainly aimed high; the President was none other than Patrice de Mac-Mahon, Marshal of France, Duc de Magenta. "It will cost a lot of money," said Mme Gautier without batting an eyelid, "but I'll get her for you." Mademoiselle de Mac-Mahon, she explained, was a pupil at the Convent of the Sacré-Coeur. It would take time to contact her and persuade her to come to the establishment.

Mme Gautier had on her list a tall, distinguished-looking girl who, because of her blue eyes and fair hair, was known as Missy. She was presented to the snob as the President's daughter, and the man was so overcome that all he could do was to bow and kiss her hand. When the girl saw that even playfulness had no effect on him, she had practically to drag him to the sofa. "So you will really go to bed with me?" he timidly murmured. She nodded her assent and he burst into tears. Mme Gautier received a huge money present. At his next meeting with Missy, he approached the subject he had at heart. His valet, who had killed his faithless wife, was under sentence of death. Could Mlle de Mac-Mahon intercede with her father? Missy said she would try, but could hold out no hope as her father was an austere man who did not allow his family to interfere in matters of state.

Since coincidences do happen, a few weeks later the valet received the President's pardon. The snob hastened to Mme Gautier to thank Mlle de Mac-Mahon, who received his thanks graciously. "Mademoiselle," he cried, "will you marry me?"

That was going too far.

"I can't," she replied. "I am betrothed to King Alfonso XII of Spain who lost his dear Queen only recently. I am now very busy with my trousseau, which means I won't see much more of you. Soon my father will accompany me to Madrid, and after the wedding you will come out and I will make you a Grandee of Spain. In the meantime Mlle de Nemours of the House of France will take my place at your side."

Unfortunately Mlle de Nemours was not up to the mark. She was a simple girl and not good at lies. Mme Gautier was only too aware of this, but could find no other girl with the wit and presence of Missy. As the snob was hard of hearing, she decided to be present at the first meeting, and to whisper the answers from behind his back.

"Where were you born, Mlle de Nemours?" he asked, an understandable question since the Bourbons were exiled from France.

"During a short journey to France," instructed Mme Gautier.

"During a journey," said the simpleton.

"During a journey?" asked the snob. "I don't follow you."

"During a short journey to France, you idiot," shouted Mme Gautier.

"During a short journey to France, you idiot," said Mlle de Nemours.

Mme Gautier nearly fainted, but the snob was delighted to be called an idiot by a Royal Princess.

Business was brisk during the First World War. The brothels, which had closed at the outbreak of war, quickly reopened. When Big Bertha shelled or the redoubtable Zeppelins bombed Paris, the girls were sent to shelters, usually the métro stations. As the sirens sounded, so the girls in their flimsy dresses rushed into the stations. One evening a dance band also sought refuge in the métro, and the musicians decided to cheer up the crowd, among whom there were, of course, plenty of ordinary folk. Still, it was war-time with its mood of madness, so everybody danced, husbands at first with their wives, then with the lightly clad girls. Nobody minded; death lurked above, and conventions were thrown to the wind. In short, a good time was had by all, except the brothelkeepers, who even under the circumstances could not forget their vocation; and running from one dancing couple to the other, they distributed their business cards with the addresses of their establishments.

After the war the old complaint about amateurs was revived. In 1810 there were a hundred and eighty brothels in Paris; by 1924 their number had shrunk to twenty-nine. On the other hand, the number of maisons de rendez-vous had risen to three hundred. After the Second World War, in an upsurge of moral indignation, the Deputies passed an act closing all brothels for good. The result was the same when Glatigny was destroyed and Hueleu uprooted.

XIV

The Vendôme Column & the Napoleonic Cult

The ground on which the Place Vendôme was planned had originally been the property of César, Duc de Vendôme, natural son of Henri IV by Gabrielle d'Estrées. It was sold by his descendants to Louis XIV whom the Marquis de Louvois, Superintendent of Finance, had in 1686 persuaded to turn the site into a "grand ornament of the Town of Paris". Louvois ordered the construction of houses in the Corinthian style. He wanted to instal in them the Academies, the Royal Library and several embassies, but he died before his plan could be effected, and frightened by the expense, Louis XIV stopped further construction and assigned the land to the Town of Paris, which in turn sold the still vacant sites to private buyers, who had to conform to the original plan when building their mansions.

Jules Hardouin-Mansard and Germain Boffrand designed an equestrian statue of Louis XIV, to be erected in the centre of the square. The model was the work of François Girardin and cast in bronze by Balthazar Keller. It weighed over sixty thousand pounds, and twenty men could have sat around a table inside the horse's belly. The statue was unveiled in the presence of the Duc de Gesvres, Governor of Paris, and the square was named Place Louis-le-Grand.

The buildings, which now house the Ministry of Justice (numbers 11-13), were built by two revenue farmers (traitants), Bourvalais and Villemarecq, whom the Regent, Philippe d'Orléans, suspected of having manipulated sums due to the Revenue. He seized the houses, and in 1717 the Marquis de Dangeau turned them into the Paris residence of the Chancellors of France.

In 1763 the mountebanks from the fair of Saint-Ovide invaded the square and built booths and wooden stages. People of quality came to applaud Harlequin, visit the Café Royal to taste the wines of Burgundy, take part in chariot races and drive around in elegant coaches. Plebeians were not encouraged to join in the fun.

On August 10, 1792, the Assembly decreed the destruction of all royal statues. An eager, vociferous crowd appeared in the square to do their duty. It was not easy, for the heavy bronze resisted nobly, so ropes were thrown round the statue to which were harnessed men of revolutionary zeal. A woman called Rose Violet, who had been a vendor of Marat's *L'Ami du Peuple*, made herself conspicuous with her noisy encouragement of the work. When the enormous statue collapsed, part of it crashed onto her. Three days later Louis XVI, accompanied by the Royal Family, was forced to stop in his coach in front of the demolished statue of his forebear. The square had already been renamed Place des Piques.

On September 23, 1806, Napoleon laid the foundation stone of the Column of Austerlitz on the spot where Louis XIV's statue had stood. The column rose a hundred and forty feet and was decorated from top to bottom with the bronze of twelve hundred cannons taken in six weeks from the Austrians and Russians. It was an exact imitation of the Trajan Column in Rome with the difference that the Parisian monument was one-twelfth larger in dimension. Two hundred and seventy-four plates of bronze bore a set of bas-reliefs, exquisitely achieved, ascending in a spiral line, and representing the most famous actions of the Campaigns of the North. The pedestal was ornamented with ensigns and machines of war extremely well executed. The designs, on which thirty-one sculptors co-operated, were chiefly by Gérard, Renaud, Beauvellet and Bergeret. The Emperor dedicated the column to the glory of the Grnade Armée. It was surmounted by his statue in a toga. With the erection of this statue the tribulations of the Column began.

On April 4, 1814, a crowd of zealous Royalists burst into the square, shouting, "Down with the Usurper, long live the King!" On this occasion the Marquis de Maubreuil took the place of the late Rose Violet. This was a better organised affair, however, and no one came a cropper. Horses were attached to the ropes, skilled workmen were used, and on the fourth day the Emperor's statue reached the ground. During the Hundred Days he refused to reinstall it, and it was melted down. After the Battle of Waterloo and during the years of the Restoration, the white flag of the Bourbons floated on top of the Column.

Yet the Column remained associated with the glory of the French army and the man who had led it. At the Congress of Vienna, Metternich asked Lord Dudley of Ward what he thought of Napoleon. "I think," he replied, "that he has made all past glory questionable and future impossible." The Parisians felt the same and even the best Royalist intentions could not overlook the past. In *A Tour Through Paris* (during the reign of Louis XVIII), the anonymous author writes:

"The French Military forms a distinct corporation in the state, and is governed by its own code. As the Romans, to evade the law that forbade the putting to death of a Roman citizen, declared him no longer a citizen before they inflicted extreme punishment, the French endeavour to save their military uniform from disgrace in the same manner, by first degrading the soldier into a private man. Accordingly, the first operation of punishment is to deprive the criminal of all that distinguishes the profession of arms. If it be an officer, they tear away his epaulettes and other military decorations. If a soldier, he is stripped of his regimentals and

obliged to make his appearance in the dress of a convict . . . the
Place Vendôme has been chosen as the theatre of these punish-
ments, whether the offender be condemned to pay the forfeit of his
life, or be consigned to the hulks, the place seems to have been
chosen in order to render the punishment more exemplary and
impressive.

"It is at the foot of the column, which excites an extraordinary degree of enthusiasm among the veteran military, that
the culprit is expelled from the ranks of his late companions in
arms."

Came the July Revolution and Louis-Philippe, King of the
French, tried to bask in the sun of Austerlitz as though it shone on
him too. He ordered a new statue, and the Emperor was again
hoisted to the top of the Vendôme Column, this time wearing his
redingote and the famous petit chapeau.

In 1865 his nephew Napoleon III, who was well acquainted with
the Place Vendôme, so called since 1799, as he had stayed at the
Hôtel du Rhin (numbers 4-6) before he became President of the
Republic, thought that his uncle should again be represented as a
Roman Caesar and not as the Little Corporal. Down once more
came the Emperor, then up he went again, his new statue sporting
a toga of such unfortunate cut that the surviving veterans of the
Grande Armée who came to lay wreaths at the foot of the Column
did not recognise their Emperor, dressed up, as some observed,
as a laundryman. The statue of the Little Corporal was taken to
Courbevoie (Seine-Saint-Denis) and set up at the Rond-point de la
Défense.

The painter Jean-Désiré-Gustave Courbet, under whom Edouard
Manet studied, developed an implacable hatred of Napoleon III.
As early as September 1870, a few days after the defeat of Sedan,
he wanted the Column to be taken down and re-erected at the Hôtel
des Invalides minus the uncle of the hated man. At the time no one
listened to him. However, when the Commune burst into being—

Punch published a drawing of Paris, a fair woman assailed by jackals while a Prussian soldier looks on with folded arms—Courbet was elected delegate of the Committee of Fine Arts, along with Manet, though he was then at Oléron and returned to Paris only towards the end of the Commune. On May 11, 1871, Courbet led a large mob to the Place Vendôme, where there had been a fusillade on March 22 among soldiers on their way to military headquarters. Fifty had perished in what was one of the curtain-raisers of the Commune. The inhabitants of the square barricaded themselves in their houses as Courbet and the throng arrived. There was no longer any argument about dismantling the statue. A carpet of dung and straw was prepared to receive the great Napoleon. As the statue came tumbling down, the head was badly damaged. The Column itself followed.

The crash could be heard as far as the Boulevard de Batignolles. An eyewitness from the rue de Rome saw the statue disappear. The crowd in the street duly celebrated the downfall of "military apotheosis, symbol of false glory". The bronze tablets were too heavy to be taken home as souvenirs, but the statuette of Victory, which Napoleon had held in his hand, vanished for good.

In 1873 Adolphe Thiers, President of the Republic, who had put down the Commune, ordered the Column to be raised again. Courbet was held responsible for having pulled it down and was sentenced to six months imprisonment and fined 350,000 francs, roughly the sum that its re-erection would cost. The fine ruined him, and when he left prison he sought refuge in Switzerland, where he died in 1877. It was not too difficult to repair the Column as most of the bronze had been left in the square, and the repaired laundryman still watches over the jewellers' shops in the Place Vendôme.

The statue of the Little Corporal at Courbevoie was lowered into the Seine on the orders of the Government of the Third Republic on September 17, 1870, the day the Prussians took Versailles. It was brought up in the following year and left in a mason's yard until

1911, when it was erected in the cour d'honneur of the Hôtel des Invalides.

In the 1830s and '40s, Bassero, a famous kettle drummer, kept his audience in thrall in a large booth in front of the Cirque-d'Hiver in the rue Amelot. The scenery on the stage consisted of old bits of sails painted in striking colours. There were twenty kettle-drums, and Bassero darted from one to the other. People from as far away as Ménilmontant and Montrouge joined the workmen of the neighbourhood and concierges and their families, to make up the audience, along with soldiers and servant girls. Bassero's outstanding solo performance was the Battle of the Pyramids. He beat the drums, then the battle began:

"Ladies and gentlemen, now you will hear the glorious battle. I beg you to give all your attention as I am the only man in the world who is capable of executing it.

"The camp awakes (crescendo rolling), the soldiers shoulder arms, General Bonaparte gives his orders, the soldiers rally round his grey redingote and little hat. (The drums imitate an army on the march.)

"'Soldiers! From the top of these monuments forty centuries and ten thousand nurserymaids watch you!'

"(The trot, the gallop, the thunder of cannons, the rolling of drums, collapse of houses.) Ladies and gentlemen, you hear the wailing of women, the shrieks of children, everything is in ruins, the massacre is general, the sun shines down on the field of carnage.

"The battle is won! I have the honour to thank you for your attention. Long live the Emperor!"

He gave a military salute to his swooning audience, which withdrew in deep silence. As the new spectators came in, he shouted, "On parade!"

In the last century the Boulevard du Temple was referred to as the Boulevard du Crime because its many theatres like l'Ambigu, la Gaieté, les Funambules, Cirque Olympique, le Petit-Lazari, Comique and Délassement produced crime plays when not bowing to the fashion of putting on plays with the Emperor as hero.

Actors like Gobert and Taillade made their fortune because they resembled Napoleon. Briand, a far from successful actor, remembered in his old age the days when he had played Sir Hudson Lowe in a play about Napoleon:

"In all my career as an actor I never had such reaction from the audience. After every performance they nearly lynched me before chucking me into the nearest fountain."

XV

Saint-Germain-des-Prés

When Childebert I returned in 543 from the Siege of Saragosa, he brought back a fragment of the True Cross and relics of St Vincent. Germain, Bishop of Paris, persuaded him to found the Abbey and Church of Saint-Croix-et-Saint-Vincent to house the relics. Childebert gave the Abbey the fief of Issy, which comprised all the land between the Petit-Pont and Meudon (Seine-et-Oise). The limits in Paris were the rue de la Huchette, the Carrefour Saint-Michel, and the rue de la Harpe as far as Porte Saint-Michel (Porte Gibart then); beyond the city gate, it took in Vanves, reaching the Seine above Meudon.

Germain was born in Autun or somewhere nearby. He studied in Avallon, then led a life of meditation at Lucey in Côte-d'Or. He was ordained priest, and when he was about forty years old he was elected Abbot of the Monastery of Saint-Symphorien in Autun. Childebert appointed him Bishop of Paris around 550, or perhaps earlier. He was over eighty years old when he died in Paris on May 28, 576, the only accurate date concerning him on record.

Already in his lifetime he was known for his miracles. He prayed once in front of a burning house and the fire subsided. Yet his most famous miracles came only after his death. On the day of his burial, as the procession passed in front of a prison, the coffin sank into the earth and could not be moved before all the prisoners were freed. He was buried in the Church of Saint-Croix-et-Saint-Vincent, which after his canonisation became the Church of Saint-Germain, des-Prés added to it because of another church of Saint-Germain in the Cité, Saint-Germain-le-Vieux.

In July 754 it was decided to transfer his coffin in the presence of King Pepin le Bref from the crypt to the sanctuary, but the sarcophagus remained stuck to the floor of the crypt. The King immediately promised to have the Abbey enlarged. The saint made no further difficulties.

By the first quarter of the ninth century the number of monks in the Abbey was one hundred and fifty. According to Abbot Hilduin his monks needed fourteen hundred muids of pure leaven a year, two thousand of wine, a hundred and eighty of vegetables, a hundred and sixty of cheese, four of butter and a hundred of salt; plus seven setiers of honey and two pounds of beeswax monthly, not forgetting an unspecified quantity of poultry and eggs for Christmas and Easter. A muid was an ancient French measure that varied in different regions. In Paris a muid of wine comprised eighteen hectolitres, a muid of oats about thirty-seven hectolitres, of salt twenty-four, and of coal and wood about forty-one hectolitres. A setier was about half a litre.

The monastery was self-supporting. All the labour of the serfs was dependent on it. As monks alone could read and write, they were the only people capable of undertaking and managing schemes on a scale beyond the ordinary man's conception for the exploitation of the land. In the Merovingian age a flourishing abbey like Saint-Germain was a direct descendant of the Gallo-Roman "villas" around which many French villages had developed.

The Normans first attacked Paris in 835. Each time they returned, they pillaged the monastery. In 863 the monks began to repair and rebuild the Abbey, but in 866, when all the churches of Paris were sacked, the Normans destroyed both Church and Abbey. In the first half of the tenth century Abbot Morard laid the foundations of the present church. He was the twenty-ninth Abbot of Saint-Germain. Church and Abbey were surrounded by high walls behind which lived about a thousand souls.

The domain of Saint-Germain, that is to say the Seigneurie de l'Abbaye, became known as the Bourg Saint-Germain. In the fourteenth century noblemen and burghers, drawn by the good air and the pleasant woods, built residences in the meadows, which were destroyed during the Hundred Years War, and during the sixteen years of English occupation (1420 to 1436) rebuilding was not encouraged. The area was still thinly populated when Nicolas Vauquelin, Seigneur des Yveteaux, chose around 1630 to build a house and lay out a garden in Saint-Germain, on the site of the present rue Visconti, formerly rue des Marais-Saint-Germain. His was the only house in the neighbourhood, and his friends nicknamed him the Last Man, also the Man who Lives at the End of the World.

Vauquelin was born in 1559 and lived to be ninety years old. He had been Lieutenant-General of Caen before he became tutor to the Duc de Vendôme. Vauquelin fell into disgrace, which decided him to exile himself from Paris, so he went to live at the end of the world!

His walled-in garden and park extended to the east beyond the present rue Bonaparte. Tallemant des Réaux described him in *Historiettes* as a grand seigneur in his seraglio. That was an exaggeration, as his sole vice was strolling in the garden with Jeanne du Poy, his harp player, a good-looking girl he had rescued from poverty. They enacted mythological scenes: she carried a shepherd's crook decorated with flame-coloured ribbons; in spite of his seventy years, he dressed as a young shepherd, wearing a straw hat lined with red satin; and guarding imaginary sheep they strolled in the garden, he reciting poetry, she playing the harp, and both of them fiercely defending the flock from imaginary wolves.

To the west of his garden extended the Pré-aux-Clercs. Two lanes cut across the fields, one leading to the Chapel of Saint-Pierre or Saint-Père (now rue des Saints-Pères, which separates the sixth arrondissement, that is Saint-Germain-des-Prés, from the seventh, the Faubourg Saint-Germain), the other used by carts bringing stones from the quarries of Vaugirard to be ferried across the Seine for the construction of the Castle of the Tuileries. The road leading to the ferry was called Grand Chemin du Bac, which after 1620 became the rue du Bac. Beyond Vauquelin's garden, the fields ran down to the Seine. Cows grazed in them, and ditches separated the small cultivated patches, but not a building was to be seen between house and river. Not far from his property, along the Chemin du Colombier (now rue Jacob), rose garbage heaps and refuse dumps. South of the property stood the imposing mass of the Abbey, surrounded by walls with turrets.

The Pré-aux-Clercs stretched from the Abbey to the Champs de Mars, taking in all the uncultivated land from the present-day rues de Seine and Bonaparte along the rues Jacob and de l'Université, the Quais Malaquais, Voltaire, Anatole France and d'Orsay to the Quai Branly. University students were called clercs (clerks), in the same way as ecclesiastics. There were two prés (fields): the Petit Pré near the Monastery, and the Grand Pré, which disappeared, so to speak, in the wasteland of the Champs de Mars. These fields belonged to the Abbey, but part of them had been ceded to the University, which noble gesture the monks were soon to rue, for with the students came noise, debauches, fights and duels. True that on summer evenings solid, peace-loving citizens were brought over in the ferry to enjoy a stroll and the country air; however, when the curfew chimed they hastened back to the ferry. It was not so much the students as the ruffians swarming all over the place who made life dangerous at night.

Until the sixteenth century the couvre-feu was chimed by the bells of every Paris church. Couvre-feu was originally the name given to one of Notre-Dame's church bells, because when it sounded one had to hasten home to bank up the fire and put out the lights. As the bell chimed the children chanted in unison: "Bonsoir mon père, bonsoir ma mère; le dernier couvre le feu." After the sixteenth century, curfew was rung in Notre-Dame only, at seven in the evening.

There were several Jeux de Paume (real tennis courts) in the Pré. Roistering and theatrical performances also helped to disturb the monks who, in accordance with the Rules of St Benedict, were enjoined to live in peace, prayer and study. The students loved fights and now and then came to blows with their benefactors. In 1163 the scholars and the monks had such a noisy quarrel that the matter was brought before the Council of Tours, where seventeen cardinals and one hundred and forty-four bishops had assembled. They decided in favour of the monks, and the scholars were condemned to perpetual silence. In 1192 came a new outbreak of fighting, and in a pitched battle a student was killed and several wounded. The sporadic fights continued until the Abbey withdrew the grant, and houses and gardens appeared in the Pré-aux-Clercs only after the University had been dislodged.

The students never accepted their defeat. In 1548 they appeared in the Pré, led by a certain de Ramus or de La Ramce, and rooted up trees and tore out vines. When evening came they withdrew with their booty, which they burnt in front of the Church of Sainte-Geneviève-du-Mont near the University.

The monks complained to the tribunals, but judgment this time went against them. The scholars had based themselves on some charter of Charlemagne, which they would certainly have been unable to produce, proving that the Abbey had usurped some of the land, including, of course, the Pré-aux-Clercs. The monks had to return half of their cultivated land in the Pré-aux-Clercs but in its pristine, uncultivated, unfenced state. Not content with their victory, the University's attitude remained belligerent, and six years after the judgment the war flared up again, this time led by another student, Baptiste Crocoezon, a native of Amiens. The students lost whatever sense of proportion they had and burnt down the houses of the substantial burghers who lived in the Pré. Unfortunately for the students, and especially for Crocoezon, one of the houses belonged to Jean Baillet, the King's Commissioner. Crocoezon was sentenced to be burnt, but as an act of mercy he was first strangled. His fellow students took his charred bones to the Chapel of Saint-Père, where several Masses were offered up for the salvation of his soul, and one of the students passed his hat round among the people who had witnessed the execution to collect enough money for Masses to be said for Crocoezon in perpetuity. The hat was filled.

Duellists found the Pré-aux-Clercs to their taste as there was little fear of being interrupted or arrested. In 1602 a duel was fought between two Protestant gentlemen, Villemor and La Fontaine, as a result of a quarrel they had had at tennis. They arrived in the field, put their swords on the ground, and searched each other for extra weapons; finding none, they shook hands, knelt and prayed together. They had with them a single witness, a lackey mounted on a fine steed. It was agreed that the survivor should take the horse after the duel. It was the lackey, however, who returned on horseback: the two duellists remained in the field, both dead.

After the Pont-Neuf was opened, more and more Parisians visited the Pré-aux-Clercs, much to the annoyance of duellists and students, and eventually Saint-Germain-des-Prés was attached to Paris in the reign of Louis XIV.

The pillory of the Abbey was situated where the rues de Buci du Four, des Boucheries (swallowed by the Boulevard Saint-Germain) and de Sainte-Marguerite (now rue Gozlin) met. The Abbey prison took up the whole length of the present houses in the Boulevard Saint-Germain between numbers 135-137 on one side and 166 on the other. It dated back to the fourteenth century and faced the main entrance of the Abbey. It was surrounded by some ramshackle buildings, one of them the Inn of the Chapeau Rouge.

In 1635 a transaction took place between the Abbot and the architect Gamard. Among other works for the Abbey, the architect undertook to build a new portal for the church and rebuild the prison. The new prison was a square building with turrets at each corner. If his aim had been to construct one of the most disagreeable prisons in Paris, Gamard certainly excelled at his work. The low-ceilinged dungeons were like oubliettes in which the prisoners could not stand up and so perished in a short time. By the eighteenth century the dungeons were no longer used, but the cells remained so abominable and damp that the soldiers—it had become a military prison—had on release to be taken straight to the Hospital of Val-de-Grace to recuperate. The walls were filthy and nothing was ever done to clean them. The courtyard, where prisoners were exercised, was so small that men stood pressed against each other, hardly able to move; and no fresh air entered it. The cells were overcrowded. One palliasse and one blanket were all a prisoner was given, and even the prison officials, whose rooms were comfortable, had no place for exercise. Before the Revolution the prison was mostly used for the detention of soldiers of the Gardes-Françaises, a crack regiment raised in 1563 which guarded the royal castles of Paris until the end of the old régime.

Room was also found in the overcrowded prison for debtors, whether noblemen or officers, who had not paid their debts of honour. Prison could, however, also be the jumping-off ground for the ambitious or the lucky. Pierre Broussel, Councillor to the Parliament of Paris, was put into the Abbey prison in 1648. In the following year he left it, nominated as Governor of the Bastille.

During the Revolution the Abbaye, as the prison was known, was filled with the unfortunate "enemies of the people". On September 2, 1792, sixteen persons were taken there in fiacres. The mob stopped the carriages at the Carrefour de Buci. Four of the passengers were killed even before they could leave their seats. The others were hauled out, and nine of them were butchered on the spot. Drunk with blood, the mob rushed to the Convent of the Carmelites in the rue de Vaugirard, where a hundred and sixteen souls were slaughtered. Not yet satisfied, the mob hurried back to the Abbaye, and formed a tribunal presided over by Maillard, a bailiff. Three hundred and fifty-seven prisoners were dragged before it; three hundred and fourteen of them were assassinated, some in front of the prison, the majority inside. The day became known as the September Massacres.

Among those held in the Abbaye during the Revolution were Mme Rolland, Clavières, Labédoyère and Charlotte Corday, who was taken there on July 12, 1793, but transferred to the Conciergerie a few days later. After her death a young man, Adam de Lux, Deputy Extraordinary of Mayence, published a leaflet in praise of her, proposing to have a statue erected to her with the inscription, "Greater than Brutus". He was locked up in the Abbaye. As he entered the prison he cried out joyfully, "I will die for Charlotte Corday." He did.

During the Restoration of the Bourbon dynasty, the Abbaye was used for the detention of soldiers waiting to be court-martialled. Five out of six detainees were acquitted. Those who were convicted left either for the gallows or to serve long sentences in irons.

On the same September day when the prisoners were being mas-sacred, in one of the dungeons a poor parish priest awaited his turn to die. Suddenly a capital idea came to him, namely to make himself clothes with the rags lying around him. When Maillard's tribunal sent for him, he appeared before it wearing the rags. When asked why he was detained, he replied because he was a beggar who had been arrested while begging for his bread. He played his part so well, and the rags looked so convincing, that he was set free. He lived near the Louvre, and reaching his street he cried with joy. The first two people he ran into were neighbours of his, one of them a butcher.

"Congratulate me, my good friends, my dear neighbours, for I escaped the massacre," said the happy priest, then explained the stratagem he had used to bamboozle the awful tribunal.

"But you won't escape us, citizen," shouted the two men, and the butcher cut his throat on the spot.

On the site of the Institut de France stood a sinister tower, part of the Enceinte of Paris, and named after Philippe Hamelin, Provost of Paris. When Jean de Nesle built his mansion, the Hôtel de Nesle, in the rue Guénégaud, the tower was renamed Tour de Nesle. In 1308 Philippe le Bel bought the house from Amaury de Nesle. The King had three sons who married three cousins, Marguerite, Blanche and Jeanne de Bourgogne. The three women, who led licentious lives, received their lovers in the mansion. One day Isabelle, daughter of Philippe le Bel and wife of Richard II of England, recognised the aumônières, purses attached to the belt, worn by two noblemen at Court. The purses were presents she had given her sisters-in-law. She rushed to her father who locked up Marguerite and Blanche in the Castle of Gaillard des Andelys. Their lovers, Philippe and Gaultier d'Aunay, were drawn and quartered, then beheaded, and finally hanged by their shoulders and left to be pecked by birds. Jeanne was incarcerated in the Castle of Dourdan.

Ten years later Blanche took the veil in the Abbey of Maubuisson and Marguerite was killed on the order of Louis X, her husband, because he wished to remarry. Jeanne was set free and given the Hôtel de Nesle when her husband, Philippe V le Long, mounted the throne. Still young and pretty after her husband's death—his reign lasted only six years—she decided to take lovers, but having learnt from bitter experience that men were indiscreet, she had them killed once she tired of them. The form was to give the lover a good meal, then throw a sack over his head, take him up to the Tour de Nesle, and hurl him into the Seine. One of the lovers was

Jean Buridan, a shining light of the University. He too, according to legend, met his end in the river. Villon believed the tale:

> Où est la reine
> Qui commanda que Buridan
> Fût jeté en un sac en Seine?

However, Buridan survived the widowed queen, who died in 1329, and was, in fact, Rector of the University in 1348. Dismissing the entire legend in his *Paris* (six volumes, published between 1869-1875), Maxime Du Camp observes: "Nowadays husbands are so good-natured that great ladies no longer need to throw their lovers into the river."

The tower was pulled down in 1662, The legend persists.

"In the old days in Paris," wrote Henri Sauval, "there were two fairs at Saint-Germain. At present there is only one. All I know of the first is that in the twelfth century it opened fifteen days after Easter and lasted for eighteen days. The Abbot and the monks were the proprietors of it for reasons I am unaware of."

The second fair, which lasted until the second half of the eighteenth century, became the most important fair in and around Paris, and no Parisian, however rich or poor, failed to attend it. Provincials flocked to it from every corner of the land. The duration of the fair varied from age to age. In 1485 Charles VIII decreed that February 3 should be the opening date and that the fair should last for eight days. Eight years later he allowed it to open for the four days following the feast of St Mathew. In the troubled times of the League no fair was held, but in 1595, by consent of Henri IV, it remained open for three weeks. In Sauval's time in the seventeenth century, the fair started on February 1 and lasted as long as it pleased the King. By then Parliament, the Abbot and the Provost of Paris no longer had any say in the matter. The Court, the nobility and the rich were generally in Paris towards the end of winter and the beginning of spring during the bad weather, and consequently the fair did not close before their departure.

Originally the fair was held in a large field, teeming with booths and stalls, in the vicinity of the Abbey. Wine, horses and sheep were sold. Later two booths were built in the field, each a hundred and thirty feet long and a hundred wide, little pavilions on their own with shops and passages. The limits of the field were the rues Guisarde, du Four, des Boucheries, des Quatre-Vents, de Tournon and des Aveugles (rue Saint-Sulpice). There were seven doors of entry, each from the rue du Four. In front of the pavilions was a vast, empty square.

The first eight days of the fair were set aside for the sale of cloth, sheets, serge and their kind. The following week it was the turn of porcelain, crockery and similar merchandise. Then came the best, for crowds were at their happiest in the shops and booths of the goldsmiths, silversmiths, haberdashers, milliners and painters, who did a brisk trade until the fair closed. The painters were much sought after because of "the infinite number of their paintings". Linen, cotton and lace and all other objects "of vain luxury and sensual pleasure," says Sauval, "were assembled by merchants who at the risk of their lives went to find them at the extremities of the Indies, in China and the New World." The shops of the goldsmiths were like Aladdin's cave.

The type of visitor to the fair changed twice a day, as though there were two separate fairs. During the day the ordinary people filled it, but by nightfall they had vanished, their place being taken by the quality; even great ladies and the King himself appeared in the fairytale lights of lustres and torches.

The fair catered not only for the common people and their betters. Gambling dens and cabarets were filled with ruffians, mountebanks, jugglers, fortune-tellers and cardsharps. Turks sold rosewater and balm straight from Constantinople—so they said. Portuguese hawked amber and porcelain, and Armenians offered tea, coffee and chocolate. Among the attractions was a "huge devil of a woman", to quote Mme de Sévigné who saw her at the fair in 1671. In 1749 the star of the fair was a rhinoceros, the first that Parisian eyes had ever beheld. Theatrical performances became fashionable in the seventeenth century.

The fair closed its seven doors in 1786.

The ferry to the Louvre used to be tied up at the bottom of the rue des Saints-Pères. One evening in 1598, shortly after the signing of the Treaty of Vervins, Henri IV on his way back from a shoot and accompanied only by two gentlemen, appeared on the landing stage and hailed the ferryman, who did not recognise him because of the simple clothes he wore. While they crossed, the King asked the ferryman what he thought of the peace treaty. In a grumbling voice, the ferryman declared that he for one had no time to think of it as he had enough worries with the taxes he had to pay; not even his wretched boat was exempt. Henri IV asked him whether he had confidence in the King, who would surely right such matters now that the war had ended.

"The King," said the ferryman, "is a good fellow, but he has a mistress who needs fine dresses and it is we who have to provide the money for them." He added that she had other lovers beside the monarch.

The King was amused, and the next day sent for the ferryman and made him repeat his words in front of Gabrielle d'Estrées. The royal mistress became so angry that she wanted the man to be flogged. The King restrained her with the words, "You are mad. He is a poor, luckless wight whose ill-humour is caused by misery. I won't let him pay any more taxes, and tomorrow, I promise you, he will shout 'Long live Henri IV and charming Gabrielle'."

The ferryman, exempted from further taxes, left the Louvre with a purse containing 25 écus.

Until the middle of the sixteenth century Paris had only four bridges: Petit-Pont, Notre-Dame, Saint-Michel and au Change.

By then the need for a new bridge to connect the Right Bank with the Bourg Saint-Germain had become evident. Thus was born the Pont-Neuf. The first stone was laid by Henri III on the very day he attended the funeral of Quélus and Maugiron, his favourite Mignons. He came straight from the Church of Saint-Paul-des-Champs in the rue Saint-Paul, and was in such a lachrymose mood that Parisian wags wanted the bridge to be named Pont-des-Larmes, bridge of tears. The bridge was constructed between 1578 and 1607. Its buildings, and particularly its shops, which did not disappear until the 1850s, drew the people almost more than the prospect of visiting the fair at Saint-Germain or strolling in the Pré-aux-Clercs. If one wanted to find a friend, all one had to do was to spend an hour or so on the bridge, for no self-respecting Parisian let the day go by without putting in an appearance on the Pont-Neuf. Police agents and spies went straight to the bridge when searching for a person they wanted to arrest or trail. If on the fourth day he was still invisible, they reported that the quarry was absent from Paris.

Recruiting sergeants frequented the bridge, for colonels, as L. S. Mercier put it, needed men to sell to the King. The sergeants were up to any old trick, such as employing low women to entice the men or cabaret-keepers to get them drunk. On the eve of Shrove Tuesday and the feast of St Martin, they carried poles from which hung turkeys, chickens, quails and leverets, in the hope that where women and drink had failed ravenous hunger would succeed. They were seldom wrong. The poor dupes, loitering near the Fountain of the Samaritaine, who had not had a square meal in their lives, succumbed to the temptation. Another trick of the sergeants was to shake their moneybags, rattling the coins. "Who wants some?" they shouted. The price for a prospective hero was 30 livres, but if he were a hefty fellow he received more. Good profit could be made out of the sons of tradesmen. The recruiting officers or sergeants, having filled them with wine, signed them on, and it cost the desperate parents 100 écus to buy them out. The recruiting offices were actually in the vicinity of the bridge, and they flew their regimental flags, one of which was embroidered with a line from Voltaire:

Le premier qui fut roi, fut un soldat heureux.

But the message had no appeal, for most of the recruits could neither read nor write.

Until the reign of Louis XIII the statues of French Kings were to be seen only on their tombs or as decorations on church porches. Louis XIII broke with tradition when he erected a statue on the Pont-Neuf to his murdered father, Henri IV. The foundation stone of the monument was laid on June 20, 1614. The figure of the dead King was cast by Guillaume Dupré. The horse that bore him had been presented to Marie de Medici, his widow, by Giovanni di Bologna. As a work of art, the horse was superior to the rider.

On August 11, 1792, the mob destroyed the statue of the man who for nearly two hundred years had been regarded by the people of France as the best King they had ever had. In order to incite the mob the story was invented that Ravaillac had murdered him because the King had raped Ravaillac's sister. The smashed statue was thrown into the Seine. In 1809, with the Empire still in full bloom, the foundation stone of an obelisk was laid on the same spot. It was to be a hundred feet high and consecrated to the glory of the French nation, but the Empire passed without the obelisk being erected, and with the Restoration Henri IV returned to the Pont-Neuf in the shape of a plaster-cast. Public opinion clamoured, however, for a bronze statue, the money for which was raised by private subscription. Inside the pedestal were deposited documents relating to the inauguration of the first statue, documents relating to the new one, several books—among them *L'Henriade* of Voltaire and a life of Henri IV—the Charter of 1814, the Peace Treaty of 1814, and coins and medals. Moreover, Mesnel, a workman on the statue who was a rabid Bonapartist, inserted into the right arm of the King a statuette of the Emperor, and placed in the horse's belly anti-royalist writings and songs, which are still inside it. The statue was unveiled on

August 25, 1818, in the presence of Louis XVIII and the happy people who might easily have included some of those or their sons who had, in Restoration parlance, laid sacrilegious hands on the original. The new statue cost 350,000 francs.

The Cour de Rohan has no connection with the family of that name; it was the courtyard of the Paris mansion of the Archbishops of Rouen. Time had turned Rouen into Rohan. It joins the Cour du Commerce near the bookshop where Doctor Guillotin tried out his invention on sheep. Contrary to general belief, the doctor, who was described by his contemporaries as a quiet, sweet-natured man, did not invent the instrument; he simply brought it up to date. It had been used as far back as the fifteenth century in Italy and the south of France, when it was called mannaja, but the doctor's improvements made it far easier to operate. He was satisfied with his experiments on sheep. "A puff of air on the neck," he said, "and all is over." He called it a philanthropic engine. It started as a labour of love, for he did not see to what commercial advantage he could put it, yet he continued with his improvements and the heads of sheep rolled in the Cour du Commerce.

At number 9 lived a German carpenter named Schmidt who assisted the doctor in his philanthropic work. He was a willing helpmate, but when the Revolution put the guillotine to use, poor Schmidt took to drink, bitterly blaming himself for having helped the doctor, in whose defence it must be said that he too had not foreseen the consequences of his experiments. Schmidt died, during the Empire, of delirium tremens brought about by wine laced with remorse; and the mild doctor also, again contrary to general belief, never felt the puff of air on his own neck: he died in his bed in 1812 at the respectable age of seventy-four.

To the south of the Cour du Commerce stands the statue of Danton, on the Boulevard Saint-Germain in the exact spot where he had an apartment of seven rooms. He used to cross the courtyard on his way to the Café Procope to meet other revolutionaries of the neighbourhood.

Originally the rue Visconti was called the rue des Marais-Saint-Germain, and for a while it was referred to as Little Geneva because of the Calvinists who lived there. In the long narrow street between rues Bonaparte and Seine have resided several famous men, among them Bernard Le Bovier de Fontenelle, writer and Secretary of the Académie des Sciences, who in his hundredth year said to a pretty young girl, on being introduced to her, "If only I were ten years younger!" Marshal de Saxe, Voltaire and Jean Racine also lived in the street.

Racine lived and died at number 24, but it used to be believed in the street that he had lived at number 13 because he planted a vine there. The street was not yet as narrow as at the present time, and the playwright's house faced the gardens of the de la Roche-foucauld mansion. Racine was already fifty-three years old when he moved to the rue des Marais. He had given up the theatre fifteen years earlier, his only preoccupation now the salvation of his soul. He recollected with horror the days when he had frequented actresses and often sobbed over his "scandalous life", which had covered his great creative years. In the course of those fifteen years away from the theatre his wife, Catherine de Romanet, had given him eight children. In spite of the presence of the smaller ones, the house in the rue des Marais remained austere in its silence.

The house was on three floors. The walls of the rooms and even of the passages were hung with Flemish tapestries. Gloomy Racine loved red. When he went out, he wore a scarlet overcoat and short pink jacket. On his return he put on a red velvet cap and cried over his sins.

At the age of sixteen Jean-Baptiste, his eldest son, evinced a desire to go to the Opéra. Racine counselled him to read Cicero instead, and as an Easter present wrote him a sermon on death. He wanted Jean-Baptiste to enter a monastery: the boy ended up in the Ministry of Foreign Affairs. Racine was deeply influenced by the Jansenist Convent of Port-Royal, where his eldest daughter, Marie-Catherine, was brought up. Nanette, his second daughter was educated in the convent of the Ursulines at Melun; the third, Babet, was with the nuns at Variville-en-Beauvaisis; the fourth, Fanchon, was waiting at the time of her father's death to be old enough to join Nanette in Melun; the youngest, Madelon, like Fanchon, lived in the parental home, together with the two small boys Lionval and Louis. Of amusements there were hardly any. Once the children were taken to the fair at Saint-Germain, where the sight of the elephant gave Lionval convulsions, an added reason not to indulge in outings.

In the summer of 1698 Racine fell ill. The medicos bled him copiously, and by October he was on his feet again, though he complained of feeling exceptionally weak. Still, he had the energy to travel to Melun to see Nanette take the veil. He sobbed throughout the ceremony. The following January he went for a stroll with his wife as far as the Tuileries, but acute pain in his back forced him home. He never left the house again, and died on April 21.

Sir George Brydges Rodney, Bart., Rear Admiral of Great Britain (elevated to the peerage as Baron Rodney in 1782) lived for a while in 1775 in the rue Visconti, driven to Paris by his creditors. He kicked his heels in his lodgings in the narrow street, thinking of the war raging in America while he, like a laid-up ship of the line, was anchored in peaceful Saint-Germain. He complained to his French friends, declaring that if only he could pay his debts and be on the high seas again, he would quickly put an end to French successes.

"If it only depends on that," said Marshal of France Baron de Biron, "I charge myself with their payment."

And he paid them. Soon it was the turn of the French Admiral, the Comte de Grasse, to complain.

In spite of all the other famous men who lived there, the rue Visconti seems most attached to the memory of Honoré de Balzac, who came to number 19 not to write, but to print and publish books. He had already done a stretch of four years as a writer, however did not feel there was enough money to be made in that profession. His mistress, Mme de Berny, who was twenty years his senior, set him up as a publisher. "Only a woman's last love can satisfy a man's first love," he wrote. He had an excellent idea, the only snag being that he thought of it before its time. He planned to publish the works of Molière, La Fontaine and other classic writers in single volumes, illustrated with woodcuts. His formula became enormously successful after he gave it up. There was not at the time a large enough public for cheap books. The literate still preferred their writers in six or more volumes. Madame de Berny paid his debts after the two-year venture failed. In 1828 Balzac went away and back to writing. The printing press remained, and can be seen at number 19 in the ground-floor workshop, now used for binding books.

In the rue de Bourbon-le-Château, which gives on to the market of the rue de Buci, a murder was committed in 1850 which, because of the rapid apprehension of the assassin, entered the annals of Saint-Germain-des-Prés. At number 1 rue de Bourbon-le-Château lived a Mlle Ribault, a spinster, who was draughtswoman at the *Petit Courrier des Dames*, edited by a Monsieur Thierry. She was killed in the afternoon of December 23 by her employer's assistant, Laforcade, while the happy throng was doing its Christmas shopping in the market. Loath to leave this life without denouncing her murderer, the old maid crawled to a screen and, with her finger dipped in her own blood, she wrote on it, "The assassin is the assistant of Monsieur Thi. . . ." Respectful to the last, she gave her employer his title though she lacked the time to complete his name.

XVI

Latin Quarter

When in 1855 the Boulevard Saint-Germain reached the Place Maubert, the square lost its personality and importance. The old houses were pulled down, and nowadays there is nothing but a circus where the Boulevard and the rues Monge and Lagrange meet. For seven centuries the square had been associated with the University, and, as one knows from an ordnance of 1546, a bread market was already established there at that date. Paris had four bread markets in all: Place Maubert, Halles, Cemetery of Saint-Jacques (Place Baudoyer) and rue Neuve-Notre-Dame (Place du Parvis-Notre-Dame). By the middle of the seventeenth century, the bakers who sold in these markets numbered one thousand five hundred and eighty. Roughly one-third of them baked their bread in Paris and the faubourgs; the rest of the bread came from surrounding villages, as far away as Saint-Germain-en-Laye.

On the Plan of Paris of Oliver Truschet and Germain Hoyau, drawn in 1552, the Place Maubert was marked with a little gibbet from which hung a little body, for the square was used for burning, drawing, quartering and hanging. To confess the condemned was the privilege of the Doctors of the University, but the Cordeliers thought it was their right too. A certain poor girl, who was to be hanged for theft, stood beneath the gallows. As a Cordelier began to confess her, an irate Doctor appeared, telling him that he had no business to do so. An unedifying row ensued. The Franciscan and the Doctor came to blows. The girl, watching them with detached interest, seemed to enjoy every brief second. The Doctor prevailed and the monk withdrew. The victorious Doctor then heard the girl's confession and gave her absolution. Then she was hanged.

The square owed its name to Jean Aubert, second Abbot of the Abbey of Sainte-Geneviève in 1161. The Abbey owned all the land in the district. The first colleges of the University were built around 1180, modest dwellings, providing roof and food for the scholars, who rose early and after Mass went to the Place Maubert and the rue du Fouarre where they listened to the lectures, sitting on the ground or on straw, beneath the open sky. Until the reign of François I the teachers were lodged and fed, but received no emoluments except from private pupils. In the colleges Latin alone was tolerated, execrable Latin spoken with a French accent. Even the servants had to speak in Latin. The custom persisted until the Revolution and earned the district the name of the Latin Quarter. In 1257 a college was founded by Robert de Sorbon for poor theological students. Later the whole faculty of theology came to be known as Sorbonne. Nowadays the whole University of Paris is called after him.

Philippe-Auguste established the organisation of the University, but the corporate body of teachers and scholars known as the University, which meant "Universality of the Sciences taught in Schools", did not come into being until the time of St Louis. It had four sections: three for the French and one for the English, Irish and Scots. The English College was given to German scholars during the Hundred Years War.

The students were a turbulent lot. In 1200 a German visitor sent his German servant to a cabaret in a street adjoining the Place Maubert. The servant was ill-treated. German students arrived to avenge their fellow countryman and gave the landlord an awful beating. Led by Thomas, Provost of Paris, the local burghers appeared on the scene and killed five German students. The Rector of the University complained to Philippe-Auguste who had the Provost and his friends locked up for life.

In 1221 the students were in trouble again. Considering themselves immune from persecution because of the privileges granted them by the King, they took to fornication, abducted married women, robbed and murdered. Guillaume de Seignelay, Bishop of Paris, excommunicated all students who carried arms. The ordinary citizens came to hate the students to the extent of fighting a pitched battle with them in 1223 in which three hundred and twenty students were killed, and their bodies thrown into the Seine. The Doctors took their complaints to the Pope; none the less the attacks on students continued until, led by the Doctors, they left Paris for a time, the colleges and faculties remaining empty. When they returned, trouble returned with them.

In 1275 on the feasts of SS Nicholas and Catherine the students marched through the streets of the Latin Quarter in the deep of night, carrying torches, dancing and shouting, and creating such disorder that further outings were finally forbidden by the Assembly of the University which met in the Church of Saint-Julien-le-Pauvre. A century later the rampaging started again. In 1367 the students chose a bishop from among themselves, dressed him up in ecclesiastical vestments and followed him through the streets with lighted torches, creating havoc. The Watch stopped them and one of the students was wounded. When Parliament heard of the affray, the Captain of the Watch was sent to the wounded youth, who not only banged the door in his face, though knowing that he was an emissary of Parliament, but set his friends on him. The Watch overpowered them and the students had to make penance in the Convent of the Mathurins (20-22 rue du Sommerard, demolished during the Revolution), and beg pardon on bended knees from the King, the Bishop of Paris and the Rector of the University.

In 1468 on the day after Epiphany the students elected a king whom they called the King of Fools and under whose aegis they made a terrible din, molesting people they met in the streets and keeping peaceful citizens awake. The following year, Kanedi, the Rector, assembled the Faculty of Arts in the Church of Saint-Julien-le-Pauvre and admonished the Doctors to keep their students in order. He sent representatives of the Faculty to wait on the Provost of Paris to ask him to arrest all students wearing a mask or carrying a stick in the street, and to send them back to their teachers who would mete out exemplary punishment. A year later, again on the day after Epiphany, the students misbehaved once more, but though they were punished, nothing seemed to stop them from indulging in scandalous behaviour during the feasts of Epiphany, SS Martin, Nicholas and Catherine. In 1488 a new order was issued by the Rector and the Faculty of Arts which permitted only decent recreations. On Sundays after Vespers the students were now allowed, even encouraged, to partake of innocent amusements, and if they felt the need of perpetrating practical jokes they were to ask the consent of their teachers who would grant permission only if they considered the jokes harmless.

In practice this decree had little effect. In 1525 on the feast of St Nicholas a woman was dragged along the narrow streets by students, some disguised as devils, others as Doctors of the University. François I was so incensed that he complained to the President of Parliament, who ordered such masquerades to be suppressed.

Excesses were not the prerogative of the Faculty of Arts. In a circular letter sent by the Faculty of Theology to all the Bishops of France, bitter complaint was made about theological students who went to church dressed as buffoons or even women, all wearing masks, singing bawdy songs, bringing their food with them and consuming it while the priest said Mass, playing dice in church, using foul language, and after Mass running round the streets like madmen. Now and then the students went even further. They elected a Pope of Fools who blessed the people he passed in the street. If someone remonstrated with them they spoke, says Henri

Sauval, "as though they were such good Christians that those who forbade their antics deserved to be excommunicated."

The colleges surrounding the Place Maubert included de Tournay, des Lombards, de Navarre, de Presles, de Boncourt, de Saint-Michel, de Montaigu, de la Marche and de Laon. In 1206 one of the first colleges of Paris was founded in the Impasse Maubert: the Collège Constantinople or Collège Grec. The Impasse Maubert, originally known as rue Sans-Bout, changed its name in the fifteenth century to Cul-de-sac d'Amboise after a private mansion of that name. It had an infamous reputation, for wherever students gathered, ruffians and prostitutes also made their appearance. The students hobnobbed and fought with them. In their wake came tramps and beggars. A low tavern in the Impasse Maubert, where one drank and slept until two in the morning when all clients were thrown out for fear of the police descending, acquired special fame in the eighteenth century because three female poisoners who practised there died from the fumes of the furnace in which they brewed their potions.

In the square the gibbet remained busy. On September 19, 1528, a young man of twenty was hanged, accused of having murdered his master with the complicity of a fellow servant. After dangling for half an hour on the gallows, he was cut down by the hangman, who pushed him into a cart to take him to the charnel house of Montfaucon. The young man moved his legs and tried to rise. The hangman took out a knife to cut his victim's throat; however, the women, who were always in the majority at executions, shouted "Miracle!" The young man began to shout too, claiming that he had been dead but was told to return to life by Notre-Dame-de-la-Recouvrance whose chapel stood on the south side of the square. He was taken to the Convent of the Carmelites, where he recovered within two days. A sergeant had remained at his bedside to arrest him the moment he could move. The Carmelites waited on François I, begging him to pardon the young man, which the King did, observing that he could not be less generous than Our Lady. A fresh investigation proved that the murdered man had been killed by his wife.

The square was used as a place of execution until the middle of the eighteenth century. One François Masson, who had stolen the goblets of the Church of the Cistercians, was hanged there on June 12, 1752. "It rained considerably and the gutters overflowed," said a police report, "none the less there was a large concourse of people."

In the nineteenth century the square was taken over by the needy and the homeless. Cigarette stubs, stale bread, leeches and fleas were sold. In the rue d'Ecosse and in houses adjoining the square, goats were raised. Cheap, dirty lodging-houses polluted the district until the coming of the Boulevard put an end to them. The poor of the Place Maubert moved into the streets between the square and the river.

The rue Maître-Albert, which until 1844 was called rue Perdue, took its name from the great theologian St Albert le Grand who, like St Thomas Aquinas, was one of the shining lights of the University in the thirteenth century. In 1815, at 13 rue Maître-Albert lived Zamor. He was Mme Du Barry's blackamoor, or more strictly he was a Bengali who had been brought to France when only seven years old by the captain of an English vessel. Blackamoors were much in fashion in the eighteenth century, and he became the Du Barry's possession. She educated him, spoilt him, lavished a fortune on him and dressed him up as a hussar. Because of the importance she attached to him, even Louis XV found him amusing. During the Terror, Zamor was the first to denounce her, and was one of the chief witnesses against her. "I often remonstrated with her because of the aristocratic world she moved in," he said. The story that he had been her lover when only a boy of ten is almost certainly untrue, for had it been the case, Zamor would have been the first to bring it up at her trial.

"One little minute more, Monsieur le bourreau," she pleaded on the scaffold.

In the rue Perdue, as it still was, Zamor eked out his existence giving lessons to children, whom he beat whenever he had a chance. "He was very nasty," said the local people, who yet went on sending their children to him. He taught them to read and charged little.

He paid 60 francs a year for his room. Charles Vatel, the historian of the Du Barry, called on Mme Lejeune, daughter of the proprietor of the house where Zamor had lived. He asked her to describe him.

"He was very small," she said, "no taller than I, less than five feet. He was a puny mulatto of a disagreeable yellowish colour with a flat nose and sparse greying hair. He would have had enough to live on had he not fallen in love with a milliner to whom he gave all his money, which she lost on a business venture."

One morning in 1820 a neighbour found him dead in bed. Three francs, all he possessed in the world, lay on his bedside table; and when he was buried not a single person accompanied his coffin to the Cemetery of Vaugirard. Twenty-seven years after the Du Barry had been guillotined, a long enough period, one would think, for a veil to have been drawn over the past, the people of the district said, "We are not going. He betrayed the Du Barry."

The rue de Bièvre already bore that name in the thirteenth century. It took its name from the river Bièvre which was linked to a canal dug about 1150 to carry water to the gardens of the Abbey of Saint-Victor. The canal, into which the inhabitants of the neighbourhood flung their refuse, ran parallel to the street, its water foul and smelly. The canal was covered in the seventeenth century to the displeasure of the local people, who demolished the brickwork in several places so as to be able again to throw their rubbish into it. Dante stayed in the street during one of his two visits to Paris.

Before the twelfth century medicine was taught and practised only in the monasteries. The physicians therefore were all monks. Their medical knowledge was not extensive, and was also limited by the celibate existence they led. In 1135 the monks were forbidden to continue practising medicine. Pope Alexander III threatened to excommunicate any monk whose studies went beyond purely theological subjects. As a result Paris remained for nearly a hundred years without physicians. In 1220 small lay schools of medicine opened their doors to lay students. In 1331 Philippe VI founded the Faculty of Medicine, which was attached to the University. The faculty's seat was at 13-15 rue de la Bûcherie which today houses offices of the department of the Seine. The street owed its name to the Port aux Bûches (port of logs) where timber for construction and wood for heating arrived. It was the most important port of Paris. The street, which then was no more than a lane, skirted the river.

At number 16 rue de la Bûcherie, Restif de La Bretonne died in 1806. Though his work comprised over two hundred volumes, he died in dire poverty. Even his small police pension had been suspended. As there was no money to pay for a decent funeral, men of the neighbourhood carried his coffin to the Cemetery of Sainte-Catherine (56-66 Boulevard Saint-Marcel). Today his books are obligatory reading in French lycées.

The oldest sign in Paris, the bas-relief at 42 rue Galande, mentioned as early as 1380 as "the house under the sign of Saint-Julien", shows Saint-Julien-le-Pauvre and his wife ferrying his Divine passenger across the river. The depth of mediaeval feeling is beautifully reflected in the bas-relief, which originally was above the portal of the Church.

Julian was of noble descent. One day, while hunting a stag, the stag suddenly stopped, turned round and spoke: "You who hunt me will one day kill your parents." Impressed by the speaking stag and frightened by the prophecy, Julian left his parents and exiled himself far from them. In the distant land where he took up his abode, he was befriended by the King, who gave him one of his castles. His parents, searching for him, found out where he was and hurried to him. They arrived at the castle while Julian was out hunting. Their daughter-in-law received them with great courtesy and gave them the conjugal bedroom. She then went out to find her husband. Night had fallen, and Julian came home without meeting his wife, and unaware of his parents' presence. He went straight to the bedchamber and in the darkness touched two strangers lying in his bed. In his fury he killed them both. When his wife got home she told him that he had killed his parents.

Julian gave up all his worldly goods, and with his wife went to live in a hut near a river, where he succoured the sick and the poor, and ferried them free of charge across the river. One evening a leper came to the hut and asked to be taken to the other bank. As Julian and his wife rowed him across the water, an aureole appeared over the leper's head. It was Christ, who had brought Julian remission of his sins. Gustave Flaubert relates the legend in his *Trois Contes*.

The Church of Saint-Julien-le-Pauvre existed as long ago as 507. Sacked by the Normans in 886, it was rebuilt in the twelfth century and given to the Abbey of Longpont. It became the parish church of the University in the days when lessons were given in the open air between Place Maubert and rue Fouarre. SS Albert le Grand and Thomas Aquinas worshipped there. The Assembly of the University was held in the church, the election of the Rector Magnificus took place there, and every two years the Provost of Paris came to Saint-Julien-le-Pauvre to swear to respect and uphold the privileges of the University. The great era ceased when new colleges were built on the Montagne-Sainte-Geneviève. The students became increasingly disenchanted with their rectors, who viewed them with dwindling indulgence, and since the rectors were elected in the church, in 1524 the students broke the windows and destroyed everything inside on which they could lay their hands. The Parliament of Paris decreed that future elections should be held in the Convent of the Mathurins.

In 1651 the Church was restored and attached to the Hôtel-Dieu. Under the Revolution it was used as a warehouse. It was restored to the cult in 1801. Robert Auget, Baron de Montyon, was a benefactor not only of the Church but also of the Paris hospitals and the poor of the city. He left large sums to charity when he died in 1820. First buried in the Cemetery of Vaugirard in 1838, he was reburied under the peristyle of the Hôtel-Dieu, and in 1877 found final rest most appropriately in the Church of Saint-Julien-le-Pauvre.

Nowadays it is the church of the Greek Catholics in Paris.

There were two saints called Séverin: one, Séverin, Abbot of Argaune in Valais, who was summoned in 504 to Paris by Clovis to cure him of a malignant fever; the other, Séverin the Solitary, who in the reign of Childebert I, son of Clovis, retired to lead a solitary, saintly life to the spot, then well beyond the southern city gate, where the Church of Saint-Séverin was to be built.

One knows that after a short stay in Paris the Abbot of Argaune left for Château-Landon in the Gatinais, where he died about 506. It seems unlikely that he could have had time in Paris to found a chapel on the left bank of the Seine. On the other hand, the Solitary lived there for a long time among fishermen and boatmen, setting them a shining example with the austere, pious life he led. They were witnesses to the miracles he performed after his death, and raised a chapel in his honour. The Normans burnt it down, but it was rebuilt in the eleventh century.

The present Church of Saint-Séverin was begun on the same site two centuries later. The clergy of Saint-Séverin found it difficult to choose between the two saints. In 1738 the parish priest tried to turn them into one: having been an anchorite in Paris, according to his version, the saint became the Abbot of Argaune. This theory had no success. Eventually both saints came to be venerated in the church and both their feast days celebrated, the Abbot's on February 11 and the Solitary's on November 23.

The clergy of Saint-Séverin took up their abode in the street which was first called rue de l'Archiprêtre, then rue aux Prêtres, and finally rue des Prêtres-Saint-Séverin. The street in front of the Church was referred to in the fourteenth century as a warren of women. A century later the College of Lisieux was installed there, but moved later to the rue des Grès (now rue Cujas), then to the rue Jean-de-Beauvais. The Cemetery and charnel house were beside the Church.

Because of the colleges and the narrowness of the streets (which included rues des Grands-Degrés, de l'Hôtel-Colbert, du Haut-Pavé, des Trois-Portes, de la Huchette, Saint-Séverin, de la Harpe, du Fouarre, du Petit-Pont and the alleyways round the Church of Saint-Séverin), life teemed in the Latin Quarter. The crowds in the neighbourhood were always dense. Monks begged in the streets in the name of "Jésus, notre Sire", itinerant vendors hawked their wares, and students and travellers pushed their way into cook-shops. The people were summoned by the bells of over twenty churches which called them to Mass or Vespers, to weddings or funerals, or to celebrate with a Te Deum the King's latest victory. But when the bell of Saint-Séverin rang out the curfew, everybody hurried home, closing the shutters and locking the doors against the night. One of the reasons why decent citizens so disliked the students was the young people's disregard of the dangers of the night to which, incidentally, they added with their turbulent roistering.

It was foolish to venture out at night in the unlit streets, for the Devil stalked them, and woe to the man he caught. Life was short and full of perils. The Devil did not reign alone in the dark: pestilence, assassins, robbers and other ruffians shared his rule. Moreover, carnal sin waited at every corner in the shape of prostitutes. Darkness was also the ally of death.

Even at home death did not leave you alone. The clocheteurs des trépassés saw to that. The bellringers of the dead, dressed in white, their coats embroidered with black skull and bones, ran through the streets ringing their hand bells until they were sure that all the inhabitants had been wakened, when they shouted:

> Réveillez-vous, gens qui dormez,
> Priez Dieu pour les trépassés.

The custom persisted well into the seventeenth century. There was no chance to forget or try to overlook the shortness of life and ever-present death.

The night, however, served medical students well. They used the hours after dark to steal corpses. Their purpose was not ghoulish: they were rarely given more than the odd corpse or two a year, and they could not study medicine without cutting up the dead. In that thick conglomeration of streets everyone knew about everybody's movements, including their deaths and burials. The medical students needed comparatively fresh corpses. Before nightfall an accomplice would hide among the tombstones of the Cemetery of Saint-Séverin who would later open the gate to his student friends. They did not need to take many precautions, for most of the people who were abroad at night were up to no good, and would not, therefore, interfere with them. The Watch seldom passed and if it came they could in any case hear it.

When the cemetery gate was unlocked, the students hurried to a fresh grave—they chose the graves of the poor, who had no coffins but were interred in shrouds—dug out the corpse, then carried it to the medical school, or in the seventeenth and eighteenth centuries to a house in the rue de la Harpe where many of them lodged. It goes almost without saying that one night Restif de La Bretonne followed such a procession to the rue de la Harpe, climbed the stairs unseen, and hidden in a dark corner, watched the students at work. He recognised the deceased, a girl of eighteen who had died the night before and whose parents he knew. Though filled with sorrow, he did not denounce the students. "Why are they not given the corpses of criminals?" was the pertinent question he asked himself.

However, there was an occasion when medical students saved a life by robbing a grave. A young girl had been duly buried, and the students had carried her away to be dissected, but by the time they reached their house the girl had revived. The students believed that the fresh earth on her shroud had brought her back to life. They gave her a drink, and as she had no idea where she was or what had happened, they tactfully explained that she had been very ill and that her parents had put her in their care, assuring her that she had recovered and was no longer in danger of death. They took her home before dawn. Her parents were out, for in their misery they had gone to spend the night with friends. The students put the girl to bed, told the servant maid to give her a hot broth as she had caught a chill in the grave, and at seven in the morning sent the servant to fetch the parents. While she was gone the students disappeared.

One was not always so lucky. At 12 rue Saint-Séverin lived for a time the Abbé Prévost d'Exiles of whose hundred and seventy works only *Manon Lescaut* is remembered. In 1763 he went for a short visit to Croix-de-Courtail, a small village in the forest of Senlis (Oise), where he died of a stroke. Death having come so suddenly, the authorities ordered a post-mortem. As the surgeon brought his scalpel to the Abbé's head, the Abbé came to life. The scalpel had struck the forehead with such strength however that a few minutes later he died of the wound.

At 33 rue Saint-Jacques stood the Chapel of Saint-Yves who was born near Tréguier in Brittany in 1253. As an ecclesiastical judge he acquired renown for his integrity and kindness to the poor. He gave up his office to become the protector of the poor, who referred to him as the father and defender of destitutes, widows and orphans. He died in 1303, and was canonised in 1347. The construction of the chapel began the following year under Philippe IV and was finished in the reign of Jean le Bon in 1357. It adjoined a college for poor scholars from Brittany, and was demolished during the Revolution.

Lawyers took St Yves as their patron saint, and on May 19 every year a Mass was celebrated in the Chapel for the eternal rest of the lawyers who had died the year before. Nowadays the Mass is celebrated in the Sainte-Chapelle. It is worth noting that the painters of Paris offer up a Mass on Ash Wednesday in the Church of Saint-Germain-l'Auxerrois for the souls of the painters who will die in the course of the year. But lawyers prefer to act on evidence.

There is a story that when St Yves arrived at the gate of Heaven, St Peter refused him entry, thinking that he was a professional lawyer. The saint waited for the next batch of arrivals, and, hiding among them, entered Paradise in their company. However, St Peter spotted him and told him to be gone. St Yves retorted that he would leave only if a huissier, a process-server, brought him an expulsion order signed by a judge. St Peter went in search of a hussier and a judge, but could find no one in Paradise belonging to the legal profession. So St Yves remained.

The Church of Saint-Etienne-du-Mont in the Place Sainte-Geneviève was built on the land annexed by Philippe-Auguste from the Abbey of Sainte-Geneviève in 1220, during the building of his Enceinte. The Church was first named Saint-Jean-du-Mont and renamed in the sixteenth century. When it became too small for the rising number of worshippers, it was pulled down, and construction of the present Church began in 1517, though it was not completed until the reign of Louis XIII. The first stone of the portal was laid in 1610 by Marguerite de Valois. The sarcophagus of St Geneviève was placed in the church, and on her feast, January 3, large crowds filled the church. By tradition on that day the sarcophagus was carried in procession as far as Notre-Dame. At first monks shouldered it, but from 1525 onwards, sixteen members of the Parisian high bourgeoisie were given the privilege of carrying the reliquary, which was so heavy that ten strong men were needed to lift it. Later twenty-four burghers who had held office as provost or alderman were granted the honour. Eventually their number rose to forty.

In 1793 the sarcophagus was melted down and the relics were burnt in the presence of happy sans-culottes, another victory over bigotry. In 1802 the original stone coffin in which the saint was buried in 551 was discovered in the crypt of the church of the Abbey of Sainte-Geneviève. Her bones had been removed from it and hidden by the monks at the time of the Norman invasion. Later a more ornate sarcophagus was made for them, so that the coffin was no longer needed. But now that there were no relics left, the original coffin was transferred to Saint-Etienne-du-Mont and surrounded by an imposing reliquary. On January 3 pilgrims still crowd the church and pray beside the coffin that the Normans failed to destroy.

The graveyard behind the Church was sold in 1784, but when the dead Mirabeau and the dead Marat fell in disgrace (the first in September 1794, the second in February 1795) and were expelled from the Panthéon (Church of Sainte-Geneviève before the Revolution) across the road, their coffins were taken to the graveyard. Mirabeau's coffin was delivered to his sister in 1798, but she refused to accept it, and it disappeared without trace, like Marat's.

The Church was restored to the Archdiocese of Paris in 1803. Its troubles were not yet over, for when on January 3, 1857, Marie-Dominique Sibour, Archbishop of Paris, arrived at three in the afternoon for the feast and novenna of Sainte-Geneviève, an unfrocked, demented, priest, Jean Verger, stabbed him to death.

XVII

From Montparnasse to the Jardin des Plantes

In the sixteenth and seventeenth centuries students of the University used to visit the hill south of the Sorbonne, where they read poetry and played music together. They gave it the name of Mont Parnasse. Montparnasse became one of the four districts of the fourteenth arrondissement when it was annexed to Paris in 1860.

In 1704 Louis XIV decided to urbanise the hill, which until then had consisted of meadows, orchards and fields, and boasted enough windmills to make Montmartre jealous. The plan of the present-day Boulevard du Montparnasse was traced in 1714; but construction did not begin until 1761. The knoll where the students used to meet—at the corner of Boulevards Raspail and du Montparnasse—was levelled down, though a small mound remained there until 1816.

The Boulevard du Montparnasse formed, with the Boulevards de l'Hôpital, Auguste-Blanqui, Saint-Jacques and des Invalides, the Boulevards du Midi, so called because they were south of the city. The Boulevard du Montparnasse stopped at the rue d'Enfer (Avenue Denfert-Rochereau) before the Avenue de l'Observatoire existed. The new thoroughfares were soon flanked by imposing private mansions with large gardens, among them the houses of Mademoiselle de Condé-Bourbon, Marshal of France Baron de Biron and the Ducs d'Orsay and Laval. During the early years of the Revolution, public feasts, dances, firework displays and "aeronautical experiences" were held in the gardens of those who had either succeeded in fleeing from, or had perished on, the guillotine. The Boulevard itself remained peaceful. In 1828 it was still described as an admirable but solitary place to promenade. It ceased to be solitary when guinguettes with arbours and swings, catering specially for lovers, came to line it.

In 1820, Choron, a theatrical impresario, established an academy of dramatic art in the Boulevard. He had the entry into several schools, where the masters introduced him to pupils who were making no headway in Greek and Latin. Such pupils were known as cancres (dunces). Choron took them under his wing. "They will soon be good for work," he said and carried them off to his academy. After a few lessons he called on their parents whom he persuaded to let their offspring embark on a theatrical career since they seemed no good for anything else. Nine out of ten agreed. When the pupils were, in his opinion, ready to be launched, he invited the aristocracy of the Faubourg Saint-Germain to witness their excellent performances. Now and again the pupils' first appearance was before empty seats, however, for the inhabitants of the Faubourg considered Montparnasse as the back of beyond.

There was another sort of academy on the Boulevard, its premises in a guinguette. The singer Anatole Lionnet gave this description: "At the other end of the room sat an aged man before a table, a small wooden hammer in his hand. He would call, 'The turn of our friend so and so . . .' and a man, usually a workman, rose in the audience, approached the table and sang a ballad or a song. Some did not sing badly and received thunderous applause. Others, naïve or pretentious, were laughed at, though also applauded. It was moving to see all those decent people who, after a day's hard work, came to that room to enjoy themselves simply and honestly, singing gay songs and sentimental ballads."

A dance hall, the Bal de l'Ermitage, was in 1848 the meeting place of female socialists and sans-culottes. Another dance hall, the Bal de l'Elysée-Montparnasse was frequented by students and artists. Yet another, the Grande-Chaumière, was frequented by anybody who could get in.

The Grande-Chaumière began modestly enough: a few small thatched huts in a garden, where drink was served and dancing was allowed. It was started in 1783 by an Englishman called Tickson, who later took a tavern-keeper, Fillard by name, as his partner. They pulled down the huts, built a house two storeys high, and laid out the gardens; there were flower beds, an arbour, swings and a shooting-booth. Under the Restoration, the place became enormously fashionable. Admirers of Corot gave a banquet there for the painter in 1826. (Corot was not the first painter to climb Montparnasse: in the reign of Louis XIV, when it was still a wilderness, the painter Hyacinthe Rigaud used to hunt there.) Benoît, Fillard's son-in-law, inherited the Grande-Chaumière and installed a switchback. Lobster salad, switchbacks and the theatre were, according to a saying in the early nineteenth century, the three passions of the grisette.

After Benoît came père Lahire, another son-in-law, an old Grenadier of the Imperial Guard, a man of immense physical strength. He persuaded the authorities to leave the maintenance of order in the establishment entirely to him. The police, who used to irritate and provoke students, were no longer allowed in, and under his rule fights and tussles ceased. In 1843 the polka was danced for the first time in Paris in the Grande-Chaumière. When Jules Favre, Horace Vernet, Emile de Girardin and Adolphe Thiers were university students, they regularly frequented the place.

In 1855 the Grande-Chaumière closed its doors. The Closerie des Lilas took over its clientele.

Another dance hall, the Arc-en-Ciel, founded in 1800, reached the heights of fame in the 1830s. It had a good orchestra, and Laurent Filiberti, the landlord, was a composer of romances and waltzes, *Brise de Soir* and *Rosita* being the best known. However, Filiberti's

fame was based neither on his work nor on the excellence of his
orchestra, but on a popular tune that he did not compose:

> Toi qui connais les hussards de la Garde
> Connais-tu pas l'trombone du régiment?
> Il a l'air vaillant quand il vous regarde,
> Eh bien, ma chère, il était mon amant.

When Filiberti had done his military service, he had been first
trombone in the fifth Hussars, so his customers sang the tune whenever he appeared among them. Associated with it in their minds,
he became as popular as the tune.

Painters gravitated to Montparnasse, but they were still French
painters until after the Franco-Prussian War. When Montparnasse
became cosmopolitan, the old painters looked back nostalgically on
the days when only French was heard there. They sighed as foreigners filled the cafés that had so completely been theirs. One night,
a few years before the First World War, two Polish artists flew at
each other's throats in a café in the Boulevard du Montparnasse.
They could not be separated, and the police were called. The Poles
were taken to the police station.

"Why did you fight?" asked the inspector in charge.

"To repay an old insult in Warsaw," said one of them.

"So that's why you travelled the whole way to Montparnasse,"
sighed the inspector.

The oldtimers had another grievance. On Sundays the military
barracks of Lourcine, in the Boulevard de Port-Royal, disgorged
its soldiers, who spent their day swaggering up and down the
Boulevard du Montparnasse, pushing people out of their way,
accosting women and filling the air with their country accents.
These soldiers were from regiments from the reliable, traditionalist
West (Sarthe, Anjou and Brittany), for the governments before the
First World War still feared that another Commune might be
attempted.

On the Boulevard de Montrouge (now Boulevard Edgar-Quinet) facing the rue de la Gaîté, stood for a time a long wooden hut, a wax museum, containing, it boasted, a hundred and sixty statues in wax. The life-size statues had been shown at the Paris Exhibition of 1855 and the Lyons Exhibition of 1872. "Everything here is magnificent, sumptuous and grand. The likenesses are perfect," declared a notice over the entrance door. The most striking statues and scenes were:

Marshal of France de Mac-Mahon, President of the French Republic and Madame de Mac-Mahon.

The Sultan Mohammed II entering his seraglio, where he finds his favourite Sultana poisoned by her jealous companions.

The Republic in all its glory, Goddess of Liberty, General Garibaldi offering her his sword.

H.M. Victor-Emmanuel II; H.E. Count Cavour.

The great reception given by Marshal of France Pélissier when he was appointed Governor of Algeria, and all the important people who assisted at the reception, including Madame la Maréchale.

The unfaithful slave and the Pasha's vengeance.

Béranger, Voltaire and other poets.

The Treaty of Paris. In this group can be seen H.M. the German Emperor, M. de Bismarck, General de Moltke and a number of other Prussians.

The Imperial Families of Russia, Turkey and Brazil.

The German Emperor's Dream.

The Royal Families of England, Spain, Portugal and Belgium.

The Indian Venus.

And a large number of other lifesize figures.

"Inside the Museum," the catalogue continued, "our employees will give all the explanations the visitors require. The Museum is lit by gas and worthy of receiving the best of Society.

"M. Serlin, the Manager, deserves the public's confidence and begs his esteemed clientele not to confuse his Museum with any other that has been set up in Paris, since his is beyond comparison!

"Anybody can visit this remarkable Gallery, where he will find nothing offensive to morals and decency. Open every day until 10 o'clock at night. Entrance fees: first-class 30 centimes; second-class 15 centimes.

"The Indian Venus is the masterpiece of the Academy of Florence, made of heavy wax, the Goddess lying on a bed. This masterpiece will not offend ladies. The masterpiece can be dismantled to satisfy the visitor's curiosity at a private session for 15 centimes."

In 1840 was built Montparnasse's first railway station, a humble building at the corner of the Boulevard de Vaugirard and the Avenue du Maine. It had one single-track line that connected Paris with Versailles. On May 8, 1842, a large crowd of Parisians travelled in several trains to Versailles to see the fountains play. At half past five the returning crowd filled eighteen small wooden coaches, too heavy a load for *Mathieu Mursay*, the little railway-engine. Instead of dividing the train into two sections, the stationmaster had a second locomotive—a real monster with six wheels—coupled to the train. Halfway to Paris *Mathieu Mursay's* axle broke and the large engine reared straight into the little one. A fire broke out in both engines and caught the wooden carriages, which were soon burning fiercely. There were hair-raising scenes inside the coaches. Most of the passengers were burnt to death. Among the few who managed to escape were a giant of a Prussian who broke open the door of his carriage and a blind man who carried his wounded brother to safety on his shoulder. When the débris was cleared a locomotive brought to Montparnasse Station a railway truck containing forty-two corpses, including those of Jules-Sébastien-César Durmont-d'Urville, sailor and explorer, and his family.

On October 22, 1895, towards four in the afternoon, a train was approaching the new Montparnasse Station in the Place de Rennes (now Place du 18 Juin 1940). It was the express from Granville, travelling at the imposing speed of sixty kilometres an hour. At the height of the rue du Château the brakes gave way, and despite the efforts of the engine driver, the train rushed at full speed into the station. The guard at the rear managed to apply the Westinghouse brake, saving the lives of the hundred and twenty-three passengers, for only the engine and the tender smashed through the glass wall and crashed into the Place de Rennes, killing a poor old woman who was selling Maurice Barrès's paper *La Cocarde* in which Barrès advocated "aesthetic nationalism". The hippomobile (horse-drawn tram) was passing as the engine—with its red apron, as André Salmon put it—broke through the glass. Luckily for the passengers, the frightened horses bolted with such speed that the engine missed the tram.

A postcard was issued depicting the accident. It sold remarkably well.

After selling his country seat, Vallée-aux-Loups, Chateaubriand returned to Paris with his wife, who, needing distraction and respite from his politics and love affairs, in 1819 founded at 86 rue d'Enfer (92 rue Denfert-Rochereau) a home, Infirmerie de Marie-Thérèse, called after the Duchesse d'Angoulême, who became its patron. It was for old priests and for widows and daughters of impoverished noblemen and of officers of the old régime. The fields and meadows belonging to this charitable institution contained a farm where cattle, goats and chickens were reared. Twenty-three cedars, two oaks and a drive flanked by chestnuts graced the property. Next to the home stood a chapel.

"I do not see a single house," wrote Chateaubriand. "At two hundred leagues from Paris I would be less separated from the world."

For financial reasons the Chateaubriands gave up looking after the home in 1838. In a letter to a friend, Madame de Chateaubriand boasted of having left it in a prosperous state. They went to live at 112 rue du Bac (now number 120), where they died, she on February 9, 1847, he on July 4, 1848. She was buried under the altar of the chapel of the Infirmerie de Marie-Thérèse, he in Grand-Bé at St Malo.

When the Boulevard Raspail was constructed, the house at 11 rue Notre-Dame-des-Champs (now number 27) was demolished. The newly married Victor Hugo lived there from the spring of 1827 until the spring of 1830. It was there that he wrote *Ballades, Cromwell, Les Orientales*, part of *Les Feuilles d'Automne, Marion de Lorne* and *Hernani*. Coming from the street, in order to reach the house, one went past a lodge, then under a dark ogival vault into a long open-air passage. The Hugos lived on the first floor, their flat comprising kitchen, dining-room, drawing-room, study and two bedrooms. The landlady, who lived on the ground floor, gave them the run of the garden. Young writers, painters and engravers, all belonging to the Romantic Movement, came continuously to visit the Hugos. A fortnight before *Hernani* came off the stage for the second time, the landlady bade her tenants be gone. She wanted less noise and bustle in her house.

"The corpses which the Hôtel-Dieu vomits up daily are taken to Clamart," wrote Louis-Sébastien Mercier in *Tableau de Paris*. A vast cemetery spread at Clamart (now in arrondissement de Sceaux), and the dead from the Hôtel-Dieu were wrapped in shrouds—no coffins for them—and as the hospital beds were urgently needed for new arrivals, the patients were lifted from them before they had time properly to expire, and, so the story goes, the hospital attendants in their hurry occasionally threw those still alive into the cart bound for Clamart. Some woke up or came round in the fresh air and shouted from among the corpses that they were not dead.

The cortège consisted of a cart pulled by twelve men, one priest, one bell and one cross. It left every morning at four. The bell awoke the good people who slept in the houses along the road. In times of epidemics, the cart made four journeys a day between the hospital and the cemetery. On All Souls Day relations of the dead visited Clamart, prayed at the nameless graves, then went to the taverns.

When the Cemetery of the Innocents was closed in 1785, Lieu-tenant of Police Lenoir hit on the idea of disposing of the bones in the old, disused quarries of Montsouris. A house called Maison de la Tombe Issoire was bought. Its deep well, which communicated with the quarry, was bricked up, and on April 7, 1786, with pomp and ceremony, the first bones arrived. The name Catacombes was given to the ossuary which was consecrated by the Archbishop of Paris. Many people protested against the name, including a journalist who was sent to the Bastille for a year to cool down. Over the gate was an inscription: "Memoria Maiorum"; on the door, "Stop, this is the empire of the dead."

Exaggerated figures have been given of the number of skeletons in the Catacombes, but six million seems a reasonable guess. The ossuary lies beneath the rues Dareau, d'Alembert, and Hallé and the Avenue du Parc-Montsouris, and is over eleven thousand square yards in size. Nightly a load of skeletons arrived, each convoy accompanied by a priest. They came not only from the Cemetery of the Innocents but also from the churchyards of Saint-Eustache, Saint-Etienne-des-Grès, Saint-Landry, Saint-André-des-Arts and others. At first the bones were simply dumped into the old quarry. During the Empire, they were grouped according to the cemeteries and churchyards from which they hailed. The bones were trans-ported in funeral carriages, but this custom ceased in time, and they

were taken in ordinary carts without priest or any form of ceremony. The last loads were delivered in 1859 following excavations
and the closing of more cemeteries.

After the Catacombes stopped receiving new skeletons, the
bones were arranged systematically, often in the shape of a
cross, with the skulls mostly on the walls, in a straight line above
them. A fountain near the gate leading to the rue Dareau was
known either as the Fountain of Lethe or the Fountain of the
Samaritaine. The Catacombes have a small stone chapel and a
small monument, supposed to have come from the tomb of one,
Gilbert.

> Au banquet de la vie infortuné convive
> J'apparus un jour et je meurs!
> Je meurs, et sur la tombe où lentement j'arrive,
> Nul ne viendra verser des pleurs.

The Catacombes were opened to the public during the Empire,
then closed for a time, but from 1874 onwards they could again be
visited, though only twice a month.

When in May 1871 the Government troops from Versailles
crushed the Commune, many of the insurgents tried to save themselves by hiding in sewers, quarries and in the Catacombes. They
were all caught, most of them killed resisting their pursuers; those
who surrendered were taken as prisoners to Versailles. The Battle
of the Catacombes was fierce. One contingent of Versaillais entered
from the Barrière de l'Enfer (Place Denfert-Rochereau), another
from the Plain of Montsouris (Avenue du Parc-Montsouris).
Carrying torches, they attacked the refugees, killing all who resisted.
In the red light of the torches, the fight raged for several hours.
The dead on that day did not enjoy the rest that had been promised
them. "Here they rest, waiting for life eternal", was inscribed above
one of the doors.

A more peaceful event was a concert given by fifty amateur
musicians on April 1, 1897, in front of a hundred guests. The

orchestra performed Chopin's *Funeral March*, Saint-Saëns's *Dance Macabre* and the Funeral March from Beethoven's *Eroica*.

The Avenue du Maine, so called since 1877, was previously known as the Chemin du Petit-Montrouge, and it led to Sceaux, originally Sceaux-du-Maine, the property of the Duc du Maine. Louis-Auguste de Bourbon, Duc du Maine, son of Louis XIV and Madame de Montespan, acquired the Château de Sceaux in 1699 from the Marquis de Seignelay, son of Colbert, who had spent a fortune on it and had several times acted as host there to Louis XIV.

The Duc du Maine was brought up secretly with his sister, who died in infancy, by Madame de Maintenon, the widow Scarron as she then was, in a house at 108-110-110 bis rue de Vaugirard, which Mme de Montespan rented from 1670 to 1674. It was on the estate of César de Vendôme, whose gardens reached as far as today's rue du Cherche-Midi. In 1692, at the age of twenty-two, the young Duke married Louise de Bourbon-Condé, the grand-daughter of the Great Condé. Sceaux became his small, personal Court. His wife gave many feasts, from which he escaped whenever he could, either going for a walk that was never long because he had a clubfoot, or hunting on horseback on his vast property, which skirted Paris. He was always happy when he reached the town where he had been brought up. In order to be even more on his own, he built the Château du Maine, more a shooting-lodge than a castle, on the very edge of his estate. The entrance was on the present site of 142-46 rue du Château. After his death in 1736, the Château du Maine slowly crumbled, changed hands several times, and was eventually demolished.

Around 1850, the grounds of the Château du Maine were taken over by a commercial enterprise with the aim of democratising the once ducal shoot. A few rickety stags and some bewildered hares were imported, to be loosed on shooting days for the benefit of the customers. The company was named Société des Chasses de Plaisance. The Nimrods of Paris gathered at the gate. There were two entrance fees: one for the guns, the other for the spectators. On Sunday afternoons, such was the din of hunting horns that one could imagine onself in the heart of the Forest of Fontainebleau. With hardly any game, and with their first excitement spent, the customers who, according to a contemporary, were more adept at hunting bedbugs than stags, ceased to patronise the place. The Société des Chasses de Plaisance went bankrupt, and thus ended the last cycle of the ducal shoot.

The Plateau de Montrouge was arid, waterless and honeycombed by quarries. Chateaubriand referred to it as a plain. He wrote in 1833, "When I tire of my gardens the Plain of Montrouge takes their place. Twenty-five years ago when going to the Vallée-aux-Loups I used to go through the Barrière du Maine; there were windmills right and left of the road, cranes at the openings of the quarries, and the nursery gardens of Cels, the old friend of Rousseau."

In time several guinguettes were built near the windmills, which stretched from the Barrière du Maine to the Barrière du Montparnasse. Acacias were planted on the plain, then travelling circuses set up their tents, and slowly a village came into being. Where today the Avenues du Maine and du Général-Leclerc meet, stood the hamlet of Petit-Montrouge, also surrounded by windmills and quarries, its inhabitants poor and living in wretched huts, and eager to rush to Paris whenever there was a chance to take part in a rising.

The hamlet of Montsouris, belonging to the parish of Montrouge, was another conglomeration of guinguettes near the Barrière Saint-Jacques. The Parc Montsouris was created by Napoleon III, who wanted to provide parks and public gardens to make Paris as green as the London he had known during his long exile.

The Parc Montsouris had its own philosopher, Emile Sauvage, who from 1872 onwards taught his disciples in the park. Seated on a bench, he discoursed on philosophy, mathematics and religion. He was a dreamer, a harmless anarchist and something of a dandy. He had no love for women, and he went home if a woman joined the open-air assembly. In winter as in summer he sat on the same bench, wearing a top hat and patent-leather boots. He defined himself as a psychologist and man of letters. He lived at 33 Avenue Reille, where he died in 1929 at the age of ninety-five.

The park was once associated with a political scandal. In 1891 a senator took a walk there. It was mid-winter and snow lay heavy on the ground. In one of the deserted lanes he came upon a statue of Marat. The senator was horrified. Who were the coarse, shameless men who had dared to erect in a public park a statue to a murderer? It later transpired that the statue had already graced the park for four years. The local authorities swore that they knew nothing about its existence. When the matter was raised in the Senate, the Government professed ignorance too. The senator persisted, however, and one night the statue was taken away in great secrecy and replaced by another—Tiger Fighting a Serpent by the sculptor Georges Guadet. Nevertheless, on March 4, 1891, the Government was censured in the Senate for having provoked decent citizens by inflicting on them the statue of Marat, which had in fact been found in a shed by the head gardener who, ignorant of history, had put it up in the park, which he considered short of statues.

In *Dames Galantes*, Brantôme relates the story of François I visiting the Royal Menagerie in the rue des Lions-Saint-Paul (now rue des Lions). He was accompanied by several noblemen and ladies, one of whom threw her handkerchief into the pit where two lions were fighting, then asked the Seigneur de Lorges, who was in love with her, to show his devotion by fetching it. He retrieved the handkerchief, and flung it into her face, saying he would never speak to her again. Brantôme got his site wrong, for the Royal Menagerie was no longer in the rue des Lions-Saint-Paul in the reign of François I: it had been removed to the Maison royale des Tournelles in 1490.

For centuries the Kings of France had owned menageries. They were less interested in plants. In 1626 Jean Hérouard, the botanist, succeeded in persuading Louis XIII to open a botanical garden in Paris, similar to the one in Montpellier, which had existed since the previous century. Hérouard's aim was to fill the garden with medicinal plants "for the use of those whose state of health required them", and to help the medical students of the University in their studies. Guy de La Brosse, colleague of Hérouard, was instructed by the King to purchase land for the garden. He did so from the Abbey of Sainte-Geneviève on February 21, 1633, for the sum of 67,000 livres. The land was outside Paris, on the edge of the Faubourg Saint-Victor (now 40 rue Geoffroy-Saint-Hilaire). It was first known as Jardin royal des Plantes médicinales, after the Revolution simply as Jardin des Plantes.

The University was opposed to the scheme, yet within ten years both botany and anatomy were being taught in the Garden, which began its career with sixteen hundred different plants. In time the University had chairs on twenty-one different subjects, including zoology, mineralogy, botany, anthropology and palaeontology.

In 1792, Bernardin de Saint-Pierre, Director of the Garden, decided to establish there a menagerie. He thought about the Royal Menagerie in Versailles, which Louis XVI wanted to get rid of, but since in all only one zebra, one buffalo and one rhinoceros were left, the deal collapsed. Next year the Commune de Paris came to the Director's rescue by having all wild beasts belonging to circuses and travelling menageries sent to the Garden. After the victories in Holland, the entire menagerie of the Stadtholder was brought there. In 1793 the Museum of National History was erected in the grounds.

Jack was the first orang-outang in the Garden. He came there in 1854, his fame having preceded him. Negroes, so Parisians were told, were convinced that orang-outangs were men who refused to speak because, if they did so, they would be forced to work. Jack arrived from Sumatra. On the voyage to France he was allowed to roam the ship, spending most of his time climbing the masts and helping the stokers. When they reached Le Havre the seamen were in tears at the thought of losing their Jack. In the Jardin des Plantes, Jack became everybody's favourite. Children doted on him and he on them. He took his meals with his keeper, using a spoon but he never mastered the fork. He was fond of women and of men's hats, and when he died Paris was heartbroken.

After him came Jacqueline, a young chimpanzee, as intelligent as Jack, and even more affectionate. She brushed herself before going to bed. She had a real bed with sheets and blankets which she shared with a dog and a cat, both of which she loved. A visitor to the Garden brought her a pair of gloves; she pulled the right one on the left paw, the left one on the right, but once her keeper had demonstrated how she should wear them, she never made the mistake again. She washed herself every morning in cold water. Her cleanliness was her undoing: she died one winter of pneumonia. She was stuffed like Jack before her, and given a place of honour in the Cabinet de Zoologie.

The Garden possessed two giraffes, the taller given in 1829 to Charles X by the Pasha of Egypt. There were two elephants, one called Marguerite, of an extraordinarily sweet disposition. The same could not be said of Martin, the brown bear, who killed two people, the first an Englishman, the second an old pensioner of the Invalides. The Englishman was in his cups and wanted to box with the bear. He jumped into the pit when nobody was looking. It was six in the morning and he lived but a few seconds longer. The pensioner's case was different: he had watched Martin playing from time to time with what he thought was a louis d'or that someone must have dropped into the pit. The old man could not resist the sight of it. Besides, it was of mighty little use to a bear. So he hid on the premises, and in the depth of night climbed noiselessly into the pit. Martin had already retired to his lair.

The old soldier picked up the shiny piece: it was a button. He cried out in his disappointment. This woke the bear, and the brave warrior, who had faced a thousand deaths at Wagram and Jena, found his swift end in the pit. A lament was written in his memory. The last verse went:

> Tout ceci doit vous apprendre,
> Enfants, vieillards, jeunes gens,
> De ne jamais, pour de l'argent,
> Chez un ours la nuit descendre.
> Car il ne respecte rien,
> Ni l' envie d'avoir du bien . . .

XVIII

Britons in Paris

In the mid-eighteenth century there lived in the rue des Cordeliers (now rue de l'Ecole-de-Médecine) a prosperous citizen who used to listen respectfully in the Luxembourg Gardens to a priest who was no friend of the English. The abbé had a simple formula. "Thirty thousand men must be raised, embarked, and disembarked in England. It might cost us thirty thousand men to take London. A bagatelle!"

The citizen fell ill and knew that his end was approaching. He remembered the dear abbé who had predicted the end of England. As he too disliked the English, he left the priest a legacy. "I leave to the Abbé Thirty-Thousand-Men 1,200 livres a year. I know him only by that name. He is a good patriot who proved to me in the Luxembourg Gardens that the English, a ferocious race who regularly depose their sovereigns, will soon be destroyed."

The benefactor died, and after the Courts had heard several witnesses who also frequented the Luxembourg Gardens, Abbé Thirty-Thousand-Men received his legacy.

After the Battle of Waterloo, when the Allies entered Paris, the Guards bivouacked in the Bois de Boulogne, which at the time was a wild, pathless, swampy, entirely neglected wood. The Prussians were under tent nearby, and did as much senseless damage as they could, cutting down the finest trees and setting the Bois on fire at several points. Three thousand Guards were the neighbours of ten thousand Prussians. "Our camp was not remarkable for its courtesy towards them," wrote Captain Gronow of the Grenadier Guards in his *Reminiscences*. He was one of the first of the British Army to penetrate into Paris. He had entered by the Porte Maillot and passed the Arc de Triomphe, which was then being built.

Scots regiments bivouacked in the Champs Elysées, which then contained only a few scattered houses. Parisian women were shocked by the kilts and did not hesitate to declare that the want of culottes was most indecent. The roads were ankle-deep in mud, and Gronow found the pavements imperfect. The stepping stones "were adopted to display the Parisian female ankle and boot in all their calculated coquetry," and the people in the streets appeared sulky and stupefied. He dined that day at the Café des Anglais on the Boulevard des Italiens, where to his surprise he found several brother officers. He had soup and fish, which was anything but fresh, then, according to English taste and predilection, "beef-steak and pommes de terre".

The Palais Royal was much visited by British and other allied officers, even if they went there in some fear and disgust. On the ground floor were jewellers' shops, where diamonds, pearls and emeralds were sold, it being the aim of a successful gambler to give these "to some female friend who had never appeared with him at the altar of marriage." Alongside a shop one might find a very dirty staircase that communicated with a café on the floor above, presided over by a very décolletée lady, laden with jewels, where the best of male society met, Britons included, holding long conversations exclusively about gambling and women. Next door might be a gaming-room. "Those gambling houses were the very fountain of immorality," wrote the captain, yet hurried daily to them with his brother officers.

An officer in the Grenadier Guards, on leave of absence, took apartments in the Palais Royal, at the time the only well-lit place in Paris. He was asked by his friends on his return to England whether it were true that he had never ventured outside. "Of course it is," he replied, "for I found everything I wanted there, both for body and mind."

The English flocked to Paris after the Restoration. There was a popular London song called *All the world's in Paris*. "Our countrymen and women," wrote Gronow, "having so long been excluded from French modes had adopted fashions of their own quite as remarkable and eccentric as those of the Parisians and much less graceful. British beauties were dressed in long, straight pelisses of various colours; the body of the dress was never of the same colour as the skirt; and the bonnet was of the bee-hive shape, and very small. The characteristic of the dress of the gentleman was a coat of light blue, or snuff colour, with brass buttons, the tail reaching nearly to the heels; a gigantic bunch of seals dangled from his fob, whilst his pantaloons were short and tight at the knees; and a spacious waistcoat, with a voluminous muslin cravat and a frilled shirt completed the toilette. The dress of the British military, in its stiff and formal ugliness, was equally cumbrous and ludicrous."

Fox, the Secretary of the Embassy, spent his days in bed, and his nights at the Salon des Etrangers at 6 rue Drouot, the most fashionable gaming-room in Paris, always full of British officers and officials. Fox was usually out of luck, but one night he won sixty thousand francs at dice, after which he was not seen again at the Salon. Gronow went to the Embassy with his passport, for a visa. He found Fox in bed in his room, which was crowded with Cashmere shawls, silks, Chantilly veils, bonnets, gloves and other articles of ladies' dress.

"Why, my dear Gronow," Fox explained, "it was the only

means to prevent those rascals at the Salon winning back my money."

The Salon des Etrangers was run by the Marquis de Livry, who presented an extraordinary likeness to the Prince Regent of England, who sent Lord Fife over to Paris "to ascertain that momentous fact".

The Hon. George T—— came regularly from London, bringing a substantial letter of credit, to gamble at the Salon des Etrangers. He contrived to lose his last penny at rouge et noir; and when he had lost all he possessed in the world he got up and exclaimed in an excited manner, "If I had Canova's *Venus and Adonis* from Alton Towers, my uncle's country seat, it should be placed on the rouge, for black has won fourteen times running."

German soldiers were much less popular than the British in Paris, where Bavarians and Wurtembergers behaved particularly badly. At Saint-Cloud, Blucher "bivouacked" his dog on Marie-Louise's sofa. The British and the Russians had better discipline than the Prussians. On November 24, 1815, on the frozen Canal de l'Ourcq, several English soldiers fell through the ice. Courageous Parisians rushed to their rescue and saved their lives. They might have felt less courageous had the soldiers been German.

Still, as Gronow relates, there was occasional trouble between occupiers and occupied. At the Théâtre des Variétés on the Boulevard de Montmartre, a piece entitled *Les Anglaises pour rire* was marvellously performed by two famous actors, Potier and Brunet. A number of Allied soldiers were admitted to the theatres free of charge. One night a party of Guards, composed of a sergeant and a few men, went to the Théâtre des Variétés. In the play, Englishwomen were ridiculed. This gave great offence to the Guardsmen, who decided to stop the show, which they did by hoisting themselves on the stage and chasing away the actors. The police were called, and wanted to imprison the men, but "they soon found to their cost that they had to deal with unmanageable opponents, for the whole posse of gendarmes were charged and driven out of the theatre."

"It must be remembered," adds Gronow, "that the only revenge the Parisians were able to take upon the conquerors was to ridicule them, and the English generally took it in good humour, and laughed at the extravagant drollery of the burlesque." Nevertheless, there were plenty of duels fought between the French and the English.

English soldiers generally walked about in parties of a dozen, and were quiet and well-behaved. Their favourite pastime was to gather in the Boulevard du Temple to watch the mountebanks and jugglers. Throughout the entire time that the British troops remained in Paris, only one of them was murdered in the streets, in sharp contrast to the fate of the Prussians.

Captain Rees Howell Gronow remained in Paris, in fact died there in 1865 at the age of seventy-one. He had become a friend of Shelley at Eton, and his mother was supposedly a friend of Mrs Jordan, mistress of the Duke of Clarence (King William IV), which was how he received his commission in the Grenadier Guards. In Paris he married a dancer from the Opéra. He was a short man with dyed hair, and was never seen without a gold-knobbed cane. Even among the snobs of his day he was considered an outstanding one. His life centred round the fashionable cafés and the boulevards. He is often mentioned in French memoirs of the last century, but without affection.

The Ecole Militaire was founded by Louis XV in 1751 for the education of five hundred young men whose fathers, in consequence of having sacrificed their fortunes in the defence of the realm, might find themselves unable to give their children an education becoming their rank and rendering them useful to the state. In front of the school was the Champs de Mars where Louis XVI took the oath to the Constitution, and where Napoleon reviewed his troops, at times as many as fifty thousand of them. The space was dug up in the shape of an amphitheatre in 1790 by the Fédérés, frightened by a rumour that it has been mined by the Royalists for the purpose of blowing them all up on the day of Federation.

On the other side of the river at the foot of Passy—the Highgate of Paris as English visitors called it—was the site intended for the palace of Napoleon's son, the King of Rome. It would have faced the Ecole Militaire, to stimulate the boy's imagination and to foster in his mind the love of military glory. When rising in the morning, he could have watched the evolution of troops in front of the school. After the Restoration, the government decided on the demolition of the foundations of the palace, which was as far as the building had gone. Tenders were invited, and an Englishman won the contract. French people accounted for this by observing that no Frenchman could have undertaken such an anti-patriotic task. As a matter of fact, the Englishman's tender was the lowest.

In the 1820s, British visitors formed part of the daily life of Paris. They liked strolling beside the Seine, admiring the washing-barges. "Through the lattice-looking openings," wrote a traveller, "one sees the flapping white caps, richly coloured handkerchiefs and bare, fleshy arms of hundreds of washerwomen, all dragging and dabbling their linen in the Seine, and casting sparkles of water up in their laughing eyes."

On the feast of St Louis the visitors observed the manners of the people, which, they regretted to see, stemmed from revolutionary habits. There was a lot of pushing at the wine fountains, where free wine was served to the masses. The gendarmes had often to expel from the crowd men who abused their superior strength in order to monopolise a good place. The expelled parties, however, were not long in forming again in column and returning to the charge. But if an old soldier, particularly an "invalide", appeared in the crowd, he was let through and at once given wine.

In the Tuileries Gardens, the Britons noticed that reading the

Public Journals was a major pastime of a Parisian. The original newspaper kiosk, which once had been sufficient to gratify the curiosity of all Paris, was established on the western side of the Gardens, and because it was exposed to the sun in all seasons, it acquired the name of Petite Provence. It had now become merely a meeting place of nurses and politicians of the lower class, fashion having abandoned it for the vicinity of the orange trees and the more frequented walks of the promenades.

"Of all the newspaper readers," wrote the anonymous author of *A Tour through Paris*, "there is not one upon whom this mode of commencing the day does not exert a great influence; but the Parisian cockneys are more fastidious than they used to be. In former times, if the Public Censor had but a poor devil of an author served up every morning to be devoured with his chocolate, he returned home perfectly contented; but now he requires the dishing up of Battles, Constitutions, Earthquakes, the Yellow Fever and the Elections. However, it must be admitted that we should get tired of newspaper reading, did not the complaisant Editors sometimes insert accidents in default of their being sent by Providence. Some offices have their portfolios for crimes and offences; the latter are put up for competition, and when they are well told, the insertion is paid to the last farthing. How many honest prose-grinders, who would not kill a fly if they could help it, live with perfect indifference on fires and murder?"

It would deeply have shocked the Britons strolling in the Gardens had they been told of the footman who in the reign of Louis XIV made a strange bet there. The Gardens were then frequented by people of quality, while their lackeys waited at the gates, at times as many as four thousand in number. The footman in question wanted to prove to his colleagues that he was a better man than they, so he bet a bottle of wine that he would raise the skirt of the first lady who emerged from the Gardens and whip her. He won his bet. Two ladies, Mlle d'Armagnac and the Marquise de Villequier, came out first. He raised Mlle d'Armagnac's skirt and whipped her, much to the merriment of the other footmen. Other ladies however ran to her rescue and held the footman until the Watch arrived. He was taken to prison. Just escaping the hangman's noose, he was condemned to the galleys.

John Scott in his *Picturesque Views of the City of Paris and its Environs* made some pertinent observations on the public gardens. ". . . public gardens are such favourites at Paris, and it must be admitted that they are, in general, handsomely embellished with casts from the antique, and ponds containing gold and silver fish. Their whole style is indeed very different from that of Hyde Park or Kensington Gardens; but the Parisians would not relish these latter. The walk to them would be found fatiguing; and when they had reached them the *picturesque* character of these noble spots would not be felt. The grandeur of the trees at Kensington would not be thought a compensation for the absence of the Apollo de Belvedere; and the free and open aspect of Hyde Park would be deemed too bare of ornament, too destitute of jauntiness and *agrémens*. The French, generally speaking, form their notions of what is fine and agreeable by some distinct reference to what is powerful, or curious, or celebrated; and without a recollection or a rule derivable from history or poetry, or present fact to guide them, their sense of the sublime and of the beautiful is at a loss. A happy combination of the effects of nature does not strike them so forcibly as the view of a palace, or of a pillar, or of a bust. As they know that an avenue has been cut out for the purpose of opening a grand vista; that a pond has been sunk to give the idea of coolness and magnificence; that a fountain has been contrived to sparkle and amuse; they are prepared at the sight of all such indications, to call up the corresponding sentiment, and to feel the due degree of delight and admiration. But, without such significant and intelligible hints, they would not know what to expect or what to experience: in candour, however, it ought to be stated, that no nation has a quicker sense of the acknowledged glories of history, of the accredited beauties of poetry, or pays the tribute of admiration more disinterestedly to the imposing circumstances of existing authority."

English travellers in the 1820s were obsessed by the Revolution which, they believed, had affected a considerable change in the French character, mingling gloom, austerity and suspicion with the politeness of the old régime, though, they admitted, a peculiar sort of politeness remained the most prominent feature of the Parisian. The dustman and the milkmaid saluted each other in the street with all the scrupulous and ceremonious punctilio that would be practised in an English drawing-room.

A drive through Paris made it obvious to the English that the French had no idea of comfort, but sacrificed everything to display. The most admirable feature of London was the excellent, constant supply of water, whereas the filth of the dwellings in Paris revealed the scarcity of supply of that necessary liquid. The English had a poor opinion of water carriers and their irritating shouts of "Eau-eau!"

Still, the boulevards exhibited a constantly enlivening scene, from an early hour in the morning until late at night. They abounded with theatres, coffee-houses, billiard halls, dancing-rooms, pleasure gardens and baths. The stalls sold toys, lace, earthenware, prints, drawings, fruit and poultry. Savoyards tormented the promenaders with their eternal strumming, but on the other hand hairdressers twisted the most wiry hair into pliant corkscrews. A "female professor" was ready for a fee to perform any given operation on one's dog. In places, chairs could be hired for a small sum per hour, and at times as many as a hundred well-dressed persons were seated in a row, some busily employed in staring or being stared at; others gossiping and indulging in the never-ending chit-chat for which the French were so renowned. The spectators themselves were part of the spectacle. They sat to be looked at, and none more so than the beaux, who with determined anxiety for the repose of their limbs, occupied three chairs at once.

The line of exhibitors in the boulevards was interminable, what with beggar bards, fortune-tellers, merry andrews, tragic actors, dancing children, performing dogs, white mice, learned monkeys and "militant canary birds". The dealers in tisane carried fantastic machines on their backs.

"Hurrah! Hurrah! Hurrah!" wrote National Guardsman Alphonse Balleydier. "The English offer us their hands, that is they offer them across the Channel. The immense English nation, that proud queen of the seas, this magnificent race of men now wants only one kind of rivalry between us, the rivalry of friendship. England is waiting for us on her happy shores; the wind is with us, the sky is blue and the sea calm. Let us go!"

And the French National Guard, twelve hundred strong, infantry, cavalry and sappers, not to mention pretty canteen-girls, set sail for Dover. It was October, 1848. The reception in Dover was most enthusiastic with loud shouts of "Vive la France!" answered by "Vive l'Angleterre!" Captain Gonnet, one of the leaders, an officer with many decorations, visited all the public houses, where at the sight of him everybody doffed his hat, and clasped his hand in burning, cordial friendship. At the banquet, toasts were drunk to the union of England and France. London was the final destination. Among the marvels of London, the French visitors saw real Chinamen, whom they found more impressive than the Turks of the rue Mouffetard in the fifth arrondissement.

They were received by the Lord Mayor. At a reception, M. Rougier, an old soldier of the Empire, met a one-armed Englishman. M. Rougier had a wooden leg.

"Where did you lose your arm?" the Frenchman enquired.

"At Waterloo."

"That's where I lost my leg. Let us embrace."

"Hurrah!" shouted One Arm, embracing Wooden Leg.

The French visitors were taken to Madame Tussaud's, which they praised, declaring that the wax figures were real works of art. Before their return to Paris they invited their English hosts, the Volunteers, to return the visit. An English committee was formed for the purpose. Its members were (as given by Balleydier):

MM Lloyd (Francis) esq; Beaufort Lodye Chelsea
   Nind (Francis) esq; Sablonière, hôtel Leicester square;
   Bulloch, esq; Chester street, Belgrave square;
   Brown, esq; Martiham, square Chelsen;
   Hible (Charles) esq; North Terrace Mount, grand West-
   minster nord.

At Easter the English contingent arrived in Paris, and their hosts were most anxious to show them the real Paris of their day, which, according to Balleydier, consisted of the boulevards, the rues de Richelieu and Vivienne, some streets of the Faubourg Saint-Germain, and the Chausée d'Antin, where virtue rubbed shoulders with vice.

In the Boulevard des Italiens, almost at the angle of the rue de Richelieu, stood the Hôtel des Princes. Though Paris could boast of two thousand hotels, yet the Hôtel des Princes was the only one worthy of the distinguished guests whom the National Guard awaited. Every reigning prince of Europe had visited the hotel, where incidentally Meyerbeer had written *Robert-le-diable*. In 1848 the hotel was the general headquarters of the committee formed to celebrate the new Constitution. Monsieur Privat, the hotel's admirable manager, had recently opened the sumptuous dining-room, which seated three hundred, and which was decorated in a striking Moorish style reminiscent of the Alhambra of Granada. Slender columns bore the coats of arms of all the European powers.

In the reading-room, newspapers of every country were displayed. There was a billiard-room, a smoking-room and bar, a salon de conversation, and a bathroom. There were large and small rooms for private banquets and intimate meals, and a ballroom for concerts and other fashionable gatherings. In the breakfast-room daily notices advised the guests on how to spend their day. Every evening the table d'hôtes, renowned for its perfect meals and choice wines, was filled with fashionable society. One reserved a place by inscribing one's name in the guest book during the course of the day, but tradespeople were not admitted to the table d'hôtes. The hotel boasted several interpreters.

The accommodation was in three sections, one reserved for families, the second for couples, or single people, and the third for the commercial travellers who were known as the nomads of the railway age.

A list of the most fashionable shops was drawn up for the English visitors:

"The elegant temple of Doucet, 17 rue de la Paix, for linen and cravats.

Humann, 83 rue Neuve-des-Petits-Champs (rue des Petits-Champs and rue Danielle-Casanova), tailor. No foreigner can afford to leave Paris without visiting his spacious premises.

Boivin, 8 rue Castiglione for gloves.

Ville, Passage de l'Opéra (Boulevard des Italiens) for inimitable boots. 'I have the honour of making boots for several crowned heads.'

Pinaud, the Caesar of Fashion, 87 rue de Richelieu for beautiful hats.

Audot, 81 rue de Richelieu, goldsmith, for travelling cases."

The hosts thought of everything. When the English visitors arrived, the reception committee established its headquarters in the Hôtel des Princes, where most of the English guests remained during their memorable stay. There were sixty male Britons, some of whom were accompanied by their wives and daughters. The clientele of the table d'hôtes became almost completely English. Claret and champagne flowed by the gallon, and one toast followed the other; yet, one is assured, there were no excesses, and decorum and exquisite politeness reigned. From the dining-room the English moved to the salon de conversation, where punch was drunk to the indissoluble union of the two nations.

On the second evening a causerie cordiale was given by the National Guardsmen who had been to London. At ten o'clock a large number of them, many in uniform, gathered in the Moorish Room to receive the distinguished guests. The admirable orchestra of the indispensable Monsieur Strauss was at the ready. As the Britons made their entrance, the signal was given, and the Moorish walls and ceiling echoed the magnificent tune of *God Save the Queen*. The British ladies joined with their menfolk in declaring their feelings of esteem and sincere friendship for France. All hands were grasped in deep affection, all eyes sparkled with happiness, and everybody expressed the same sentiments. At long last the Entente Cordiale had become a reality.

A speech from the English side contained the words: "It is supposed that the sea separates us. Perhaps it was so in the past, but I am glad to be able to say that now that our two nations know one another better, even the sea no longer separates us, and all the old prejudices which blinded us so often have ceased to exist. Oh, what state of happiness the English and the French have reached in witnessing this frank cordiality.

"We speak the language of Shakespeare, Walter Scott and Franklin, you the language of Voltaire, Rousseau and Fénelon, therefore no rivalry can exist any longer between us, and are we not all brothers and friends?"

Deeply moved, all those present drank to the union of North and South, meaning England and France.

After the speech and the toasts, the door of the dining-hall opened. Richly laid tables awaited the Britons. There was only one snag; not one Frenchman had brought his wife along. The English expressed their regret and disappointment, but during the whole week of festivities not a single French wife or daughter put in an appearance. An Englishman observed that it was probably better like that, since otherwise the bachelors among them might lose their heads and hearts. The French did not take the hint.

One Englishman became the hero of the party. When a National

Guardsman asked him whether he had seen the exiled French Socialist leader Louis Blanc in London he replied, "You mean that tiny fellow? I saw him between the legs of a Guardsman." The reception lasted until nine in the morning.

An Englishwoman asked Monsieur Strauss for his autograph. The next day he sent her an album of his prettiest waltzes.

The English were taken to a gala performance of the Opéra. The entire chorus sang *God Save the Queen*, which struck the French as a deeply religious anthem, and some of the National Guardsmen shed a tear for France, which had become a republic. "Vive la reine Victoria!" they shouted in unison.

On the following day the visitors were received by the Prefect of the Seine Department. Champagne flowed in the drawing-rooms of the Préfecture. The Prefect's toast was to the two most civilised people on earth. From the Préfecture the English were driven to the Café Tortoni, then back to the Hôtel des Princes, where they drank without excess until ten the following morning.

The last night of the visit was spent in friendly smoking and drinking punch and grog.

It was certainly not of the National Guardsmen's guests that Monsieur Charles de Forster was thinking when, in his *Quinze Ans à Paris*, published in 1849, he gave a picture of the foreigner in Paris, who, he said, never stopped in the streets to look at a building, for he found none worthy of his gaze, and in fact made a habit of noticing nothing, apart perhaps from throwing a cursory glance at a famous monument. The foreigner thought the royal palaces mean, the Arc de Triomphe de l'Etoile too low for him, and the Park of Versailles too small. If you showed him the Panthéon, he spoke of the Vatican; and as for the Louvre, everything was so much better in the British Museum. At the Opéra he put cotton wool in his ears, and thought of La Scala and San Carlo. If you spoke of David, Foyatier and Dantan, he would mention Thorwalden and

Flaxmann. In short, he came to Paris to praise other towns and their achievements.

After the Franco-Prussian War the English came back in even larger numbers. By then the British visitor was, as it were, under the aegis of the much admired Prince of Wales, the future King Edward VII. The Heir Apparent's popularity was such that every short and fat Parisian who had any self-respect tried to resemble him. Beards à la Prince de Galles were grown, frock coats were cut in the English fashion, and top hats had the same princely gloss. In a maison de rendez-vous frequented by just such a self-respecting Parisian, the manageress was aware that nothing gave her client more pleasure than being mistaken for His Royal Highness. Whenever the customer came to her establishment in the rue Taitbout, the manageress told the girl of his choice to ask him whether he were . . . she wouldn't dare to say who. A new girl who had no worldly manners put the question bluntly: "Are you the Prince of Wales?"

"Promise not to tell anyone?" he whispered. "Yes, I am. I hope I can count on your discretion because if it leaked out, it could lead to international complications."

In the eighties the English frequented mostly the Boulevard de la Madeleine. They wore yellow jackets, noted a boulevardier, had bandy legs and their faces reflected their spleen. They ambled from one railway or steamship agency to another. The Boulevard was in fact infested with travel agencies. There were so many Britons about that the poor boulevardier imagined himself in London on his way to Buckingham Palace. The sons of gay England, as he called them, were to be found also in large numbers in the rue Neuve-Saint-Augustin (rue des Filles-Saint-Thomas). The nearer you got to the Church of the Madeleine, the shabbier the Boulevard became. The cheap dairy shops and fruiterers in the area belonged to retired valets and cooks who had invested in them their life's savings; their customers were fellow servants, and at every step one encountered a man in a red waistcoat or wearing a white tie or dressed as a groom. These places were not for the British, but the flower market beside the Church which smelt of gardens and fields did give joy to the spleen-ridden sons and daughters of Albion.

There were many Fenians in Paris. They met at the Irish-American Bar near the Madeleine, and also at a cheaper place in the Faubourg Saint-Honoré known as the Irish Ambassadors. The Fenians' leaders were James Stephens, called the Head Centre of Fenian Brotherhood, and Eugene Davis, a writer and journalist. J. C. Millage, the Paris correspondent of *The Daily Chronicle*, wrote sensational articles on the Fenians in Paris who in fact led quiet lives, wanting only to earn a living. As a result of Millage's articles, Scotland Yard descended on Paris after the explosion in the Houses of Parliament in 1885, and since relations were excellent between England and France, Stephens, Davis and all other harmless, grousing Fenians were expelled without the slightest proof of complicity against them.

During the Exhibition of 1889, Sir James Whitehead, the Lord Mayor of London, gave a banquet in the Guildhall style at the Grand Hôtel. He was accompanied by Sir Polydore de Keyser and other celebrated City men. The Lord Mayor's banquet brought together W. T. Stead, fresh from his "Modern Babylon" campaign, Colonel Villiers of the British Embassy, the British press in Paris, and a crowd of Frenchmen, chiefly businessmen, but some from the fields of art and literature. When W. F. Lonergan of *The Daily Telegraph* entered the banqueting hall, "it was some moments before I could define to myself precisely whether the chairman or president of the function was the Lord Mayor, Monsieur Tirard, then head of the French Cabinet, or Mr W. Beatty-Kingston, the Special Correspondent of *The Daily Telegraph*. Mr Kingston, in truth, occupied a most commanding position at the table. He was able to see and to be seen by everybody." Then to his relief Mr Lonergan discovered that the powdered footmen stood not behind Mr Kingston but near the Lord Mayor and M Tirard. The banquet, thought Mr Lonergan, could not have been beaten in the City itself as far as food and wine were concerned. The speakers, though ponderous and dull, were fortunately brief in their utterances, and the banquet was a great success and a happy occasion.

Not so happy was the visit to Paris of the Sirdar, Sir Herbert Kitchener, after the Fashoda Incident in 1898, when Kitchener had ousted Major Marchand from the Sudan. A strong wave of Anglo-phobia came in the wake of the Incident. On October 26 Kitchener arrived in Paris from Marseilles, where he had landed on his return from Egypt. The entire British press in Paris went to the Gare de Lyons to see him arrive. To their surprise, they found the station crowded with enthusiastic Frenchmen, who had come however not to meet and applaud Kitchener but to acclaim Captain Baratier, one of Marchand's companions in the trek from West Africa to Fashoda. The British journalists were under the impression that it was not mere coincidence that Baratier was on the same train as Kitchener: it was a diabolic French machination to humiliate the English. Baratier and some of his brother officers were in the middle carriage, and were at the windows as the train came in. They were loudly cheered, the tempest of vivats continuing for a quarter of an hour. Kitchener, Sir Henry Rawlinson and Captain Rawson were in a carriage at the rear of the train, and when they alighted only the British press and Monsieur Lemoine, Thos. Cook & Son's agent, were there to receive them.

Kitchener looked curiously at the crowd of men and women who were cheering Baratier, then he turned away. Monsieur Lemoine swiftly took him and his party to one of Cook's hotels, the windows of which overlooked that outpost of England, the Gare du Nord.

Selected Bibliography

Alphand, A. *Les Promenades de Paris*. J. Rothschild, 2 vols., Paris, 1867-1873.

Andrieux, L. *Souvenirs d'un Préfet de Police*. Jules Rouff & Co., Paris, 1885.

Anonymous. *A Tour through Paris*. W. Sams, London (n.d.).

— *Notice sur les Prisons*. H. Fournier (n.d.).

Arbousse-Bastide. *Mes impressions à Paris*. C. Meyrueis, Paris, 1857.

Auberive, Ch. *Voyage d'un curieux dans Paris*. V. Sarlit, Paris, 1860.

Babize, E. *Le XVIIe arrondissement à travers les âges*. Published by the author, Paris, 1930.

Bachelin, H. *Collines et Buttes parisiennes*. Firmin Didot & Co., Paris, 1944.

Balleydier, A. *Visite rendue par l'Anglettere à la France*. Office général des chemins de fer et navigation, Paris, 1849.

Beaurepaire, E. *Paris d'hier et d'aujourd'hui. La chronique des rues*. P. Sevin & E. Rey, Paris, 1900.

Boisson, M. *Coins et Recoins de Paris*. Editions Bossard, Paris, 1927.

Boulenger, J. *Dans la vieille rue St. Honoré*. Firmin Didot, Paris, 1931.

Boutet de Monvel, R. *Les Anglais à Paris, 1800-1850*. Plon-Nourrit, Paris, 1911.

Brossays Du Perray. *Remarques historiques et anecdotes sur le château de la Bastille*. 1774.

Cain, G. *Coins de Paris*. Flammarion, Paris, 1905.

Cuisin, P. *Les Nymphes du Palais Royal*. Roux, Paris, 1815.

Deroye, L. *Le XIVe arrondissement, son origine, sa formation*. J. Mersch, Paris, 1898.

Deslys, Ch. *Paris historique, pittoresque et anecdotique. Le Jardin des Plantes*. G. Havard, Paris, 1854-1855.

Doniol, A. *Histoire du XVIe arrondissement de Paris*. Hachette, Paris, 1902.

Drumont, E. *Mon vieux Paris, hommes et choses*. Charpentier, Paris, 1878.

Du Camp, M. *Paris, ses organes, ses fonctions et sa vie dans la seconde moitié du XIX siècle*. Hachette, 6 vols., Paris, 1869-1875.

Dulaure, J.-A. *Singularités historiques, contenant ce que l'histoire de Paris et ses environs offre de plus piquant et de plus extraordinaire*. Baudouin frères, Paris, 1825.

Fegdal, Ch. *Choses et gens des Halles*. Athéna, Paris, 1922.

Fegdal, Ch. *Dans notre vieux Paris*. Stock, Delamain, Boutelleau & Co., Paris, 1934.

Forster, Ch. de. *Quinze Ans à Paris*. F. Didot frères, 2 vols., Paris, 1849.

Fournier, E. *Chroniques et légendes des rues de Paris*. E. Dentu, Paris, 1864.

Funck-Brentano, F. *La Bastille des comédiens*. A. Fontemoing, Paris, 1903.

Girault de Saint-Fargeau. *Les 48 Quartiers de Paris*. F. Didot frères, Paris, 1846.

Gronow, Captain Rees Howell. *Celebrities of London and Paris*. Smith, Elder & Co., London, 1865.

Gronow, Captain Rees Howell. *Reminiscences*. Smith, Elder & Co., London, 1862.

Hillairet, J. *Dictionnaire historique des rues de Paris*. Editions de Minuit, 2 vols., Paris, 1964.

Hillairet, J. *Gibets, piloris et cachots du vieux Paris*. Editions de Minuit, Paris, 1956.

Huysmans, J. K. *La Bièvre et Saint-Séverin*. P. V. Stock, Paris, 1898.

Laffitte, J. *Un coin de Paris*. Hachette, Paris, 1897.

Lenotre, G. *La Petite Histoire: Secrets du vieux Paris*. Grasset, Paris, 1954.

Lenotre, G. *Paris et ses fantômes*. Grasset, Paris, 1950.

Leroy, B. *Mémoires*. H. Kistemawckers, Bruxelles, 1895.

Leroy, J. *Saint-Germain-des-Prés, Capitale des lettres*. A. Bonne, Paris, 1952.

Lock, F. *Paris*. F. Didot frères, Paris, 1850.

Lonergan, W. F. *Forty Years of Paris*. T. F. Unwin, London, 1907.

Lurine, L. *Les Rues de Paris*. G. Kugelmann, Paris, 1844.

Mercier, L. S. *Tableau de Paris*. Virchaux, 2 vols. Hambourg, 1781.

Mercier, L. S. *Le Nouveau Paris*. Fuchs, C. Pougens et C.-F. Cramer, Paris, 1798.

Minerath, M. *Histoire du XIVe arrondissement de Paris*. Lefebvre, Lille, 1928.

Pessard, G. *Paris nouveau et ancien*. Sauvaitre, Paris, 1892.

Piton, C. *Paris sous Louis XV*. Société du Mercure de France, Paris, 1908.

Poëte, M., Henriot, G., and Burnand, R. *Paris sous la République de 1848*. Bibliothèque historique de la ville de Paris, 1909.

Redesdale, Lord. *Memories*. Hutchinson, Vol. I & II, London, 1916.

Restif de La Bretonne, N.-E. *Le Pornographe*. J. Nourse, London, 1769.

Restif de La Bretonne, N.-E. *Les Nuits de Paris*. Smith-Lesouëf, London, 1788-1794.

Sauval, H. *Chronique scandaleuse de Paris*. H. Daragon, Paris, 1910.

Sauval, H. *Histoire et recherches des Antiquités de la Ville de Paris*. C. Moette, 3 vols, Paris, 1724.

Sauvan, M. *Picturesque Tour of the Seine from Paris to the Sea.* R. Ackermann, London, 1821.

Scott, J. *Picturesque Views of the City of Paris and its environs.* Longman, Hurst, Rees, Orme & Brown, London, 1820.

Stern, J. *Lord Seymour dit Milord l'Arsouille.* La Palatine, Paris–Geneva, 1954.

Tallemant des Réaux, G. *Historiettes.* A. Levasseur, Paris, 1834.

Villemessant, H. de. *Mémoires d'un journaliste.* E. Dentu, Paris, 1873.

Virmaître, Ch. *Paris-documentaire: Trottoirs et Lupanars.* H. Perrot, Paris (n.d.).

Watin, fils. *Le provincial à Paris,* 1787.

Wiriot, E. *Paris de la Seine à la Cité universitaire.* Tolra, Paris, 1930.

Index

STREETS, SQUARES, Etc.

MONUMENTS, BUILDINGS, Etc.

INDEX

239

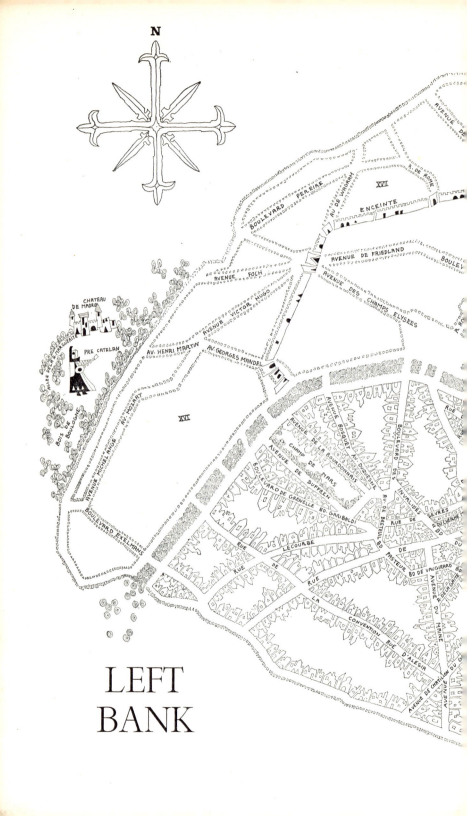

LEFT
BANK